THE BIOGRAPHY OF J.R.R. TOLKIEN

the biography of

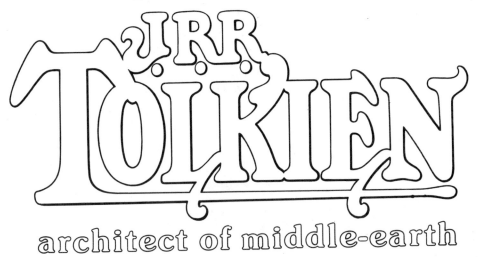

J.R.R. TOLKIEN

architect of middle-earth

by Daniel Grotta

Running Press
Philadelphia, Pennsylvania

Copyright © 1976, 1978 by Running Press
All rights reserved
under the Pan-American and International Copyright Conventions
Printed in the United States of America

Distributed in Canada by John Wiley & Sons Canada, Ltd.
22 Worcester Road, Rexdale, Ontario M9W 1L1

International representatives: Kaimon & Polon, Inc.
2175 Lemoine Avenue, Fort Lee, New Jersey 07024

9   8   7   6   5   4   3   2   1
Digit on the right indicates the number of this printing.

SECOND EDITION

Library of Congress Cataloging in Publication Data

Grotta, Daniel, 1944–
The Biography of J.R.R. Tolkien

First edition © 1976 published under title:
J.R.R. Tolkien

Bibliography: page 189
Includes index
1. Tolkien, John Ronald Reuel, 1892–1973—Biography.
2. Authors, English—20th century—Biography.
I. Title
PR6039.032Z65   1978   828'.9'1209   B   77-29209
ISBN 0-89471-034-6 Library binding
ISBN 0-89471-035-4 Paperback

Printed and bound by Port City Press, Baltimore, Maryland
Typography: Garamond, by CompArt, Inc., Philadelphia, Pennsylvania

Cover illustration by The Brothers Hildebrandt
Cover calligraphy by Robert Petrick
Cover art direction by James Wizard Wilson
Interior design by Peter John Dorman

This book may be ordered directly from the publisher.
Please include 25 cents postage.

Try your bookstore first.

Running Press
38 South Nineteenth Street
Philadelphia, Pennsylvania 19103

ACKNOWLEDGMENTS

I am grateful to the many people who kindly assisted me in my research, without whose help there would not have been a book. I would like to give special mention to Mrs. Allen Barnett, Mrs. Vera Chapman, Owen Barfield, Father Gervase Mathew, Professor Przemyslaw Mroczkowski, Dr. Clyde Kilby, William Cater, Geoffrey Woledge, Mavis and Charles Carr, Professor David Abercrombie, Professor T.V. Benn, Father Phillip Lynch, Howard Rosenblum, Frank Beckwith, Shireen Billimoria, and Professor William Walsh. Also, for access and information, the staff of the British Museum Reading Room, the *Sunday Times,* the *Daily Telegraph* library, the *Times* library, the *BBC* Archives, and the *Oxford Mail.*

I wish to thank the following for permission to reproduce materials from their publications: *The Collected Poems of Wilfred Owen;* © 1964; New Directions. *The Dethronement of Power,* by C.S. Lewis; published by the University of Notre Dame Press. "The Elvish Mood" in Talk of the Town, January 15, 1966 issue of *The New Yorker;* reprinted by permission of *The New Yorker.* "The Fantastic World of Professor Tolkien," by Michael Straight; reprinted by permission of *The New Republic,* © 1956, The New Republic, Inc. *Farmer Giles of Ham,* by J.R.R. Tolkien; published in the United States by Houghton-Mifflin Company. *The Image of Man,* by William White; reprinted by permission of Abingdon Press. "J.R.R. Tolkien, RIP," by Guy Davenport; appeared in *National Review* issue September 28, 1973; permission to reprint given by National Review editorial office, 150 East 35th Street, New York, N.Y. 10016. *Light on C.S. Lewis,* edited by Jocelyn Gibb; reprinted by permission of Harcourt Brace Jovanovich, Inc., New York. *The Lord of the Rings,* by J.R.R. Tolkien; published by Houghton-Mifflin Company. *Modern Heroism,* by Roger Sale; copyright © 1973 by The Regents of the University of California; reprinted by permission of the University of California Press. "Oo, Those Awful Orcs," by Edmund Wilson; reprinted with the permission of Farrar, Straus, and Giroux, Inc., from *The Bit Between My Teeth* by Edmund Wilson; copyright © 1956, 1965 by Edmund Wilson. "The Prevalence of Hobbits," by Phillip Norman, *New York Times Magazine,* January 15, 1967; © 1967 by The New York Times Company; reprinted by permission. *The Problem of Pain,* by C.S. Lewis; published in the United States by MacMillan Publishing Company, Inc., 1943. *The Road Goes Ever On: A Song Cycle,* by Swann and Tolkien; published by Houghton-Mifflin Company. *Three Selected Literary Essays,* by C.S. Lewis; reprinted with permission from Cambridge University Press, New Rochelle, New York. Excerpts from an essay by Clyde Kilby in *Shadows of Imagination,* edited by Mark Hillegas; published by Southern Illinois Press. *Tolkien: A Look Behind The Lord of the Rings,* by Lin Carter; © 1969 Ballantine Books, Division of Random House, Inc. Excerpts from an essay by Patricia Spacks from *Tolkien and the Critics,* edited by Neil Isaacs; published by Notre Dame University Press. *Tolkien's Crucible of Faith: The Sub-Creation,* by John Timmerman; copyright © 1974 Christian Century Foundation; reprinted by permission from the June 5, 1974 issue of *The Christian Century. The Tolkien Relation,* by William Ready; reprinted by permission of Henry Regnery Company. *Tree by Tolkien,* by Colin Wilson; copyright © 1974 by Colin Wilson; Capra Chapbook Series, Capra Press, Santa Barbara, California. "Why Frodo Lives," by Judith Christ; copyright © 1967 Downe Publishing, Inc.; reprinted with permission of *Ladies' Home Journal.*

CONTENTS

THE BIOGRAPHY OF J.R.R. TOLKIEN

PROLOGUE:
THE OLD PROFESSOR

WORKING AT HIS OLD-FASHIONED Hammond typewriter in his garage study, painstakingly recording the history of the First and Second Ages of Middle-earth, Professor Tolkien must have seemed like Bilbo Baggins himself at Rivendell, carefully chronicling in the *Red Book of Westmarch* his fantastic adventures. The room accurately reflected an author once described by his friend C.S. Lewis as a "great but dilatory and unmethodical man." Books were everywhere, in stacks and on shelves, dark-topped tobacco tins lined the shelves as well, and scattered about and stuffed into drawers were papers filled with Elvish scribblings, histories, and genealogies. A blue wind-up alarm clock sat prominently on the desk, to remind Tolkien of appointments and interviews. Everything was covered with what Tolkien euphemistically called "distinguished dust."

Tacked on the window ledge was a map of Middle-earth on which in blue-black ink the journeys of Bilbo and Frodo were marked. Over the door leading to the garden was an old kaffir powder horn from South Africa, and on the floor by the desk was an old and battered, buff-colored portmanteau. A visitor once asked what was in the portmanteau. Tolkien grinned, "It isn't there for anything at all except that inside it are all the things I've been going to answer for so many years. I've forgotten what they are."

Amid the clutter, smoking his pipe, sat the retired professor, smiling, square-faced, and silver-haired. In his later years, Tolkien could well have served as the model for an English country squire—tall, slightly stooped, and slightly plump; a fastidious dresser, with a propensity for wearing waistcoats or sweaters beneath his stylish tweed suits. More than most men, he laughed and constantly amused himself by making up jokes. Although a private, often pessimistic person, he shared his sense of humor and fair play with everyone with whom he came in contact. An English journalist once described Tolkien as "a cross between Bilbo and Gandalf," and indeed his appearance and outlook resembled closely that of his beloved hobbits. According to Tolkien's description of hobbits in *The Lord of the Rings,* their "faces were as a rule good-natured rather than beautiful, broad, bright-eyed, red-cheeked, with mouths apt to laughter, and to eating and drinking. And laugh they did, and eat, and drink, often and heartily, being fond of simple jests at all times, and of six meals a day (when they could get them). They were hospitable and delighted in parties, and in presents, which they gave away freely and eagerly accepted."

Furthermore, hobbits "love peace and quiet and good tilled earth: a well-ordered and well-farmed countryside was their favorite haunt. They do not and did not understand or like machines more complicated than a forge-bellows . . . Even in ancient days they were, as a rule, shy of 'the Big Folk,' as they call us, and now they avoid us with dismay and are becoming hard to find. They are quick of hearing and sharp-eyed, and though they are inclined to be fat and do not hurry unnecessarily, they are nonetheless nimble and deft in their movements." In addition, hobbits love with a passion tobacco and mushrooms, bright colors (especially yellow and green), and prefer a comfortable life at home to travel and adventure.

Such a description would equally have applied to Professor Tolkien himself. "I am in fact a hobbit in all but size," he once told an interviewer who had noted the similarity. "I like gardens, trees, unmechanized farm lands, I smoke a pipe and like good, plain food—unrefrigerated—but I detest French cooking. I like—and even dare to wear in these dull days—ornamental waistcoats. I'm fond of mushrooms out of a field, have a very simple sense of humor (which even my most appreciative critics find tiresome). I go to bed late, and get up late, when possible."

The fame and success that *The Lord of the Rings* brought Tolkien in his mid-70s both surprised and perplexed him. He was pleased that his books had become immensely popular, but was loathe to accept the mantle of fame his readers tried to press on him. Though occasionally accessible to admirers who requested an audience properly, Tolkien was usually quite unavailable. As his popularity grew, he withdrew increasingly from public view. Like other famous figures, Tolkien was constantly badgered with well-intentioned admirers—businessmen eager to cash in on his popularity, college students wishing to ask questions about certain passages in his books, and other interlopers. Although Tolkien was once a well-known figure on the Oxford scene, instantly recognized as he walked along the Carfax or bicycled along Merton Lane, with his long black robe flapping in the breeze, fame forced him to hide from the world.

So jealously did he guard his privacy in later years that it was easier for a journalist to obtain an interview with the prime minister than with Professor Tolkien.

Tolkien disliked academic and popular literary criticism of *The Lord of the Rings*. He thought that the critics who had tried to unravel the allegory of his greatest work had missed the point entirely, for he insisted that *The Lord of the Rings* was not an allegory. Tolkien, in fact, loathed allegory; he preferred instead a cracking good story or a straightforward saga.

Tolkien gave all the appearance of working several hours each day in his garage study at 76 Sandfield Road, Headington, a suburb of Oxford. The Tolkiens enjoyed caring for the roses they had planted shortly after moving to Headington in 1954, but in late summer and autumn the neighborhood had to contend with large sporting crowds, which choked the quiet street that led into the soccer stadium nearby. On game days, the footballers would park their cars in any unoccupied spot. In the end, Tolkien installed a gate across his driveway to keep the sports fans out.

Tolkien had a strong fear of being interrupted. The slightest unexpected intrusion upon or deviation from his prearranged daily schedule had an immediately detrimental effect on his writing. And Tolkien was lazy. His total literary output over a period of more than five decades was surprisingly small. Tolkien was a disorganized writer, an incorrigible procrastinator, a slow worker, and one who created his own distractions. When trying to write, he often doodled and drew, or worked on Elvish languages, or practiced calligraphy, writing a meticulous but almost illegible black script. He also looked forward to visits by friends or family as an excuse to interrupt and put aside his work. And yet he complained about how difficult it was for him to write. "Exhausting!" is how he once described his feelings about writing to a *New York Times* journalist. "God help us, yes. Most of the time I'm fighting against the natural inertia of the lazy human being. The same old university don who warned me about being useful about the house once said, 'It's not only interruptions, my boy; it's the fear of interruptions.'"

After Professor Tolkien's tremendous success in the United States, he gladly accepted the assistance of a series of part-time secretaries until George Allen & Unwin, his English publisher, provided him with its own part-time secretary, Joy Hill, who visited him weekly in Oxford to help answer his correspondence, put his notes in order, discuss business matters, and even assist with light housework when Mrs. Tolkien's arthritis or migraine headaches became too severe. Joy Hill eventually became one of Tolkien's principle links with the outside world. The longer she assisted him, the more invaluable she became; it was inevitable that she was one of the few intimates in the Tolkien household, above and beyond her set duties to her employer.

Oxford had changed strikingly since Tolkien first arrived in 1911, but it still retained many centuries-old traditions, buildings, and institutions. The villages and open fields of Tolkien's student days had given way to the suburban towns and factories that now surround the city. The colleges' appearances have remained virtually the same for centuries, but gone are the days when students had to wear academic robes in the town, climb into college over spiked fences and glass-studded walls after midnight, or face being sent down and struck off the college register for entertaining, unchaperoned, a member of the opposite sex in college rooms. The Oxford of the mid-60s was larger, faster, more crowded, built up, and industrialized, but it still was recognizably and uniquely Oxford.

After his retirement, Tolkien maintained contact with his old college, Merton. He was pleased to be elected Emeritus Fellow of Merton in 1963, and regularly dined at High Table during term, or chatted and sipped sherry with former colleagues in the Senior Common Room. Among the close friends whom he visited were Professor Nevill Coghill, who in 1959 had succeeded Tolkien as Merton Professor of English Language and Literature after Tolkien's retirement; Lord Halsbury, who was an amateur philologist and a keen Anglo-Saxon scholar; Dr. Elaine Griffiths, a former student and a Fellow of St. Anne's College; Alistair Campbell, a scholar who had become Bosworth and Rawlinson Professor of Anglo-Saxon after Tolkien's friend Charles Wrenn retired; Reverend Gervase Mathew, one of the surviving Inklings (a literary group of which Tolkien was a member) and a Fellow of Balliol College; Professor Norman Davis, who upon Coghill's retirement succeeded him as Merton Professor; Donald Swann, who wrote the music to Tolkien's poetry in *The Lord of the Rings* that was later made into a successful record album; and his son Christopher, a don at University College, Oxford.

Conversing with Tolkien was a demanding task because it was often very difficult to understand exactly what he was saying. He spoke in a soft, low-pitched, rapid voice, not bothering to enunciate or articulate clearly. Tolkien mumbled constantly, his speech often seemed garbled to even his most attentive listeners, and he unconsciously upset friends because they could never tell whether he was telling a joke or cursing under his breath. Another problem was that he rarely bothered to take his pipe out of his mouth; this added constant clicking and sucking noises to his already garbled conversation.

He was also bad at telling jokes and stories because he invariably muffed the punch line (or never even got to it), swallowed his words, or laughed heartily in the middle. According to one friend, Tolkien was sometimes exasperating because he would change a subject without warning, or end a thought in mid-

12

sentence and refuse to elaborate further; and once he left a subject or brought up a new one, there was no turning back. But Tolkien spoke the common language of scholarship with his colleagues (even if at times that common language happened to be Gothic, Welsh, Icelandic, Anglo-Saxon, Finnish, or even Elvish). His peculiar manner of speaking, which would have distinguished him almost anywhere else, was not that uncommon in the academic environments of Oxford and Cambridge.

Tolkien had only a passing awareness of what was happening outside Oxford and England, and only a superficial knowledge of the great events and disasters that became front-page news. For many years, he did not even read a newspaper, preferring to hear a predigested form of the news in Senior Common Room conversation or High Table communication. He refrained from political involvement, had little interest in social movements or conflicts, and couldn't be bothered with lurid crime stories or tales of scandal. And yet, Tolkien's personal storehouse of knowledge outside his own subjects of philology and mythology was enormous. He read prodigiously (although the older he grew, the less he was able to read), and spoke knowledgeably about everything from French literature (which he detested) to science fiction (which he loved), from Swiss mountain climbing to the problems in communicating with Turkish taxicab drivers, and from early Church history to latter-day ecumenical movements. Tolkien liked to tell jokes in English, to sing in Gothic, to narrate sagas in Icelandic, to chant in Elvish, and to recite poetry in Anglo-Saxon.

His life was long and generally happy, and he confided to a journalist friend that he had no regrets whatever. The shower of fame and fortune that came to him late in life did little to change his outward mode of living. Apparently the earlier years of scrimping and saving left lifelong habits of personal parsimony, since he spent frugally and counted money carefully. Nevertheless, Tolkien was generous—almost to a fault—when it came to helping family and friends and giving anonymous charitable gifts. Although he was a wealthy man by most standards, he declined to live ostentatiously or spend indiscriminately. Except for his up-to-date wardrobe and occasional holidays abroad, the Tolkiens lived almost as they had for years, living in the same house, eating the same food, and seeing the same friends.

If someone had thought to ask Professor Tolkien what more he would like to have accomplished in his lifetime, he would probably have replied that he wanted to finish his first great love, *The Silmarillion*. This work, a ''prequel'' to *The Lord of the Rings*, which covers the history of the First and Second Ages of Middle-earth, had been started in his youth, advanced in its first form during World War I, rewritten during the 1930s, put in a drawer for decades, rejected by a publisher, and only dusted off after he had become famous. Tolkien tried to rewrite *The Silmarillion* while in his mid-70s, but the two-edged sword of success and the encroaching infirmities of old age constantly retarded his progress. It remained unfinished at his death in 1973.

THE YOUNG LAD
1892–1911

JOHN RONALD REUEL TOLKIEN, the first child of Arthur and Mabel Tolkien, was born one hot Sunday morning in 1892 after a difficult labor. Arthur's middle name was also Reuel—ancient Hebrew that translates either ''friend of God'' or ''God is his friend''—and the tradition of including Reuel in each child's middle name was one that years later Tolkien himself extended to his own offspring, and as his children did to their children. The name Tolkien derives from the German Tollkiehn, an older variation of the more modern Tollkühn. Tolkien's son Christopher wrote author and critic William Ready that ''the name is German in origin, a compound of 'toll' meaning 'mad' (cognate with English 'dull') and 'kühn' [meaning] 'brave' (the English 'keen'), and so meaning 'foolhardy.' '' The name Tollkühn may also be translated as ''rash'' or ''daring,'' and can refer either to someone unwisely bold or someone who displays courage and initiative in the face of overwhelming odds. The nearest equivalent in English would be something like Rashbold.

Tolkien's ancestral origins are thought to be rooted in the Ernestine Saxon Duchies (which now form the state of Lower Saxony in the Federal German Republic, and the districts of Karl-Marx-Stadt, Erfurt, Halle, and Leipzig in the German Democratic Republic). Prior to Bismarck's consolidation of the German states into a single *Reich* in 1871, the name Saxony was used to designate a number of sovereign states ruled by members of the Ernestine line of the House of Wettin. Since the thirteenth century, the House of Wettin had ruled land acquired through war, marriage, negotiation, and a grant from the Holy Roman Emperor, Frederick II. Saxony's borders changed continually as Wettin offspring married, conquered, ceded, consolidated, or stole territories from each other. One by one, the great lines of the Hennenbergs, Albertines, and

15

Eisenbachs died out until, by the beginning of the eighteenth century, the House of Ernestine controlled all the duchies.

Like other feudal rulers, the Wettins warred constantly among themselves and with their neighbors. The Reformation split Saxony into hostile Catholic and Protestant factions, and the region frequently became a religious battlefield as powerful European armies clashed again and again. The Counter Reformation and the Thirty Years' War decimated Saxony, which was left in the end overwhelmingly Protestant. The Tollkühn family branch from which Tolkien is known to have come was at one time associated with the Elector of Saxony, who represented the region in the Holy Roman Empire. Because of the significance of the name, it is likely that one of Tolkien's ancestors may have distinguished himself in service to the Elector, and been subsequently rewarded with rank, wealth, or land. At the time, a man could often take as his last name a recognized attribute of valor or strength, a great deed, a physical or mental characteristic, a title, or a nickname. Such may have been the origin of the name Tollkiehn.

One of Tolkien's forebears emigrated from Saxony to England, probably in the first half of the eighteenth century. This was when the German Hanovers were replacing the Scottish Stuarts on the British throne.

In 1714, George I had been invited to assume the throne left vacant by the death of Queen Anne. This was a popular move at the time, but some years later King George became involved in a series of scandals that threw suspicion not only on the royal family but on many other Germans who had emigrated to England. Perhaps Tolkien's ancestor decided to Anglicize the family name in order to avoid sharing the stigma of "German George." (In 1936, when anti-German sentiment was again on the rise in England, a relative of Tolkien's, Frank Neville Tolkien, changed his name to Tolkin.)

The Tolkien family eventually settled in Warwickshire in central England, the district that happens to be furthest from the sea. By the end of the seventeenth century, Birmingham in Warwickshire was well on its way to becoming a principal focal point of the Industrial Revolution, and many thousands flocked to the city for work, wealth, and opportunity. This helped transform illiterate farmers into a large working class; it also raised up a new middle class of tradesmen, businessmen, and professionals. The Tolkiens advanced into the middle class and a comfortable, though not opulent, style of living. (At one time, Frank Tolkien's father owned a piano factory, but it went out of business some time after the mid-nineteenth century.)

The Victorian Protestant ethic, coupled with the rise of technology and modern medicine, helped insure that most nineteenth century English families were large. To help care for such households, most parents were part of an extended family in which grandmothers, grandfathers, aunts, uncles, and other relatives shared the burdens and responsibilities of providing money, looking after the young, and caring for the house. Arthur Tolkien was the first-born of a rather large family, and as such was expected to assist in bringing up his younger brothers and sisters. He left school early, went to work, refrained from leaving home, and delayed getting married until the last of the younger children had grown up.

Arthur Tolkien worked in a branch of the Lloyds Bank in Birmingham, but he felt that there wasn't enough opportunity for advancement. At that time, South Africa was just undergoing another gold and diamond boom, and the Bank of Africa needed experienced, qualified personnel from England to staff its branches in the interior. Frank Tolkien applied, was accepted, and left by ship to take up his new post some time around 1890.

Arthur Tolkien was no longer a young man when he first arrived in Bloemfontein, the bustling, booming capital of the Orange Free State. South Africa was at that time an amalgam of sovereign countries, crown colonies, and independent native lands. The most developed regions—those with the largest number of white settlers—were south of the great Kalahari Desert and east of Cape Town. The Orange Free State was in the middle of these regions, and Bloemfontein was in the middle of the Orange Free State. In the 1870s, and again in the mid-1880s, major diamond discoveries and gold strikes in the Transvaal, Natal, and the Cape Colony had lured many thousands of adventurers to Africa. Few found wealth, but most remained—as farmers, ranchers, miners, and tradesmen. Because of its strategic location, Bloemfontein became an important trading center, a town, and finally a city.

Bloemfontein had been established in 1846 as an oasis town surrounded by endless miles of semiarid desert. A farmer named Jan Bloem had discovered the spring from which flowed the Bloemspruit, the only source of water in the region for many years until a pipeline was built from the Modder river 22 miles away. The city is about 750 miles northeast of Cape Town, 250 miles southwest of Johannesburg, and approximately 300 miles west of Durban. Communication between these capital cities was both long and arduous until the railroad connecting them was finally finished in the year J.R.R. Tolkien was born.

Although Bloemfontein was the capital of a sovereign nation and the seat of the *volksraad,* or national assembly, it was still in the 1890s a frontier town. Almost a half century had passed since the Great Trek, more than twenty years since the end of the Bantu wars, and a decade since the Zulu war, but tension was growing between the Boers, who were of Dutch heritage, and the

English settlers. In 1890, the population of Bloemfontein was approximately 25,000, mostly Bechuana and Basuto; there were only 2,077 Europeans at the time, and although Afrikaans was the official language, English predominated. The word *apartheid* had not yet entered the language, although the policies of racial discrimination and double standards of justice had.

Life in the Orange Free State was quite different from life in rural England. The seasons were, of course, reversed, and the winter days could become intensely hot. It rained little during winter—even less in summer—and dry, hot winds often blew across the desert through the town. The view from the capital was of an unbroken, treeless desert, punctuated by scruffy farms and surrounded by distant hills. The town, which once had resembled a frontier town of the American West, had already begun to look like a small city when Arthur Tolkien settled there in a large, two-storey white house with both a balcony and a gallery. Bloemfontein's most impressive building was the new *Raadzaal*, where the *volksraad* met, built in Renaissance style and dominating the market square. The city streets were laid out in straight lines at right angles, with the market square in the middle. Most of the houses were surrounded by large wooded gardens, well tended by black servants. As the city thinned out, the houses gave way to shanties, which in turn gave way to native settlements and the desert.

Arthur Tolkien married relatively late in life, at age 34, but apparently he chose well. His bride, Mabel Suffield, was brought up in a religious family in the town of Evesham, Warwickshire, about twenty miles south of Birmingham. She was an educated, cultured woman, devoutly religious, a member of the Unitarian Church. She and her two sisters had been missionaries in Africa before returning to England. For a time, Mabel Suffield had tried to teach Christianity to the Sultan of Zanzibar's harem.

Mabel and Arthur had known one another in England when he was still working for Lloyds Bank, and while they had fallen in love, circumstances dictated that they wait many months before being married. But after Arthur Tolkien had made a success in South Africa, he sent for his fiancee, and the two were married in the Cape Town Cathedral on April 16, 1891. She was twenty-one years old at the time.

J.R.R. Tolkien was born on January 3, 1892. He was small and sickly, and there was naturally much concern for his health. As an infant, he reacted badly to the heat and the lack of humidity, though the climate of Bloemfontein was thought to be healthy for those with respiratory problems; it is still a rest resort for invalids and convalescents. Not long after Tolkien's birth, the Bloemspruit overflowed its shallow banks after an unexpectedly heavy rainfall, flooding some of the richer houses that had been built beside the stream. But the biggest event of that year was the opening of the railroad between Cape Town and Johannesburg by the president of the Orange Free State, F. W. Reitz. Hailed as the greatest single move to bring security and prosperity to the area, it later became a power pawn between the British and the Boers.

Bloemfontein apparently made a particularly deep impression on young Tolkien. Throughout his life he retained crystal clear memories of his earliest years. Tolkien himself believed that being born in Africa, and being uprooted to England at a very tender age, helped stimulate his imagination and memory. The contrast between the African desert plain and the gentle green hills in England seems to have triggered a spark of creativity and precocity. "Quite by accident," he once said, "I have a very vivid child's view, which was the result of being away from one country and put in another hemisphere—the place where I belonged but which was totally novel and strange." He could recall, for example, that his first Christmas tree had been a wilting eucalyptus, that when he was two he had bathed in the Indian Ocean, and how horrified he had been to see a visiting archdeacon eating mealies (ears of Indian corn) in the proper native fashion.

Tolkien also remembered a somewhat traumatic incident, one that was later incorporated into both *The Hobbit* and *The Lord of the Rings*. "I was nearly bitten by snakes and I was stung by a tarantula, I believe," Tolkien recalled years later. "In my garden. All I can remember is a very hot day, long, dead grass, and running. I don't even remember screaming." After that, he apparently had a life-long fear of spiders, which he passed on to his young son Michael by dramatic bedtime readings of Bilbo's creepy encounter with the spiders of Mirkwood from *The Hobbit*. This was later reinforced by Frodo and Sam's near-fatal struggle with Shelob in Cirith Ungol in *The Lord of the Rings*.

There was one other incident which Tolkien recalled with great amusement, though when it happened it must have caused great pandemonium. Like most other white families, the Tolkiens employed native houseboys. One of them was named Isaak, and apparently he was proud of both his position and his employers; in fact, he named his own son Isaak (after himself) Mister Tolkien (after Tolkien's father) Victor (after Queen Victoria) to show his admiration. Once, he "borrowed" Tolkien from the house for several days to proudly show the white youngster off in his native *kraal* (village). The Tolkiens were panic-stricken when they discovered that both Isaak and their three-year-old son were missing, since Isaak had neither asked permission nor bothered to inform anyone of his plans. Of course, the boy had never been in danger, but his parents hadn't known that at the time.

Tolkien's only brother, Hilary, was born in February, 1894, and he too was considered a sickly infant. At three years of age, Tolkien had not grown out of his delicate state of health; neither did he show signs of improvement. After much deliberation, therefore, it was decided that Mabel Tolkien would take her sons back to England either until such time as they were strong enough to return to the hot, dry climate, or until Arthur Tolkien resigned his position with the bank in Bloemfontein and found a similar position in Birmingham.

With great reluctance, the Tolkien family split up in April, 1895. Being parted from his father at such a tender age and under such strained circumstances was a painful experience for Tolkien. One particularly poignant memory was of watching *A.R. Tolkien* carefully being painted on the large steamer trunk. With astonishing insight and maturity, young Tolkien suddenly realized with great sadness that this was the last time he would ever see his father.

Mabel Tolkien and her two sons boarded a packet ship, the S.S. *Guelph,* bound for England via the Suez Canal and the Mediterranean. Eventually, the three settled in Sarehole, a rural village on the outskirts of Birmingham. Several months after they arrived, word came from the Orange Free State that in February, 1896, Arthur Tolkien had died of acute peritonitis. Apparently, he had been stricken with a minor case of flu that went unchecked until more serious complications arose. William Cater, a feature writer for the London *Sunday Times* magazine, was perhaps the only journalist in whom Tolkien confided family matters. According to impressions that Cater received over the course of their friendship, ''Tolkien possibly blamed himself for his father's death because he had taken his mother away from South Africa through his own ill-health. Tolkien seemed to have felt that if only they had remained there, possibly his father would have lived.'' The loss of his father was the first of several tragedies in Tolkien's early life.

Sarehole in the last decade of the nineteenth century was like an island of tradition about to be submerged in a vast sea of change. Describing England in the 1890s, a contemporary observer wrote, ''the old sobriety of mind has left our shores and we have changed from a stolid into a volatile nation.'' The winds of change gave rise to reform bills, tariff acts, trade unions, suffragettes, and ultimately war. England was about to convulse its way into the twentieth century as a country far different from what it had been scarcely a decade earlier. A few pockets of nineteenth century rural England clung tenaciously to the old ways, but only until World War I swept that idyllic world completely away.

Sarehole was Tolkien's vision of ''a kind of lost paradise.'' He once said that he had a ''strange sense of coming home'' when at the age of three he first arrived in the Warwickshire village. Sarehole had "good waterstones and elm trees and small quiet rivers." It was surrounded by open fields and farmlands, though in the distance one could see the grimy smoke of nearby Birmingham. Shakespeare was said to have visited Sarehole as a youth, and it had not appreciably changed since his day. "I could draw you a map of every inch," Tolkien said when he was seventy-four years old. "I loved it with an intensity of love that was a kind of nostalgia reversed. There was an old mill that really did grind corn, with two millers who went straight into *Farmer Giles of Ham*, a great big pond with swans on it, a sand pit, a wonderful dell with flowers, a few old-fashioned village houses and, further away, a stream with another mill."

The family lived in what Tolkien himself described as "genteel poverty," although his definition of poverty may have been shaped by the affluent state in which his family had lived in Africa. Certainly it was a comedown from a fine house with servants, and their financial situation undoubtedly worsened after Arthur Tolkien's unexpected death, but it appears that they were better off than most other inhabitants of Sarehole. In any event, the degree of poverty that Tolkien remembered does not seem to have affected him adversely, although the lack of enough money remained a chronic problem until he was well past the age of retirement.

There was a marked dissimilarity between the rustic inhabitants of the village and the middle-class Tolkien family; their dress, speech, and customs set them apart. Mabel Tolkien apparently took great pride in dressing her sons in the finery of the day: short black velvet coats and knee-length trousers, large round hats with drawstrings, frilly white satin shirts with wide collars and huge red bows loosely tied at the neck. She also made them wear their hair long and curly. According to Tolkien, the village children, who had only plain clothing to wear, "rather despised me because my mother liked me to be pretty."

Apparently the change in climate helped both Tolkien and his brother Hilary grow to good health. At seven, Tolkien was robust and tall for his age; he greatly enjoyed playing outside and taking long walks around the countryside. He was a shy, almost awkward lad, and although he never became close friends with the other children in the village, he grew to like and almost to envy them. He often watched with admiration as they played in the street, but as much as he apparently wanted to be like them, he remained an outsider.

Everything about Sarehole fascinated Tolkien. He bought candy from a toothless woman at the village stall, and liked to watch the old miller grind wheat into flour and the farmers as they went about their business in the fields. Frequent long walks around the countryside—a practice established and encouraged by his mother—instilled in him a deep, almost reverent love of nature. Sarehole was undisturbed by factories, motor cars, suburban subdivisions, and social upheavals; it was an idyllic setting in which to grow up.

Many years later, Sarehole became transformed into Tolkien's beloved Shire, and the inhabitants became his hobbits. ''I took the idea of the hobbits from the village people and children,'' he once told an interviewer, adding that ''the hobbits are just what I should like to have been but never was.'' Bag End went straight from his Aunt Jane's apple farm into the Shire, as did the harvest festivals, farmers, and other local places. ''The Shire,'' Tolkien admitted, ''is very like the kind of world in which I first became aware of things.''

Tolkien began to show considerable ability at an early age, a precocity that he later thought came from his father's side of the family. (But on the whole, he once wrote, ''though being a Tolkien by name, I am a Suffield by tastes, talents, and upbringing.'') Fortunately, Mabel Tolkien was very talented in her own right, and she took charge of Tolkien's education. She had been a governess before becoming a missionary, and while she lacked an extensive formal education (women in Victorian England did not go to unversities), was altogether qualified to instruct her son.

She quickly taught him to read and write, and then progressed to Latin, Greek, mathematics, and romantic literature. Such a regimen would have overwhelmed anyone of lesser talent, but Tolkien lapped it up. Ironically, he was a lazy student, but he learned his lessons quickly and with such ease that he began to read and study on his own. Mabel Tolkien's goal was to prepare her son for a scholarship examination for the King Edward VI School in Birmingham, the finest secondary school in the region. She hoped he would ultimately qualify for a university place.

Tolkien first became interested in language when he was seven, while learning basic Latin and Greek. It is likely that as his skill in and love for those languages increased, he began to improvise and experiment on his own. By age nine, he had become marvelously proficient at languages, and much of his spare time was devoted to creating his own. This was disconcerting to his mother, despite the intelligence and imagination that her young son easily exercised. Her one thought was to have him qualify for a scholarship—he would have no hope of obtaining any further education if he failed the examination, since there was no money to pay for it.

''I invented several languages when I was only about eight or nine,'' Tolkien proudly remembered, ''but I destroyed them. My mother disapproved. She thought of my languages as a useless frivolity taking up time that could be better spent in studying. It's really too bad. The languages were rather crude attempts, but it would be interesting to see them.''

After repeated remonstrations, Tolkien reluctantly abandoned his youthful intellectual pastime and studiously applied himself to Greek and Latin. Several years later, however, he once again picked up the practice of inventing languages, a practice that he avidly pursued throughout his life.

Mabel Tolkien also first stimulated her son's great love of fantasy and fairy stories. Reading fairy stories was a great Victorian pastime, and not only for children. The nineteenth century proved particularly rich in fantasy writers, and undoubtedly Tolkien became acquainted with many of them. As a child, he had been read fairy stories by George MacDonald, William Morris, and Andrew Lang—which he loved—and tales by Hans Christian Anderson, Lewis Carroll, and the Brothers Grimm—which he did not. On his own, Tolkien later discovered G. K. Chesterton, Hilaire Belloc, H. G. Wells, and other contemporary fantasy writers, as well as works by Malory and Spenser. In fact, Malory's Arthurian legend fascinated and fired his imagination so much that years later he began—but never completed—an epic poem about King Arthur. But of all the fairy stories that he heard or read as a child, he loved those by George MacDonald the most.[1]

Mabel Tolkien also managed to instill in her older son an "almost idolatrous" love of trees, flowers, and nature, classical mythology and marching band music. He shared her enthusiasm for festivals, pageants, parades, and fireworks, as well as her love of queen and country, thatched cottages, fresh mushrooms, and ultimately religion.

Just after the turn of the century, Mabel Tolkien was converted to Catholicism. She embraced the new religion as fervently as she had the old, and passed her zeal on to her sons. At that time, nearby Birmingham had become the scene of a resurgence of Catholicism, stimulated and spearheaded by Cardinal Newman's Oratory Fathers. Birmingham had been a hotbed of puritanical Protestantism ever since the days of the English Civil War, and although it was later the scene of various nonconformist sects and denominations (notably the Unitarians), the city was traditionally anti-Catholic. Through the centuries, there had been a number of violent riots against "popery," the last major one as late as 1867. But as Birmingham became an increasingly important industrial center, many thousands of Catholic Irish and German workers flocked to the city in search of employment.

John Henry Newman, who in 1879 became Cardinal of England, was one of the most important and influential theologians of the nineteenth century. At one time he had been a priest of the Church of England, but as the Anglican movement became increasingly liberal, he became increasingly conservative. Eventually, he left the Church of England and was ordained a Catholic priest by the Congregation of the Oratory of St. Phillip Neri, otherwise known as the Oratory Fathers. After nearly two years in Rome, where he was given a Doctor of Divinity degree by Pope Pius IX, he returned to England to establish branches of the Oratory Fathers. In 1847, Newman set up a chapter in London and then in 1851 moved to Birmingham to establish the Oratory there. His avowed purpose was "to teach Catholicism to converts, immigrants and backsliders," and because he managed to temper Romanism with Anglicanism, the order proved notably successful. Newman also established, in 1859, an Oratory school in Birmingham. St. Phillip's School was run along the lines of an English public school, and both Tolkien and his brother Hilary attended classes there.

As the years passed, Mabel Tolkien had moved from Unitarianism to high Anglicanism; ultimately she began to take instruction at St. Anne's Catholic Church in Birmingham, and she was finally accepted into the Catholic faith in June, 1900. Her sister May was converted at the same time. This was a rather courageous declaration of faith, since Mabel Tolkien and her sons heavily depended upon their relatives for friendship and moral and financial support. She correctly surmised that in becoming a Catholic she would anger and offend her family, and indeed several relatives—both Suffields *and* Tolkiens— withdrew their financial assistance. Fortunately, an uncle paid Tolkien's school fees when he was accepted at the King Edward VI School in 1900. However, Tolkien's mother was forced to withdraw her son from the prestigious school in 1902 because of a lack of money. He was then sent to St. Phillips; but because the academic standard was not particularly high, Tolkien's mother took him out of the school later that year and began to tutor him at home.

Although their conversion to Catholicism probably placed a certain strain on family relationships, Tolkien still enjoyed frequent visits to his grandmother in Birmingham. On one occasion, his ever-active imagination and early memories played tricks on his mind. "I got a perfectly clear vivid picture of a house, but I now know that it was in fact a beautifully worked out pastiche of my own house in Bloemfontein and my grandmother's house in Birmingham, because I can still remember [Tolkien was in his mid-70s when he said this] going down the road in Birmingham wondering what had happened to the gallery, the balcony."

In 1903, Tolkien finally won a scholarship to the King Edward VI School in Birmingham. He had taken scholarship examinations in 1899 and 1900, and while he failed both times, he did pass the entrance examination and was accepted as a paying student. His success in the third examination helped ease Mabel Tolkien's anxiety about school fees.

The King Edward VI School was the oldest educational institution in Birmingham. It was established in 1552 with money that had been received after

Henry VIII sold the newly confiscated lands and monasteries that had belonged to the Gild of the Holy Cross. It had been named for his son, Edward VI, and by the nineteenth century the school had achieved a notable scholastic reputation. It was not as prestigious as Eton, Harrow, or Rugby, but its academic standards were high, and a good percentage of its students won places at Oxford and Cambridge. The King Edward VI School was on New Street in Tolkien's time, and consisted of two high schools, classical and modern, both having a combined student body of approximately 500 boys. In 1896, an adjoining girls' high school with 300 pupils had been opened, although classes were not co-educational. Also, the King Edward VI School foundation operated seven middle, or grammar, schools for younger students throughout the city. These had a total enrollment of 1,900. Only the best students from these schools were permitted to continue their education at the New Street institution.

Going to school in Birmingham meant the end of the idyllic life in Sarehole, and between 1900 and 1904 the Tolkiens lived in a series of rented houses in or around the city. After the Boer War and the unsettled economic conditions it brought in its wake, Birmingham burst into the twentieth century with a vengeance. With an ever-increasing population, the surrounding villages eventually became the city's suburbs and, ultimately, became completely absorbed into the metropolis itself. This was the fate of Sarehole, and Tolkien was saddened as he saw the steady encroachments of civilization marching towards the countryside in the form of new houses, factories, and suburban railways. Years later, in the first book of *The Fellowship of the Ring,* Tolkien painted the perfect portrait of the Shire as it had been from time immemorial, and although the hobbits wished it to go on forever in the same way, cosmic events were already conspiring to irrevocably change their way of life. "I wish it need not have happened in my time," Frodo sadly tells Gandalf. "So do I," says Gandalf, "and so do all who live to see such times. But that is not for them to decide. All we have to decide is what to do with the time that is given us."

To Tolkien, both Sarehole and the Shire had been "tucked away from all the centers of disturbance," and had come "to be regarded as divinely protected, though people didn't realize it at the time. That's how England used to be, isn't it?" But, according to Tolkien, "behind all this hobbit stuff lay a sense of insecurity. I always knew it would go away, and it did."

The second tragedy in Tolkien's young life was his mother's death in 1904, when he was twelve years old. Mabel Tolkien had been unwell for some time, and when she finally was forced to go into the hospital she was diagnosed as diabetic. In those days, before the use of insulin, diabetes mellitus was invariably a fatal disease, and Mabel Tolkien, knowing she did not have long to live, began making legal arrangements regarding her sons' education and upbringing. Her greatest concern was that both Tolkien and Hilary should continue in the Catholic faith, and she feared that if the boys were given to their Protestant grandparents, they would be pressured into changing their religion. This desire presented a dilemma, however, since she had no money of her own, and so no means by which to provide for her children after her death. She decided to consult with Father Francis Xavier Morgan, a priest who had befriended the Tolkien family.

Father Morgan had been a student at the Oratory School in 1875, and joined the order after graduating in 1877. He was half Spanish, that part of his family being well-to-do sherry merchants from Andalusia. He made England his permanent home, but his brother had elected to live in Puerto Santa Maria in Southern Spain and take care of the business; Father Morgan visited Spain every other year until his death in 1935. He was known as Father Francis to his friends and colleagues, and undoubtedly this is how Tolkien addressed him. Father Morgan was a tall, silver-haired man who was distinguished rather than imposing; he had a firm but gentle manner, a keen intellect, and an unusual sensitivity towards children. He took a great liking to the Tolkien boys, and was very influential in their upbringing. In a way, he was a surrogate father to them from the very beginning.

Father Morgan offered to serve as their legal guardian, and to assume responsibility for their upbringing. Mabel Tolkien quickly agreed, since this would insure that they would remain Catholics, as well as receive an excellent education. According to Phillip Lynch, an elderly priest at the Birmingham Oratory who had known both Father Morgan and the Tolkien boys in the early 1900s, Father Morgan's guardianship was "a task he fulfilled very adequately."

After Mabel Tolkien's death in November, Father Morgan took charge of the boys and persuaded a sympathetic aunt, Beatrice Suffield, to take them in. Aunt Beatrice, unlike the other relatives, did not object to the boys' religion, and promised not to force them to convert back to Protestantism. Although Tolkien was not happy living with his aunt, her home was near the Oratory, and he and Hilary spent many hours there with Father Morgan. Another consolation was in meeting another King Edward's boy, Christopher Wiseman, who was to become Tolkien's best friend.

Four years later, when it became apparent that Aunt Beatrice could no longer handle the boys—who were by this time strapping young lads—Father Morgan obtained lodging for them at a boarding house run by a Mrs. Faulkner, who frequently was entrusted with the care of charity orphans by the Oratory.

The boarding house was an extremely modest structure in the Eddystone section of Birmingham, with a number of resident orphans—both Catholic and Protestant. The money provided for their food and care was relatively little, and Tolkien remembered living in a kind of perpetual twilight of hunger. However, he and his brother Hilary had a second-floor room to themselves.

Life in Birmingham was, of course, very different from life in Sarehole. Instead of quiet solitude and wide open spaces, Birmingham was noisy, crowded, and dirty. Its population had grown to well over a half million by 1900, partly by attracting new workers to the district and partly by gobbling up the surrounding suburbs and villages. Birmingham was known as "a community of untiring industrial activity," a title aptly reinforced by the hundreds of smokestacks that poured pollution into the grey sky both day and night. Many of the nearby districts and towns—Dudley, Wolverhampton, Walsall, Wednesbury and South Staffordshire—had also become bustling industrial centers, and the region around Birmingham was known as "the black country." Like Upper Silesia or the Ruhr today, the entire valley around Birmingham was well on its way to becoming an interconnected system of adjacent manufacturing towns that would eventually fuse into one vast industrial district, swallowing all available open spaces to satisfy its insatiable appetite for land.

To Tolkien, Birmingham was at once depressing and stimulating. He hated the squalor, but enjoyed the schools, libraries, parks, and museums. Best of all, he loved the occasional journeys with Father Morgan to still unspoiled English countrysides. Shortly after Mabel Tolkien died, Father Morgan, Tolkien, and Hilary went by railway for a fortnight's holiday in Wales. It was the first time Tolkien had been in the west country, and he developed a lifelong love of Wales and everything Welsh. As they penetrated further into the Welsh countryside, snatches of conversation and station signs with Welsh names became more and more frequent. "I heard it coming out of the west. It struck me in the names of coal-trucks; and drawing nearer, it flickered past on station-signs, a flash of strange spelling and a hint of a language old and yet alive; even in an *adeiladwyd 1887* ill-cut on a stone-slab, it pierced my linguistic heart. . . . It is the native language to which in unexplained desire we would still go home."

Years later, that impression was still so strong that he declared, "Welsh always attracted me more than any other language." Tolkien incorporated many linguistic components of Welsh into his own Elvish languages, especially the singsong, gentle Ls that roll off the tongue. And in *The Lord of the Rings,* the "music of Welsh comes through in naming mountains and other places."

Tolkien's progress at the classical side of the high school was by school standards excellent, but only passing according to his potential. He was, in his own estimation, "one of the idlest boys Gilson [Robert Cary Gilson, the headmaster] ever had." After visiting Wales, Tolkien again turned to making up languages, and also began studying Anglo-Saxon, Welsh, and even medieval Welsh on his own. This talent might have gone unnoticed and undirected if it hadn't been for George Brewton, his form-master. Brewton was a "fierce teacher," according to Tolkien, and something of a medievalist in his own right. When he discovered Tolkien struggling through Anglo-Saxon on his own, using only books found in the library, he took him in hand and shared his enthusiasm for medievalism with the teenager. The first thing he did was quiz Tolkien, in order to learn exactly how advanced he was in his private studies. Apparently the boy's knowledge was considerable, but incomplete. Having learned Anglo-Saxon straight from books, he really had no idea of correct pronunciation. Nor had he mastered the intricate grammar.

Brewton set up a regular private tutorial session to help Tolkien with his Anglo-Saxon. He was a demanding teacher—as demanding as Tolkien was lazy. But no matter how much work Brewton poured on, or at how fast a pace he conducted the lessons, Tolkien always managed to keep one step ahead of his teacher, and still had time to study Welsh, and even Gothic, on his own. After he was satisfied that Tolkien was sufficiently proficient in the language, Brewton introduced him to Anglo-Saxon literature. And it was through Brewton that Tolkien first discovered the wealth of untranslated medieval Midlands literature.

Another instructor at the King Edward VI School who had a positive influence on Tolkien was a man named R. W. ("Dickie") Reynolds. Reynolds taught English in the upper forms, and he introduced Tolkien to both literature and, more important, literary criticism. Now Tolkien was able to synthesize his love of languages with the methodology for discovering meaning in language.

Tolkien did not neglect his other studies, but he did not pursue them with great enthusiasm either. He spurned the classics for Anglo-Saxon literature, and although his Latin and Greek were excellent, his knowledge of the standard Roman and Greek works that were required for matriculation to Oxford and Cambridge was only passing. His weakness in the classics did not bother Tolkien at the time, and he continued his private pursuit of rather obscure subjects in preference to the required work. This deficiency was later to plague him during his first two years at Oxford.

By the age of sixteen, Tolkien had grown into a handsome, tall young man, much admired by the girls. He had outgrown his earlier physical frailties, and become both an active athlete and a keen sportsman. He tried out for the rugby team—the most popular school sport of the day—and played a number of matches as a member of the first team. An excellent student, and still quite shy, he was well-liked by his classmates, and enjoyed what little social life living in a boarding house for orphans could afford him. He did have several very close friends. One was Wiseman, of course, and the other was Robert Quilter ("R. Q.") Gilson, son of the headmaster. Together with three or four others from the same form, Tolkien, Wiseman and Gilson formed a clique that reveled in everything from sports to scholarship. And as was customary during that day and age, the students formed their own private clubs. At first they called themselves the Tea Club, but later they changed the name to the Barrovian Society (named after a tea shop called Barrow's). Later that name too was changed to the T.C.B.S. since the combined initials sounded mysteriously impressive to the socially conscious schoolboys. The T.C.B.S. had an extensive influence on Tolkien. It allowed him a ready platform for experimenting and expounding his philological studies and early attempts at writing.

Tolkien was probably not yet sixteen when he fell in love for the first—and only—time in his life. At the Eddystone boarding house lived another orphan named Edith Mary Bratt. Her social background was similar to Tolkien's. Edith Mary was about three years older than Tolkien, but this disparity had no appreciable effect on their blossoming friendship. Nor did the difference in religion seem important to them, through it became a stumbling block between her family and Tolkien until she reluctantly converted to Catholicism.

In time, the friendship grew into a "love match," as the Tolkien family later described it. Such a relationship at their tender age was bound to be discouraged, so it necessarily developed in secret. One of their accomplices was the housekeeper, a maid named Annie Gollins, who was enlisted by the couple to carry messages and arrange meetings. She also helped them by doing little—and sometimes not so little—favors.

Tolkien and Hilary never quite got enough at the table to satisfy their ravenous appetites. Edith Mary pleaded with Annie Gollins to help her steal food from the pantry and scraps from the kitchen to feed the brothers. Annie Gollins readily agreed to the conspiracy, and for months they had a makeshift system utilizing the dumbwaiter for smuggling food upstairs. She would load leftovers on the dumbwaiter when no one was looking and quickly hoist it up to Edith Mary's first floor room. Edith Mary's room was directly below Tolkien's second floor window; she in turn would ferry the food from the dumbwaiter to her window, tie it to a string that Tolkien would let down on signal, and then the hungry brothers would hoist it up.

This system worked well for months, but eventually the landlady became suspicious, and set about trying to discover who was stealing the missing food.

They were caught, and the entire story of their affection eventually came out. Their respective guardians were informed of the situation, and Edith Mary was banished to the house of an aunt and uncle, with whom she subsequently lived for a number of years. Not only were they separated, but they were expressly forbidden to see, visit, write, or communicate with each other in any way. This edict was not rescinded until Tolkien was at Oxford and had passed his legal majority. This enforced separation put a strain on Tolkien's relationship with his guardian, Father Morgan, especially after Tolkien and Edith Mary were discovered seeing one another after they had been forbidden to do so. But since Father Morgan's financial support was vital if Tolkien was to go to the university, he eventually acceded. Perhaps the years of waiting and anticipation helped sharpen Tolkien's love—in any event it made him much more determined to marry Edith Mary, despite the difficulties.

Father Morgan tried to spend as much time as he could with his wards, and took their religious instruction as his personal responsibility. As a gesture of respect and admiration, Tolkien taught himself to read and write Spanish (imperfectly, however, since he never successfully mastered that language), and he was delighted whenever Father Morgan told them stories about Spain. He genuinely liked Father Morgan, despite his sternness and inflexibility about Edith Mary, and both realized and appreciated the Oratory's guidance and material assistance in his upbringing.

Most of all, he enjoyed the long walks and trips through the countryside that they would take together. On one such trip, Father Morgan took the Tolkien brothers to the Devon coast, with which Tolkien was immediately and permanently enchanted. (More than fifty years later, long after Professor Tolkien had retired and become famous, he and his wife bought a modest bungalow in Bournemouth, on the Devon coast, in order to escape his admirers.) The three of them stayed at the house of one of Father Morgan's friends, the Mathews. Tolkien got to know Mr. Mathew's son slightly, but the boy was several years younger than Tolkien. Later, at Oxford, the acquaintanceship between Gervase Mathew and Tolkien was to grow into close companionship.

In early 1909, when Tolkien was still upset over his frustrated romance, he sat for a scholarship examination for Oxford University. The competition was fierce, and he failed to win a place that year. He took a similar scholarship examination the following year, and while he just missed winning a full scholarship, he was awarded an ''exhibition''—a slightly inferior kind of scholarship—to Exeter College, Oxford University, one of the colleges at which the King Edward VI School had established and funded an exhibitory.[2] The examination was highly competitive, since the school's best students were competing for the single place available at Exeter. Tolkien outscored all the others—barely—and though that in itself was considered a great achievement, he did not receive much praise from either the school or the Oratory because they knew he should have passed with a much higher margin, and should have won a full scholarship rather than an exhibition.

Tolkien completed his final form with flying colors, and as a reward, Father Morgan arranged a mountain climbing holiday in Switzerland for the nineteen-year-old and his brother Hilary during the summer before he was to go up to Oxford. It was Tolkien's first trip to the continent, as well as his first attempt at mountain climbing. He was awe-struck by the sheer majesty of the Alps, and he often expressed a desire to return (but never did). He climbed part way up one of the peaks, but inexperience and bad weather forced his party to abandon its quest for the summit. This incident was later transformed into the Fellowship's unsuccessful attempt to enter Mordor by passing over storm-bound Barazinbar in *The Lord of the Rings.*

Tolkien's early life was marred by two tragedies, the loss of each of his parents. But it was also marked by the peaceful years at Sarehole, his friendship with Father Morgan, and his strong religious faith. Despite his parents' deaths, poverty, and forced separation from his sweetheart, Tolkien reflected that "it was not an unhappy childhood. It was full of tragedies, but it didn't tote up to an unhappy childhood."

THE EXHIBITIONER
1911–1915

Y OUNG TOLKIEN first "went up" to Oxford at the beginning of the 1911 Michaelmas term[1] as a Classical Exhibitioner in Residence at Exeter College. Prior to the First World War, students at Oxford and Cambridge were officially listed as exhibitioners, scholars, or commoners. Exhibitioners and scholars were students who had been accepted solely on *proven* merit—having usually taken a competitive examination—and whose college fees were paid for from the funds of a school, college, or university. The subtle difference was that an exhibition was usually considered inferior to a scholarship "in merit, dignity, if not the amount." This was because exhibitions were usually awarded to students from middle-class high schools; scholarships were awarded by wealthier upper-class public schools. On the other hand, commoners, far from being common in the usual sense,[2] were students who paid their own college fees. Scholars and exhibitioners tended to be highly intelligent and academically able; commoners tended to be quite wealthy, well connected, and lazy. In Tolkien's day, the only *physical* distinctions among the three were the very minor variations in the black academic gowns that junior members of the university (undergraduates) were required to wear at most times outside their rooms. In practice, however, there were no academic differences among the three: scholars, exhibitioners, and commoners shared the same college staircases (sets of rooms), had the same tutors, attended the same lectures, and won the same degrees.

Tolkien, having studied classics at King Edward VI School, elected to read[3] classics at Oxford, an almost inevitable choice for someone with his academic background. In England, the classics invariably mean Greek and Roman language[4], literature, art, history, and philosophy—still the queen of curricula in prewar England—with optional courses in modern languages,

32

literature, and philosophy. The nearest American equivalent would be a liberal arts education without science courses.

Tolkien had not selected Exeter College because of any special merit, appeal, or association; it just happened to have been the Oxford college to which his exhibition had been applied. In America, students traditionally choose a particular university because of its prestige, graduate schools, science programs, location, tuition, or academic reputation. At Oxford and Cambridge, however, a student is much more likely to choose a college because of the size of the rooms, the extent of the wine cellars, the quality of the food, and the percentage of fellow students who belong to one's own social class. Such apparently arbitrary and trivial reasons help point out the vast differences between American colleges and universities and the Oxbridge' system of education. In order to understand the somewhat complicated and confusing relation of the Oxford colleges to Oxford University, it is first necessary to know, in brief at least, Oxford's history, and that of the great European universities.

Some time after the reign of Charlemagne, travel and commerce between European lands became easier, safer, and more common, and the so-called Dark Ages gave way to the Middle Ages. The Church was universal, and the common language among educated individuals was Latin. Until that time, education had been solely the province of local monasteries, but this became less common as scholars and teachers decided to seek opportunities elsewhere. Such persons, in their search for employment, naturally gravitated towards the cities. Many were accepted into rich households or local monasteries, but others remained ''free-lance,'' soliciting students however they could and instructing them for a fee. Since most of these itinerant scholars were foreigners, and so under constant suspicion by the local townspeople, they inevitably began to band together in common (fortified) lodging houses for better protection. This had the effect of creating scholars' quarters in the towns, where any lad wishing instruction could find a tutor. The lodging house where scholars lived became known as a *collegium.*

In time, when enough scholars crowded into a particular collegium, they would either add a new wing, or some would leave to build an entirely new collegium nearby. Also, as scholars became more numerous, and because most scholars in the Middle Ages belonged to religious orders, each order—say the Dominicans, or the Franciscans—wanted a collegium of its own. By the twelfth century, a number of medieval towns had relatively large districts containing numerous *collegia,* or colleges, each with its own master, rector, warden, dean, or father superior, and each competing against the others for students, noble favor, and money. Inevitably, they began to recognize common interests and created a central administrative body to oversee the college. That central administrative body was called the *universitas,* or university. It is important to note, however, that in many, if not most matters, the colleges remained independent of the university.

By the twelfth century, the most renowned universities in Europe were in Paris and Bologna, and scholars flocked to those cities to teach, study, or become students of other scholars. These included hundreds of English scholars, most of whom went to the University of Paris. But in 1167 A.D., during one of the periodic feuds between Henry II of England and Louis VII of France, Henry ordered all English scholars resident at European colleges to come home. In retaliation, Louis threw out of Paris all those English scholars who had decided to ignore Henry's edict. The predictable consequence of this royal feud was that England was suddenly besieged with as many as two thousand hungry and homeless scholars.

King Henry quickly decreed that they should move *en masse* to a small market town in the Thames Valley called Oxnaford,[6] or Oxford. This disorganized rabble descended on the town like an invasion of locusts, poverty, inflation, and even plague with them. This initial twelfth century confrontation instituted a centuries-old animosity between town and gown that was periodically punctuated with bloody pitched battles and massacres. Because of both poverty and plague, the scholars took many years to organize themselves into colleges. Many elected to associate themselves with the numerous ecclesiastical establishments and religious orders that had sprung up in the early thirteenth century. It wasn't until 1248, when Henry III issued a royal charter which gave attractive one-sided concessions and privileges to scholars and students, that the first colleges came about.

There is still considerable controversy over which college is the oldest in Oxford. University College claims that distinction, having been founded in 1249, but since it didn't have a building of its own until almost forty years later, Balliol College (1263) claims distinction as the oldest. Balliol, however, did not develop into a proper college until its statutes were written in 1282, and this allows Merton College (1264) to claim title as Oxford's oldest college. It functioned as a college since its establishment, and indeed, all later colleges at both Oxford and Cambridge were modeled upon its statutes and organization.

The actual origin of the university itself is vague, although it seems to date from as early as 1133, when theological lectures were given by a cleric named Robert Pullen. However, it didn't come to prominence until after the establishment of the first colleges, when the university was used to represent their interests in the town and to the king. Oxford University, as such, wasn't even incorporated until 1571, when Elizabeth I instituted reorganizations of both Oxford and Cambridge. Over the course of seven centuries, more than a score of other colleges have been established and officially associated with the university; as the number of colleges increased, the power and prestige of the university increased.

Today, as in Tolkien's years as a student, the colleges are primarily *residences* for students and fellows. They grant degrees, of course, but the curricula, lectures, and examinations are administered by the university. Technically speaking, no student ever *attends* Oxford University, since no such entity exists. Oxford University is not a physical structure; the buildings most people think of as Oxford University either belong to the colleges or to the Oxford Schools (colleges that are not formally associated with the University).[7] In the Oxbridge system, a student applies for admission to a particular college (whose entrance standards are established by the university), pays fees to the college (some of the money goes to support the university, the rest goes for room and board and college-related expenses), lives in his college, and receives a degree from his college. But he is also automatically a member of the university and is subject to university standards, curricula, and discipline. The distinction between one college and another is really slight; academically, they are all the same. Students from different colleges attend the same lectures and share the same tutors. Thus, the reason a student chooses one college over another is largely arbitrary, and likely to be predicated upon petty or sentimental preferences. Tolkien was fortunate in belonging to Exeter, since that particular college was much less socially conscious than many others. Had he gone to Balliol, for example, it is likely that he would have been ostracized and ridiculed for being a poor orphan exhibitioner.

When Tolkien came up to Oxford, he found himself in a town steeped in history, mythology, and legend. At the time of the Norman invasion in 1066, the town had been barely a village, but in the fourteenth century, enthusiastic Oxford scholars apparently fabricated a more ancient and noble history for their town and university. One legend, as romantic as it is untrue, is that the university had been connected, about 1000 B.C., with "Brut the Trojan" (King Mempeic) and the Druids. Another legend is that Oxford was the site of a first century Roman garrison; this sounds credible because the town rests on a strategically important peninsula having the only practical river crossing for miles. But it just so happens that the Romans bypassed the swampy peninsula and made their encampment at Dorchester-on-Thame, over seven miles away. Still another legend credits Alfred the Great with founding Oxford, and though this seems highly unlikely, archeologists have discovered coins in other parts of what was Alfred's Kingdom of Wessex bearing the name Osknaforda or Orsnaforda, which indicates that there might have been a mint in the town.

The last romantic legend surrounding Oxford's origin concerns the story of an apocryphal nun named St. Frideswide, who was said to have founded a nunnery there.

Oxford had been an occasional battlefield between the invading Danes and the English, and yet another battlefield with the arrival of the Normans. The town began to grow in size and commercial importance, prospering steadily until the scholars swarmed in, bringing in their wake a decline lasting nearly a hundred years. From the thirteenth century onward, a series of royal charters steadily eroded the townspeople's rights in favor of the university. This caused a great deal of hostility between town and gown, which occasionally broke out in murders, riots, pitched battles, and even massacres. The worst massacre occurred on St. Scholastica's Day, February 10, 1533, when the outraged townspeople, triggered by some trivial incident, butchered over one hundred students and scholars. Afterwards, they were made to pay a heavy, humiliating penalty, and another royal charter giving the university even further rights was issued. (An annual ritual forcing the town mayor to pay one silver penny in token of submission, to swear to uphold all the rights of the university, and to hold a solemn high mass in memory of the slain scholars was continued until 1825.) There were no more great massacres, but the last great riot occurred as recently as 1857, and the battle cry *Town! Town! Gown! Gown!* rallied each side for centuries.

During the Middle Ages, Oxford was a fortified town with great walls. Little of that Oxford survives today, except perhaps in such ancient street names as Magpie Lane, Pennyfarthing Street, Slaying Lane, The Turl, Little Jewry, Seven Deadly Sins Lane, Catte Street, Kybold Street, Logic Lane, and ironically, Paradise Street (where Oxford castle once stood, later the site of a prison and a place of public hangings).[8] Another reminder of older days is the iron cross in Broad Street marking the spot where Thomas Cranmer and two other bishops were burned at the stake. The great bell ''Tom'' in Christ Church College's Tom Quadrangle, Cranmer's old college, still rings 101 times for the college's original 101 members at precisely 9:05 in the evening. Students and fellows are still summoned to Hall at Queen's College by the blowing of trumpets, and Christmas day at the college is marked by the arrival in Hall of a silver platter bearing a boar's head, at which time the medieval boar's head carol is sung by all. Another ancient tradition still flourishing at Oxford is ''progging,'' when the names of misbehaving students are taken by a roving black-robed proctor (a senior member of the university) with two burly bowler-hatted ''bulldogs'' assisting.[9]

Many ancient myths and traditions still abounded in Oxford during Tolkien's student days. Undergraduates, for example, were required to wear their academic robes at lectures, tutorials, at Hall, and whenever they went outside the college walls into the town. (Later, the requirement that they actually *wear* the robes in the town was slackened and they were permitted simply to carry them; either way, it was easy for proctors and bulldogs to instantly identify and separate "gownies" from the "townies" over whom they had no authority. Attendence at Chapel was, in practice but not theory, compulsory, except for Catholics, Jews, and nonconformists, who were permitted to attend their respective religious services instead.[10] In fact, until the early nineteenth century, fellows, or senior members of the colleges, had been required to belong to holy orders in the Anglican church; indeed, it was not until 1877 that fellows were even permitted to marry. The colleges competed to offer the best food and drink at table, but students and dons[11] alike suffered from an appalling lack of basic creature comforts, and Tolkien had to use the same sort of "japanned tin sponge-bath full of tepid water" that Lewis Carroll had complained about nearly a half century earlier. "Ragging" (hazing) by upperclassmen towards new students was officially discouraged, but still endemic in Tolkien's day.

Another noble Oxford tradition that was at its zenith when Tolkien was a student was that exemplified by the hundreds of university clubs and societies. There were snob clubs, literary societies, social cliques, sporting clubs, steeplechase societies, and even dining clubs. Perhaps the most famous (or infamous) Oxford society was the Hell-Fire Club, which was founded by rich young rakes at Brasenose College in 1768, and terrorized the countryside for over a half century until its last president died of delirium tremens during a drinking bout in 1834. Another famous club was the Martlets, a literary society established during the 1600s at University College, whose total attendance at any one time was limited to twelve. (C.S. Lewis was once president of the Martlets, but later quit when they refused to admit more than twelve members.) Other clubs in Tolkien's day included the Old Etonians, the Myrmidons, and the Bullingdon. In later years, among the better-known clubs were the Wodehouse Society, the Charon Club, the Uffizi Society, and the short-lived Merton Essay Club (to which Tolkien may once have read a paper). Most students at Oxford join one or more clubs or societies during their undergraduate years, and Tolkien participated in university social life by joining the college Essay Club and The Dialectical Society and the Stapeldon (a debating society), and even starting his own clubs, the Apolausticks and Chequers.

The Oxford that Tolkien found in 1911 had not significantly changed on the surface for centuries. A few new colleges had been added to the university during the nineteenth century, but otherwise things remained much the same. The city itself was surrounded by vast open fields and pleasant villages. This delighted Tolkien, since it was such a contrast to the great industrial factories and dirty slums that typified much of Birmingham. Industry was virtually non-existent in Oxford. The largest single employer (after the univeristy) was the Oxford Press, and it had only three hundred workers. Horses still pulled the tram cars around the city, but the chief means of transportation for members of the university was the ubiquitous bicycle (Tolkien also had one). At that time, motorcars were relatively rare and then (as now) junior members of the university who wished to have them needed written permission from the proctor. This was all about to change even while Tolkien was a student. A former bicycle repairman who once had a small shop on High Street, not far from Exeter College, had recently taken to building motorcars. His name was William Morris,[12] and he would later be responsible for irrevocably altering the Oxford landscape Tolkien loved so dearly.

In Tolkien's time, there were, out of a total Oxford population of about fifty thousand, three thousand junior and senior members of the university. These Oxonians[13] lived, for the most part, a life completely divorced from that of the townspeople. In past centuries, this demarcation even extended to the courts: the town had absolutely no jurisdiction over wrongdoers who were associated with the university (including lowly cooks and bedmakers), not even if they had committed rape or murder.[14] This particular prerogative of the university had been long abrogated by Tolkien's day, of course, but the continued existence of two separate Oxfords was still manifest in many ways. For example, both town and gown patronized their own pubs and hotels. University students went to such places as the Turf, Turl, White Horse, Bear, Royal Oak, and King's Arms to drink; they ate at the Randolph Hotel and the Eastgate Hotel; and bought their pipes and tobacco at Cooke's and Colin Lunn. Town-gown romances were officially discouraged by both factions, undue fraternization was frowned upon, and black-robed students were warned against wandering into certain sections of the town alone after dark. Punch-ups and beatings were not all that uncommon in 1911, although the last pitched riot had taken place almost a half century earlier. Actually, the problems between town and gown scarcely affected Oxford undergraduates because few ever had occasion to overstep the invisible barriers or violate the unwritten laws that separated the two.

In the year Tolkien came up, two quite different but not unrelated struggles were raging in Oxford and throughout England. The final battle in Parliament for the supremacy of the House of Commons over the House of Lords had precipitated the greatest political controversy since the Chartist and Reform Bill agitations in the nineteenth century. It is quite probable that Tolkien himself had a nostalgic allegiance to the hereditary House of Lords, and regretted that chamber's vote under pressure reducing itself to impotence. Years later, he expressed his fondness for both royalty and nobility, ''I'm rather wedded to those loyalties because I think, contrary to most people, that touching your cap to squire may be damned bad for squire, but damned good for you.'' *The Lord of the Rings,* of course, depicts an hierarchical world governed by hereditary kings and lords. (''This system has never been worse than others in struggles for power.'')

The other struggle in 1911 was the beginning of the final clash between the university and the colleges for supremacy. Earlier, pressure from the university to make professors from the Oxford Schools also fellows of the colleges (and therefore reduce the influence and prestige of the tutors, who had been the backbone of the Oxbridge system for so many centuries) had prompted one college warden to threaten to withdraw his college from the university itself. This ongoing controversy was to continue until 1926, when the power of the nonresident M.A.'s[15] to directly influence the operation of the university was eliminated.

Tolkien apparently adapted quite well to both Oxford and academic life; this was in contrast to the bewildering and somewhat intimidating experiences most of the 850 new students encountered in their new environment. To many, Oxford gave them their first taste of independence after the strict discipline of the Edwardian family and English public and boarding schools. Oxbridge functioned on the principle of *in loco parentis*—acting in place of the parents. Theoretically, this meant that the college (and the university outside the college walls) closely monitored each student's behavior; indeed, many of the obligatory requirements, such as chapel attendance, gate hours, and scout (servant) supervised cold baths[16] had been established on this basis. In 1913, for example, ''Junior members of the university are required to abstain from frequenting hotels or taverns, except for reasons to be approved by the vice-chancellor or proctors.'' Furthermore, no undergraduate was permitted to play billiards in a public room before 1 P.M. or after 10 P.M., to attend horse races,[17] keep a dog in college,[18] frequent a dance during term, or even have an aviator's license. But such rules were more honored in the breach than in the observation, and most students suddenly found they had an inordinate amount of personal freedom—as well as personal responsibility.

Social life at Oxford during that decade was primarily predicated upon class, temperament, or athletic prowess. The university officially recognized only exhibitioners, scholars, and commoners, but almost all students were subject to three unofficial classifications: scholars, commoners, or toshers; fops or swots; hearties or aesthetes. Scholars were those who were studious, commoners were middle and upper-class students, and toshers was the derogatory term used for students from working-class backgrounds.[19] Fops were silly persons who put on intellectual airs, and swots were students who had little interest outside their studies. Hearties were those who were friendly, vigorous, and athletically-minded, while aesthetes were artistic and slightly effeminate. Tolkien was considered a scholar, a swot, and a heartie.

At that time, Oxford University was still considered the private preserve of the rich, the famous, and the well-connected. Steeple-chasing, fox hunting, motor racing, and weekend private parties in Paris were all activities of the select set. It was customary for the sons of the rich and famous[20] to come up to Oxford for three years to obtain their degrees at some of the more posh and accommodating colleges. Practically *anyone* who had sufficient money could obtain an Oxford degree, regardless of intelligence, academic ability, or the amount of work done. Until the Second World War, an Oxford student could receive a fourth-class degree,[21] which is roughly equivalent to a D- average at an American college or university. Oddly enough, rather than carrying a stigma, it shared the aura of an Oxford degree of a much higher category, and indeed was something of a class-conscious badge of not having worked at studies, or having been a swot. And for those rich students too lazy to even legitimately earn a fourth-class degree, some colleges offered a "Grand Compounder" degree. This was granted upon the payment of a large fee, and did not require that the student actually attend the college, much less take courses and pass examinations.

Exeter College was not oldest, the richest, the most prestigious, or the largest of the Oxford colleges, but it had a reputation for high scholarship, good companionship, and fine traditions. Exeter had been old even before Columbus set sail for America. It had been founded by Walter Stapeldon, the bishop of Exeter, in the year 1314, and had been known as Stapeldon Hall. The name was changed to Exeter College in the fifteenth century. Until 1565, when the college was extended by Sir William Petre, Exeter consisted of no more than twelve scholars and a rector. This was expanded through the years, and by Tolkien's day the number of fellows and junior members had reached almost sixty. The college building itself is jammed into the most ancient section of Oxford and borders on Balliol, Brasenose, All Souls, Jesus, and Hartford Colleges. Close by Exeter is Sir Christopher Wren's Sheldonian Theatre, both the old and new Bodleian libraries, the beautiful Radcliffe Camera, the History of Science Museum, and the Indian Institute, as well as nearly a score of other colleges. Exeter borders on the Turl, Catte Street, and Broad Street, which places it near the geographical center of the old town. Part of the original college is still extant, but the tower, library, and chapel, for example, were added over the centuries. Both the chapel and the small fellows' garden between the college and the Divinity School are especially beautiful.

Tolkien lived in the college[22] during his four years at Oxford, his room, board, and tuition having barely been paid for by his modest exhibition. At that time, some of the college fees at Exeter were:

Admission fee £5
Caution money (returnable after
      leaving the college with no debts) £25
Tuition (per term) 77s
Room rent (per year) 99s
Service charges—(coal, letter delivery, chimney
      sweep, warming and lighting of chapel, choir
      fund, shoe cleaning, etc. (Per year) £13 10s
Bedmakers (per term) £1
Degree fee for B.A. £4 12/6

These may seem low in relation to today's high cost of education, but it must be remembered that they were considerable sums then—as much as the average laborer earned in a year. As a result, Tolkien was chronically short of money. Other students at Exeter shared Tolkien's genteel poverty; the college traditionally had among its members a high proportion of exhibitioners. During Tolkien's student years, some of his fellow exhibitioners at Exeter included Michael Windle (the two became close friends), John Cardross, Orsmond Payne, Arthur Willis, George Elliot, Francis Roberts, and Louis Thompson.

Although somewhat shy and reserved, Tolkien was popular with his contemporaries and quickly made a number of friends at Exeter. He was especially close to a loose coterie of fellow students—Brown, Field, Shakespeare, Cartright, Windle, Norton, Carters, Trimmingham, Cullis, and his old T.C.B.S. friends from King Edward days, Smith and Gilson. There was also a young American Rhodes scholar named Allen Barnett. Barnett, an athletic history student from the South, possibly introduced Tolkien to the pleasures of tobacco, for throughout his life he maintained a particular fondness for Kentucky-cured tobacco. (Father Morgan had occasionally smoked a pipe, and it is possible that Tolkien had taken to tobacco long before he had ever met Barnett.) This group of friends had no particular name, but their great interests were a zest for life and a love of Oxford.

Tolkien and his friends made the most of their student years by frequenting pubs like The George and The Swains, eating at the Eastgate or the Randolph, taking early-morning coffee at the Buols or late-night tea at the Old Oaks. They played American baseball on the Christ Church Meadow, cricket at the Cricket Ground behind Ruskin College, punted on the Cherwell, cycled to distant churches and historic sites, and took long weekend walks through the Oxfordshire countryside (a tradition Tolkien was to continue into the 1930s). Together, they watched the ''summer eights'' races on the Thames, went to the cinema, attended Gilbert and Sullivan operettas, watched various sporting matches, and tried to seduce girls from the town or from the women's colleges.

Other favorite pastimes included telling stories and playing practical jokes on each other. Allen Barnett described a somewhat typical morning in 1913 when neither had any ''swotting up'' to do: ''Went back to the jolly inn in the morning with Tolkien and we both got quite merry and made awful fools of ourselves when we got back to college. He put white shoe polish in my four-in-nines,[23] but also some of his . . . Got off at the river this A.M., and visited most of the day. Went with Field and Windle for a walk and then with Carters for lunch with Barnes. It was quite a jolly affair and was largely reminiscent of our tasteful life.'' The double entendre refers to their predilection for alcohol, especially warm beer and stingers. Oxford was and always has been a drinker's town, and in past centuries the inns and pubs were the only places students could meet outside the colleges. At one point, there were more than 370 alehouses serving gin and brandy, and drunkenness was endemic among both town and gown.

Tolkien also amused himself and his friends by concocting elaborate jokes and stories. One such example of his schoolboy wit survives in a typewritten letter that he sent to Allen Barnett.

A young man wished to purchase a birthday gift for a lady friend. After much meditation and consideration he decided upon a pair of gloves as being appropriate. As his sister had some shopping to do, he accompanied her to a ladies wearing apparel shop. While he was selecting the gloves, his sister made a purchase of a pair of drawers for herself. In delivering the parcels that afternoon, by mistake the drawers were left at his sweetheart's door with a note as follows:—

Dear Velma:—This little token is to remind you that I haven't forgotten your birthday. I didn't choose it because I thought you needed them, or because you haven't been in the habit of wearing them, or because we go out evenings. Had it not been for my sister I would have gotten long ones but she says they are wearing the short ones—with one button. They are a very delicate color, I know, but the lady clerk showed me a pair she had worn for three weeks, and they were scarcely soiled at all. How I wish I might put them on you for the first time! No doubt many other gentlemen's hands will touch them before I get a chance to see you again, but I hope you will think of me every time you put them on. I had the lady clerk try them on and they looked very neat on her. I did not know the exact size, but I should be capable of judging nearer than anyone else. When you put them on for the first time put a little powder in them and they will slip on easier. When you remove them blow in them before laying them away, as they will naturally be a little damp from wearing. Hoping that you will accept them in the same spirit in which they are given and that you will wear them to the dance Friday night, I remain,

Lovingly yours:—
John

P.S. Note the number of times I will kiss the back of them in the coming year!

John

Such merry pranks and misappropriations of time did not seriously affect Tolkien's prowess as a scholar. He spent many hours by himself reading, and frequented Blackwell's and Maxwell's in search of book bargains and old lore. (He ran up a considerable bill during his stay at Oxford, and had to ask Father Morgan for additional money to help pay it.) But he was still lazy as far as his studies were concerned. Fortunately, he had several brilliant and influential tutors who helped to shape his love of scholarship and direct it towards the serious study of philology.

Tolkien's first tutor was a young fellow named Joseph Wrighty, who had arrived at Oxford in the same year as his pupil. Wrighty, a self-taught scholar from Yorkshire, had started out as an illiterate mill worker and ended up as Deputy Professor of Comparative Philosophy at Oxford and an author of some standing. He immediately discerned Tolkien's interest in languages, and helped him develop a firm foundation in the principles of philology. It is probable that he persuaded Tolkien to show him some of his early experiments in creating language, since Wrighty imparted to his student the methods by which a language with consistent roots, sound laws, and inflection could be developed.

It was through Wrighty's influence and encouragement that Tolkien first started creating what eventually became his beloved Elvish. But Tolkien's greatest impetus to transform Elvish languages from an experiment to a life-long pursuit probably came from his other English language tutor, William (W.A.) Craigie. Craigie was a world-famous philologist who had been appointed in 1910 as one of four joint editors of the Oxford English Dictionary. This was a great honor and a heavy responsibility. Besides being a philologist and a linguist, Craigie was also an authority on mythology, especially Scottish lore. It was Craigie who introduced Tolkien to the Icelandic and Finnish languages and mythologies. He also taught him correct pronunciation. The

Finnish was, along with Welsh, later incorporated into Elvish.

Tolkien had already taken the unusual step of *not* reading "Greats," which was the accepted honors course at Oxford, and led after three years to a B.A. degree in the classics. Instead, he elected to read English, which would afford him the opportunity to study other languages as well. Tolkien's relatives in Birmingham were upset by this because pursuing English meant an extra year at Oxford, and his exhibition was not likely to cover the added expense. But Tolkien stuck to his decision, so great was his love for language and so great his confidence in his ability and luck.

Unfortunately, in the year Tolkien came up, and for several more semesters, there were no tutors to be had in Anglo-Saxon. At Oxford, the examinations for the B.A. degree are two: either a pass or honors examination to determine which, if any, of the honors schools the student may attend, and the final examination that determines the class of degree the college will grant the student. This means that an Oxford student usually receives two different honors marks (or more, in some cases).

During the Easter term, 1913, Tolkien sat for his examination in Moderns (which included Anglo-Saxon, as opposed to Greek and Latin). He had pursued Anglo-Saxon on his own until E.A. Barber arrived at Oxford and became his tutor. Unfortunately, it was too late for him to develop proficiency, and he spoiled an otherwise brilliant examination, receiving second-class honors in Moderns. That it was a perfectly creditable achievement did not matter, since Tolkien was very disappointed with his performance. Apparently, he was required to attend various lectures on the Classics that were boring, repetitive, or unnecessary, and years later he complained that "my love of the Classics took ten years to recover from lectures on Cicero and Demosthenes."

Another tutor who greatly influenced Tolkien was a young New Zealander at Merton College named Kenneth Sisam. Sisam, a junior fellow who had been a Rhodes scholar, but suffered from ill health, was a specialist in fourteenth century literature. Sisam apparently inspired in Tolkien an interest in medieval English literature, adding to that which Brewton at King Edward VI School had discovered and cultivated.

As Tolkien worked on Elvish, he discovered some very important principles that were later to lead him into writing both *The Hobbit* and *The Lord of the Rings.* As he created his language, he realized that *language presupposed a mythology.* In his view, language developed from a desire to relate experience, and not merely to convey information. To tell the past is history; but to *explain* the past, and to make it meaningful to the present, is mythology. Suddenly, Tolkien realized that Elvish was useless as a language unless it too had a mythology, or a meaningful history to explain its origin and justify its existence.

Tolkien's first efforts to create a mythology to presuppose his Elvish languages were written at Oxford, but never completed. The story focused on the Atlantean legends, but even that was to be part of a greater, more complete mythology. ''The problem is to get across a whole mythology which I've invented before you get down to the stories.'' Tolkien chose Atlantis because he had ''always been fascinated by the lost continent.'' In his mythology, Atlantis became tranformed into the island continent of Numenor, in the Second Age of Middle-earth. Like the ring of power in *The Lord of the Rings,* the forbidden fruit that ultimately corrupts that Numenorians is their quest for immortality. (Tolkien once said that he was fascinated by immortality and longevity.) Tolkien actually began and worked extensively on the book he titled *Numenor.* When this was finally abandoned in 1916 after it became ''too grim,'' he modified the myth and began writing *The Silmarillion,* which shifted away from Atlantis. Later, these two early attempts at myth-making were synthesized into *The Hobbit* (originally a wholly unrelated work, it was later revised to conform with the Middle-earth myths in *The Lord of the Rings*).

The year 1914 was a fateful one. Early in the year, Tolkien still could have changed his mind and taken the examination for Greats, but he stuck to his original intention of spending a fourth year at Oxford. He was twenty-two, and while he wanted to marry his childhood sweetheart, Edith Mary, he decided to wait until after receiving his degree. Apparently her relatives disapproved of young, Catholic, penniless Tolkien, and he wished to impress them with something more substantial, such as a fellowship or a teaching post. Tolkien still played tennis, rugby, and other sports, drank beer with the boys in pubs, wandered around the countryside with Allen Barnett and went on summer holidays to Cornwall, Brittany and France, but more time was spent on serious pursuits and plans for the future.

By August, 1914, the world was going to war. Hundreds and then thousands of young members of the university flocked to the colors and accepted commissions in the Home Army. But the old Home Army was destroyed at the Marne and Mons, and the new Home Army became Kitchener's Army. At Oxford, the mood was festive and exciting. Almost all Tolkien's friends and fellow students left the colleges to enlist, trading their black robes for smart red uniforms. (Tolkien had joined a territorial horse regiment in 1912, but resigned after a few months, concluding that the army wasn't for him.)

The old rector of Exeter, Reverend William Jackson, was replaced by a newer man, Lewis Farnell. The colleges—including Exeter—were suddenly transformed into parade grounds and then soldiers' barracks. Companies of newly-uniformed soldiers drilled on The Parks, charging straw dummies with wooden rifles, then, as equipment was issued, with bayonet-tipped Enfields. Tolkien joined in these cavalry and infantry charges as part of his duties in the Officers' Training Corps. The charges up Shotover Hill and Wythan Hill delighted the spectators almost as much as did the marching bands and martial music of military parades passing down High Street.

As the war mired down in France and Belgium and the casualties began to mount, the red coats changed to khaki, the parades turned to drills, the cavalry charges became practice trench assaults, and the colleges that had become barracks now became military hospitals. The pressures on Tolkien to leave Exeter and accept a commission were great. He was virtually the only undergraduate in the entire college, and one of the few able-bodied young men at the university. Between 1914 and 1915, the student population dropped from three thousand to one thousand, and most able-bodied fellows and employees had left to enlist. Tolkien justified his decision to stay at Oxford by looking ahead to *after* the war. He thought he wouldn't be good for much of anything if he failed to take a degree, and would certainly not be an eligible suitor for Edith Mary.

One by one, the membership rolls of the college changed from ''A'' (absent, in the army) to ''D'' (deceased), but still Tolkien remained. In 1915, he sat for his final examinations, and was not very surprised when he received first-class honors in English Language and Literature. The graduation ceremony at the Sheldonian Theatre was small and muted; Tolkien was one of only two students in the entire university who received a first-class degree in English Language and Literature that year.

In 1915, the Turks began their massacre of the Armenians, the English were hopelessly bogged down in Gallipoli, the Prussians broke through on the Russian Front, gas attacks were initiated on the Western Front, and the Italians were slaughtered by the Austrians. Finally, young Ronald Tolkien, B.A. Exeter, decided to go to war.

THE SOLDIER
1915–1919 ⚜

ON JULY 7, 1915, Tolkien was commissioned a temporary second lieutenant in the 13th Reserve Battalion of the Lancashire Fusiliers. Conscription had not yet been introduced in England—the only major belligerent power still relying on volunteers. Enthusiasm and recruitments, however, had been waning since the destruction of the original British Expeditionary Force in 1914, and the more recent Neuve Chapelle offensive, which produced such horrendous casualty lists that the government fell. Winston Churchill's ill-advised invasion of the Dardanelles at Gallipoli had been a disaster, and Germany's policy of unrestricted submarine warfare had already begun. Many of Tolkien's childhood and college friends were already dead; by the war's end, all but two were.[1]

Tolkien joined his regiment after a last long holiday in Birmingham and began his final training almost immediately afterwards. As an Oxford graduate, he was automatically granted a commission in the army. The "Kitchener Armies" were formed so quickly that the traditional ranks and schedules for promotion were all but discarded. Also, the traditional British regimental system had begun to break down as a result of the constant casualties, so hundreds of thousands of volunteers (and later, conscripts) were assigned to replacement battalions, which were then attached to under-strength regiments.

To understand the significance of Tolkien's position in the Lancashire Fusiliers, it is necessary to first understand the traditional British regimental system. The word "regiment" derives from the Latin *regimentum*, or rule, and came to mean a single command or authority exercised over others. Early military regiments were under the command of a single leader; later, the rank of a regimental commander was traditionally that of colonel. After the Napoleonic Wars, and prior to World War I, British regiments consisted of two battalions; one of these was posted abroad, while the other remained in England. After a period (usually two years—shorter if there had been fighting), the battalions were rotated. Each battalion comprised ten companies (approximately 120 men and five officers each), and the companies were further divided into three equal-sized platoons.

What was most significant about British regiments, however, was that many of them were *regional:* men from Scotland joined a regiment like the Argyll and Southerland, men from Wales joined the Royal Welsh Fusiliers, and men from Ireland joined the Irish Guards. Furthermore, recruitment for battalions was usually *local;* often from the same village, town, or neighborhood. When World War I began, each neighborhood rallied around volunteer battalions, which were likely to be recruited and led by local retired officers and sergeants who had fought in the Boer War or the Sudan. These were "Kitchener's Armies," groups of local citizen soldiers—the platoons came from the block, the company from the neighborhood, the battalion from the town, and the regiment from the region.

Lord Kitchener did not foresee the tragedy this localization would produce. With friends and neighbors thrown together into battles that invariably resulted in vast numbers of casualties, each new offensive often left entire neighborhoods bereft of sons and husbands. Owen Barfield, a friend of C.S. Lewis and one of the Inklings, remembers when entire communities were in mourning and every front door in the neighborhood had a funeral wreath on it. After the Somme offensive in 1916, when this kind of regional tragedy was at its worst, the New Armies being conscripted were assigned to regiments and battalions according to need, and not according to the town, city, or shire the draftee hailed from. But the policy of replacement according to need and not neighborhood had already been instituted on a limited scale the year before.

Ordinarily, Tolkien would have joined a regiment from Oxford or Warwickshire, but he decided to go into the army at the same time as his friend G.B. Smith, who had joined the Lancashire Fusiliers. While he was successful in entering the Lancashire regiment, he was not posted to the same battalion as Smith, which was a great disappointment to Tolkien.

By 1915, with the tremendous influx of men, the typical British regiment had swelled from two battalions to as many as twenty-five. The regiments in turn belonged to brigades, divisions, army corps, armies; the armies fought on the side of the Allies from the Western Front to Micronesia, from the Southern Balkans to South Africa. Never in recorded history had war been waged on such a scale, or with such appalling destruction and loss of life. Almost no one foresaw that the introduction of machine guns and rapid-fire artillery would make frontal assaults massacres and cavalry charges suicidal, or that war would be fought in trenches where millions of soldiers faced each other across a three hundred yard no man's land stretching from the English Channel to the Swiss border. After the German army failed to reach Paris in autumn, 1914, both the Allies and the Central Powers dug trenches and settled down to a long siege. To break this military stalemate, both high commands resorted to the strategy of attrition—wearing down your enemy's resistance by killing more of his soldiers than he killed of yours—coupled with tactical offensives to produce a breakthrough.

The stalemated war of attrition periodically exploded into great battles, after which the casualty rolls exceeded the populations of many small cities. Longer battles produced more wounded and dead than many small countries' entire populations. As men fought and died, more men, and even boys, were conscripted, quickly trained, and sent in as replacements. Armies were counted in the millions, and ultimately tens of millions. War on this scale was impossible, unprecedented, unheard of. But it happened, and as a result the world was never the same.

When Lord Grey said, "The lamps are going out all over Europe; we shall not see them lit again in our lifetime," he recognized that the world would not be the same after the war, regardless of who won. Tolkien too lamented the passing of the unspoiled English countryside. "I always knew that it would go, of course, and it did," he said. "Perhaps that is why I loved it all the more."

By the time Tolkien had finished his training with the 13th Reserve Battalion, England had been put on a total war footing. Food was rationed, women were working in munitions factories, the cities were blacked out for fear of naval or zeppelin attacks, a conscription bill was being talked about for the first time, newspapers were censored, and both social and economic pressures had all but destroyed the extended family.

Tolkien fully realized that "each man will do his duty," and took his responsibilities as an officer seriously. But of the patriotic slogans and noble purposes, Tolkien later said, "I was brought up on 'the war to end all wars,' which I didn't believe at the time, and believe even less now." He particularly admired the simple working-class and rustic lads who had volunteered for the army as soon as war had been declared. They were not brave or heroic, and did not want to die, but they saw their duty and did it. "I've always been impressed that we're here, surviving, because of their indomitable courage against impossible odds," Tolkien once said. He also revealed that the single most important passage in *The Lord of the Rings* said that the wheel of the world was turned by the small hand becuase the greater was looking elsewhere, adding that it is turned because it *has* to turn, because it is the daily task. Such men fought under him in his platoon; such men were models for the small, unimaginative, but brave hobbits who did their duty against impossible odds.

On January 8, 1916, Lieutenant Tolkien was transferred from the 13th Reserve Battalion to the 11th Battalion of the Lancashire Fusiliers. Part of the regiment had served in the disastrous Gallipoli campaign, and had returned to England to regroup, rest, and prepare for assignment on the Western Front at Flanders. Tolkien decided to apply his skills in language and communication by becoming the battalion signal officer, and his training was intensified because of imminent departure for the front. There were rumors that some time that year there would be a "final push" toward the long-awaited breakthrough, and indeed the Allied commanders planned a coordinated attack on all fronts during the summer.

However, the German High Command did not run on the Allies' timetable, and decided to initiate their strategy of attrition at the French fortress of Verdun. On February 21, 1916, the Germans concentrated the heaviest artillery barrage in history against this relatively small target, and followed that with fierce infantry assaults. In the words of the German High Command, Verdun had become a "mincing machine" that would "bleed France white." The French were hard pressed to replace their losses, and indeed, army mutinies became a threat (and later a reality) due to the almost suicidal nature of the battle. As a consequence, the French leaders pressed British Field Marshal Haig to accelerate plans for a British counter-offensive to relieve the pressure on Verdun and force the Germans to break off the battle. Haig reluctantly chose a place for the offensive not in Flanders, where it would have had a good chance of success, but on the river Somme, where it was most likely to fail.

Tolkien's battalion received word that they would be leaving their Staffordshire billet for the front at the end of March, 1916. He was granted one final leave, which he used to good purpose by marrying his childhood sweetheart, Edith Mary Bratt, on March 22.

Shortly before Tolkien's twenty-first birthday, he had asked for and reluctantly received permission from his guardian, Father Morgan, to begin corresponding with Edith Mary. Since they had pledged themselves to one another, he automatically assumed that they would become engaged and marry as soon as he took his degree. But it turned out that she had, in her loneliness, become engaged to someone else. Tolkien went to visit her at her Uncle Jessup's house in Cheltenham, and convinced her to marry him instead.

Edith Mary was very active in the Church of England and was not eager to convert to Catholicism as Tolkien wished. But he pressured her into studying with a Warwick parish priest named Father Murphy, and she was received into the Catholic Church in early 1914. This estranged her from her relatives, who were staunch Protestants, and effectively ended what social life she had at Cheltenham. In later years, Edith Mary began to resent her new religion, first becoming a lapsed Catholic and then antagonistic to the church. While she later outgrew her hostility, she did not attend Mass regularly with her husband.

Edith Mary's relatives still disapproved of the match, not so much because Tolkien was a Catholic, but because he was an infantry officer about to leave for the front, and the war so far had produced its greatest number of casualties among junior officers in the field. But the young couple decided to proceed immediately rather than wait until after the war. They were married by Father Murphy at the Catholic Church in Warwick.

Following an abbreviated honeymoon, in Somerset, Tolkien joined his regiment and left for France. Shortly after arriving, his battalion was put in the front line at a small town named Rubempré, about ten miles from Amiens. Trench warfare in World War I was a Dantesque nightmare: rotting corpses in no man's land, intermittent shelling and sniper fire, constant downpours and flooded trenches, and a sea of mud reeking of death. Nighttime forays into no man's land meant daily casualty lists, surprise attacks, and dead comrades. Sleep was impossible, comfort all but forgotten; soldiers suffered from body lice, from drenched and rotted clothing, from swollen feet, from never-ending colds, and from faulty equipment. The field was alternately quiet and cacophonous; hot meals were virtually unknown; and men went weeks without even washing. Forced marches at night from one position to another were common, as were deadly surprise attacks of gas. The full horror of the trenches was captured most vividly by Wilfred Owen, a Midlands poet killed only a week before the armistice, in his poem, *Dulce et Decorum Est:*[2]

> Bent double, like old beggars under sacks,
> Knock-kneed, coughing like hags, we cursed the sludge,
> Till on the haunting flares we turned our backs
> And towards our distant rest began to trudge.
> Men marched asleep. Many had lost their boots
> But limped on, blood-shod. All went lame; all blind;
> Drunk with fatigue; deaf even to the hoots
> Of tired, outstripped Five-Nines that dropped behind.
>
> Gas! Gas! Quick, boys!—An ecstasy of fumbling,
> Fitting the clumsy helmets just in time;
> But someone still was yelling out and stumbling,
> And flound'ring like a man in fire or lime . . .
> Dim, through the misty panes and thick green light,
> As under a green sea, I saw him drowning.

In all my dreams, before my helpless sight,
He plunges at me, guttering, choking, drowning.

If in some smothering dreams you too could pace
Behind the wagon that we flung him in,
And watch the white eyes writhing in his face,
His hanging face, like a devil's sick of sin;
If you could hear, at every jolt, the blood
Come gargling from the froth-corrupted lungs,
Obscene as cancer, bitter as the cud
Of vile, incurable sores on innocent tongues,—
My friend, you would not tell with such high zest
To children ardent for some desperate glory,
The old lie: *Dulce et decorum est*
Pro patria mori.

It is difficult to accept Tolkien's assertion that none of his war experiences directly inspired some of the darker passages in *The Lord of the Rings*. Perhaps the key to resolving this apparent contradiction is that Tolkien did not *intentionally* translate his own war experiences into the book; nonetheless, they are there. For example, Frodo's journey through Moria could have been directly lifted from a 1916 newspaper account of what the Western Front was like:

Dreadful as the Dead Marshes had been, and the arid moors of the Nomen's-land, more loathsome far was the country that the crawling day now slowly unveiled to his shrinking eyes. Even to the Mere of Dead Faces some haggard phantom of green spring would come; but here neither spring nor summer would ever come again. Here nothing lived, not even the leprous growths that feed on rottenness. The gasping pools were choked with ash and crawling muds, sickly white and grey, as if the mountains had vomited the filth of their entrails upon the lands about. High mounds of crushed and powdered rock, great cones of earth fire-blasted and poison-stained, stood like an obscene graveyard in endless rows, slowly revealed in the reluctant light.

As May passed into June, Tolkien's battalion was shifted to the Somme in preparation for the big push that was expected within several months. Already great preparations were being made for the offensive, all at night in order to escape the marauding eye of the German observation planes. Artillery of every description was transported to the Somme by horse-drawn gun carriages, stripped from other divisions along the entire length of the Western Front. Several thousand gun carriages were lined up almost wheel to wheel in the greatest concentration of artillery that the world had ever known. Hundreds of thousands of soldiers were quick-marched to the sector at night and placed under cover by day. Nearby civilians were secretly evacuated to the rear, and their houses and farms used for billets. Countless supplies transported by horse and motorcar were stockpiled under camouflage netting, and great pits were dug to accommodate the expected flood of corpses. Field hospitals were secretly set up, and wood-staked cages were prepared for prisoners. Further back, cavalry divisions hid their horses in the woods, waiting for the infantry to pierce the lines and for the artillery to destroy the German fortifications. Nightly raids into no man's land in search of German prisoners were intensified and guide tapes that were to lead the soldiers to their assigned targets were unwound. New rail lines were laid for bringing up the heavy siege guns and mortars.

By accident or design, Tolkien captures this vast preparation for battle in *The Lord of the Rings:*

> But everywhere he looked he saw the signs of war. The Misty Mountains were crawling like anthills: orcs were issuing out of a thousand holes. Under the boughs of Mirkwood there was deadly strife of Elves and Men and fell beasts. The land of the Beornings was aflame; a cloud was over Moria; smoke rose on the borders of Lórien.
>
> Horsemen were galloping on the grass of Rohan; wolves poured from Isengard. From the havens of Harad ships of war put out to sea; and out of the East Men were moving endlessly: swordsmen, spearmen, bowmen upon horses, chariots of chieftains and laden wains. All the power of the Dark Lord was in motion.

C. S. Lewis noted the astonishing similarity of that, as well as other passages from *The Lord of the Rings,* to his experiences in the trenches: ''This war had the very quality of the war my generation knew. It is all here: the endless, unintelligible movement, the sinister quiet of the front when 'everything is now ready,' the flying civilians, the lively, vivid friendships, the background of something like despair and the merry foreground, and such heavensent windfalls as a cache of choice tobacco 'salvaged' from a ruin.''

It is also difficult to dismiss the marked similarity between the orcs and the German soldiers, especially the SS elite in World War II. Even the word ''orc''[3] denotes hell or death, and the SS emblem was a silver death's head. Tolkien denied that the Germans became the orcs, stating that there were absolutely no parallels between the orcs' beaked helmets, their murderous, treacherous ways, and the Germans' spiked helmets and reputation for ruthlessness. Nevertheless, he once conceded that one might easily infer from reading their description in *The Lord of the Rings* that the orcs were really Germans. ''But as I would say somewhere, even the goblins weren't evil to begin with. They were corrupted. I've never had these sort of feelings about the Germans. I'm very anti that kind of thing.''

Just before the British army began its artillery barrage on July 1, 1916, the High Command went to great lengths to convince every man at the front that the offense would really be a ''cakewalk,'' since they confidently expected the intensive, sustained barrage of artillery to destroy the German trenches, kill the enemy troops, cut the barbed wire in no man's land, and prevent the German High Command from rushing in reinforcements in time. There would be no shortage of artillery shells, as there had been the year before, and the offensive would be greatly aided by the introduction of a new secret weapon: the tank. The enemy's planes would be driven from the skies by a superior air force; each company would have one or more of the new, portable Lewis machineguns; and every soldier who went ''over the top'' would carry at least fifty pounds of ammunition, supplies, rations, trench-digging equipment, and other materials that would eliminate the necessity for immediately establishing time-consuming supply lines. Once the enemy lines were breeched and wooden spans were constructed over the trenches, the waiting cavalry divisions would cross over and capture the German Crown Prince's headquarters at Baupaume, twenty miles north of the front. From that point onward, no one in the Allied High Command really had any clear-cut idea of how or where to proceed, but apparently they dismissed their lack of planning by believing that the breakthrough itself would force the Kaiser to sue for peace.

Tolkien was only one of thousands of British soldiers crouching in their trenches on the evening of June 23 when the barrage began. During the next seven days, hundreds of thousands of shells rained continuously on German positions along the twenty-mile Somme front. Though the attack had not been entirely unexpected by the enemy, the severity of the artillery barrage forced the Germans to begin withdrawing troops from Verdun, shifting them to the Somme.

That was the only objective that was reached in the entire Battle of the Somme.

All the ministers, field marshals, and generals had been dead wrong. For one thing, the wrong *kind* of artillery shells were generally used (shrapnel rather than high explosive), and so failed to destroy the German bunkers or cut the barbed wire. The sustained barrage on no man's land was *too* intense, and only served to create more mud, which rendered the tanks completely useless. The German gun emplacements behind the line were virtually untouched, and reserves and reinforcements could be rapidly transported by rail to the sector. But the worst miscalculation was in loading down each soldier with too much equipment.

Seconds after the final barrage was lifted, hundreds of thousands of Tommies stormed over the top and began the life-and-death foot race across no man's land. As they tried to traverse the impossibly mired field between the two trenches, the German soldiers who had survived the bombardment desperately scrambled out of the deep concrete bunkers to set up their Maxim machine guns. The race lasted less than 120 seconds, but at most sectors along the twenty-mile front the British lost, and lost terribly.

Because of the mud, the mangled or missing leader tapes, the heavy backpacks, and the uncut wire, the Germans got into position first and raked the front lines with deadly, methodical machinegun fire. Thousands became "hung up on the wire," which the Germans had laid so that the British would be "herded" into deadly enfilade fire. In minutes, entire battalions were wiped out; the total number of British casualties that day was over 50,000—more than any other single day of warfare before or since. Such slaughter was almost incomprehensible, and when the first casualty figures came into headquarters, they were not believed.

Lieutenant Tolkien and his battalion had not fought in that first day of slaughter, but had been held in reserve in a rear area at Bouzincourt. They did not go into action until a week later, when the battlefield had turned into a veritable charnel house. But Tolkien remained active in the Somme offensive for months afterward, both in the front lines and in a rest area. Years later, he recalled the experience with levity, when he was extolling the virtues of thatched cottages: "People still love thatched houses; they pretend it's because they're cool in summer and warm in winter, and they'll even pay a bit of extra insurance. We found German trenches which were often very habitable indeed except that, when we reached them, they faced the wrong way about."

On the first evening following the July attack, those few companies that had captured the first line of German trenches were too tired to press their advantage. Communications were virtually nonexistent. None of the generals had any idea which sectors had been captured, and therefore could not supply or reinforce the successful troops. Elsewhere, the slaughter continued, despite impassioned pleas from the field commanders to break off the battle. Almost no prisoners were captured, and wounded survivors straggled back over a period of days. Each hour gave the Germans more strength, and made the British occupation of captured enemy trenches increasingly untenable. The British eventually abandoned the captured trenches and the battalions retreated to their own lines under the cover of darkness. Every British tank that had been thrown into the battle was either destroyed or had to be abandoned to the mud.

As each day passed and the battle continued, thousands were killed or wounded. Still the generals would not break off, so utterly deceived were they about their "success." They simply didn't believe the casualty figures. Both armies attacked and counterattacked throughout the summer and autumn. France had been mauled so badly at Verdun that she could not assist the British in any way. Finally, on November 19, 1916, the British broke off the battle and the Somme once again fell quiet.

The politicians hailed the Somme as a great victory, since it convinced them that Germany was beaten and would shortly sue for peace. To the soldiers who fought in the Somme, it was a defeat beyond belief. The British suffered more than 600,000 casualties, and the Germans approximately the same. During that battle, "Britain's finest flower of young manhood" had been slaughtered; an entire generation of the best and the brightest was shattered for a few yards of mud. England was not to launch another major offensive during the war; indeed, Field Marshal Montgomery's ultracautious military strategy during World War II is directly attributable to the great losses incurred on the Somme.

Although hundreds of thousands of Tolkien's countrymen—including almost all of his school and university friends—had been killed or wounded on the Somme, Tolkien was spared injury. He won no medals, commendations, dispatch mentions, or promotions, but he had done his duty to the best of his ability. As summer turned to autumn, the weather turned cold—colder than any year in memory. Many froze to death in October and November with the unexpected onslaught of a premature winter. Many others, weakened by the cold, the damp, and fatigue, succumbed to serious illnesses—the two most debilitating were influenza and trench fever. In late October, Lt. Tolkien contracted a serious case of trench fever while serving in the front line near Beauval.

Trench fever is a form of rickettsia, a term used to describe a group of bacteria, carried by fleas, ticks, mites and body lice, that cause serious disease in both humans and other mammals. The most common form of rickettsia are Rocky Mountain spotted fever, typhus fever, Q fever, and trench fever. Trench fever was virtually unknown before the First World War, but soon manifested itself on a large scale among the lice-ridden, water-soaked soldiers at the front. No one—not even the generals—was immune to body lice, and every soldier who was rotated out of the front line for rest was first fumigated and deloused. Some body lice carried the rickettsia bacteria, which infected thousands of soldiers on both sides.

The symptoms of trench fever closely resemble those of flu and typhus: high fever, body rash, mental disorientation, headache, small ulcers around the louse bites, and prostration. It is rarely fatal, but its victims become extremely ill, and convalescence takes months in bed, followed by extended periods of weakness. The organism itself may remain in the body for many years afterward, and cause periodic flare-ups.

Tolkien was evacuated from Beauval in November, and then transported to a hospital ship[4] for the trip back to England. On November 9, 1916, he arrived back in Birmingham at the First Southern General Hospital, which had been converted for the military sick and wounded. Tolkien's case was particularly grave, and he had to spend many months in and out of the hospital. Even after being discharged, he was never again assigned to a combat battalion.

But Tolkien used that time to good purpose by writing a long, complex story that would provide the mythology for his Elvish language. Contrary to one popular belief, Tolkien did not write *The Lord of the Rings* in the trenches; indeed, he wrote virtually nothing in the trenches. About his supposed writing at that time, Tolkien replied, ''That's all spoof. You might scribble something on the back of an envelope and shove it in your pocket, but that's all. You couldn't write. . . . You'd be crouching down among the flies and filth.''

The story that Tolkien began writing in the hospital was about three mystic gems of power called the silmarilli that were wrested from the Iron Crown of Morgoth in the First Age of Middle-earth. *The Silmarillion*, as Tolkien called it, became the ''prequel'' to *The Lord of the Rings*—a sort of ''Paradise Lost,'' or the end of the age of innocence. Tolkien spent much time in 1916 and 1917 writing *The Silmarillion*, apparently finishing a first rough draft some time in 1918 (it was much shorter than *The Lord of the Rings*, and lacked an appendix). By the time he had completed the story, it also spanned the Second Age of Middle-earth and the rise of Sauron. Many years later, when Tolkien started revising *The Silmarillion*, he had to modify the story in order to conform with *The Lord of the Rings*, but the story itself had been written almost twenty years before Tolkien's most famous work was begun. While recovering, Tolkien also decided to devote his life to the study of languages and to return to academic life once the war was over.

Tolkien was promoted to temporary first lieutenant in January, 1917, while in the hospital. Some months later, he was released and attached to the 3rd Reserve Battalion of the Lancashire Fusiliers. He did not wish to, nor did he return to active service in France. In November, 1917, he became a father for the first time when his wife Edith had a baby boy. They named the infant John Francis Reuel Tolkien—Francis in honor of Father Francis Xavier Morgan and Reuel a continuation of the family tradition.

In October, 1918, Tolkien was released from active service, and the following month he was employed by the Appointments Department of the Ministry of Labor, which handled all civilian employment in the United

Kingdom. The war officially ended about two weeks after he started his new position, but it would be several years before England returned to a prewar footing. Prime Minister David Lloyd-George immediately called for a national election (later called the khaki election, because so many of the voters were still in uniform) in order to ride on the crest of popularity; Spanish influenza began to sweep the world, and within two years, more than twenty million victims would die from the pestilence; the Irish question, which had broken out in the abortive Easter Uprising in 1916, was again threatening to erupt in national violence; and the Allies pressed their victory home by issuing the strong anti-German Versailles Treaty, which helped create postwar problems in Germany. Millions of ex-servicemen returned home, war-weary, idealistic but cynical, victorious and yet vanquished, since the world they had known before going off to the front had passed away, a victim of the times. Tolkien's beloved Sarehole had been absorbed into the city of Birmingham. William Morris' small motor works at Cowley outside Oxford, which in 1912 had begun manufacturing the famous bull-nosed Morris motorcar (the English equivalent of the Model T Ford), had become a large war factory and was beginning to gear up for large-scale postwar automobile manufacturing.

New voices in poetry and literature, like Eliot, Pound, and Joyce were being heard, and audiences were no longer scandalized by the new music of Satie, Berg, Stravinsky, and Schoenberg, or the art of Dali, Klee, or Picasso. Short skirts and wild parties, trade unions and the Labor Party Irish revolutionaries and women's suffrage were all part of postwar Britain. So too were increased industrialization, the building of motor roads, the end of the great medieval forests, ever-growing towns and cities, and a rapidly changing system of social values.

Tolkien worked for the Ministry of Labor in Oxford until the summer of 1919, anxious all the while to get away from both government and the military. He apparently took no joy in his war service, and did not claim the medals and battle ribbons that were his by virtue of having served on the Western Front during the Somme offensive; nor did he ever apply for a disability award in later years, although his trench fever qualified him for one. Apparently he had "done his duty," wished nothing in return, and did not want to be reminded of the horrors of trench warfare or of losing almost all his close friends during the four long years of war. When his time was up, Tolkien applied for a discharge and was finally released from military service on July 16, 1919. But the final formality didn't occur until November 3, 1920, when he officially relinquished his commission, retaining the permanent rank of first lieutenant.

The First World War was probably the single most important experience in Tolkien's life. It certainly fired his imagination to a degree not previously achieved and provided valuable experience and insights that were later incorporated into his mature works. In his famous 1938 Andrew Lang Lecture, "On Fairy-Stories," Tolkien himself appreciated that "a real taste for fairy stories was wakened by philology on the threshold of manhood, and quickened to full life by war." The war became a frequent point of reference in his lectures and conversations with students right up into the '50s, when the more recent horrors of the Second World War eclipsed it in interest.

Apparently the war left invisible scars on Tolkien, scars that did not manifest themselves in the sort of despair, melancholy, or cynical hedonism that marked many others of his generation, but caused him to withdraw from the outside world. He returned to a cloistered academic life and did not easily enter into close, personal friendships with his neighbors and colleagues. Nor did he seek fame or recognition outside a small circle of professional philologists, academic advancement to the degree of which he was capable, or quick and frequent publication of his stories, translations, and scholarly papers.

According to Professor Roger Sale, Tolkien "seems to have withdrawn from the wounds and terrors of the war and all we think of modern life." Sale also perceived that he had been "ravaged by the war, but in his case there was no immediate or direct response . . . . Tolkien has always spoken . . . as though only madmen or fools would contemplate the twentieth century without horror. Yet during the long years of his withdrawal, his imagination was coming to terms with the inescapable fact that he is a modern man and not an elf or an ent."

In his book *Modern Heroism,* Professor Sale attempts to demonstrate how writers like Tolkien overcame the horrors of the twentieth century by turning to myths and heroic acts of the past. According to Sale, if "despair is created by the sense that history has overwhelmed the world, then heroism will be created in defiance of that same history." Tolkien was one who managed eventually to overcome his war experiences and the grim realities of the postwar world through will power, imagination, and writing.

THE SCHOLAR
1919–1925 🚯🚰

EX-LIEUTENANT RONALD TOLKIEN returned with his small family to Oxford in 1918 to resume his interrupted academic career. Like other brilliant scholars who had been undergraduates at the Oxford colleges before the war, Tolkien had hoped to obtain one of the coveted fellowships in either Anglo-Saxon or English Literature. Competition was unusually stiff, however, and Tolkien elected instead to accept occasional work as a teacher and tutor for the English School.

The university had suffered greatly during the war, and of the 3,000 members in 1914, 2,700 had been killed.[1] In 1917, the university had dropped to a mere 350, an all time low, lower even than when the Black Plague had decimated Oxford at the end of the Middle Ages. By war's end, the academic body of the university consisted entirely of the elderly, unfit, and infirm, and the tiny student population at the colleges were either invalided veterans, neutral foreigners, or those too handicapped to serve in civilian positions.[2]

After a brief residence at 50 St. John's Street, the Tolkiens moved to an upstairs flat at 1 Alfred Street, over a shop facing Christ Church College. Ironically, the site was near the spot where William Morris once had a bicycle shop. While Tolkien worked for the English School, many of his future friends and associates who had also served in the army returned to Oxford as "mature students." They included C.S. Lewis at University College, Owen Barfield at Waldham College, Hugo Dyson at Exeter College, Gervase Mathew at Balliol College, and Nevill Coghill at Exeter College. Tolkien first met Coghill at the English School building near Merton College when the latter approached him to ask if he would consent to read a paper to an essay club.

According to Coghill, "He was senior to me, having taken his degree already, and I was only a demobilized second lieutenant, and I think he was a demobilized captain[3]—I'm not sure about his rank. I was the secretary of the college essay club, and I was deputed to invite him to read us a paper, because we knew that he was very distinguished as a philologist. So I went up to him one morning, not having been introduced to him before, and I said 'Oh Captain Tolkien, would you be so kind as to read a paper for us to the essay club?' And he said to me in his abrupt, quick-spoken manner, 'Yes, certainly.' It was extraordinarily difficult to hear what he said sometimes because he spoke so rapidly and without biting off words at the end. So I said 'Well, what will be the title of your essay,' and he said hastily, 'The Foragonglin.' And I said 'I beg your pardon,' and he said, 'The Foragonglin.' So I said 'The Follogonglin,' and he said 'Yes, that's right,' so I wrote it down, never having heard of the Gondolin[4] you see, and I spent a week trying to swot up and find out what Gondolin was, but there was no mention of it anywhere.''

It was somewhat typical of Tolkien to neglect to tell Coghill that it was a made-up word. In later years, both as an active professor and a retired celebrity, he often automatically assumed that his audience knew everything about the subject on which he was talking. For example, he once told William Cater of the *Sunday Times* in an offhanded way that ''of course the Elvish language is deliberately made to follow to some extent the same type of changes that turned primitive Celtic into Welsh.'' The journalist's reply—in print, and not to Tolkien's face—was, ''Of course!''

Tolkien was well remembered by one of his old tutors at Oxford, W.A. Craigie. Craigie had been elected to the chair of Bosworth and Rawlinson Professor of Anglo-Saxon in 1916, and was one of four co-editors of the *Oxford English Dictionary*. Craigie offered Tolkien a position as a junior editor on the project, the purpose of which was to create the most extensive and definitive dictionary of the English language. Tolkien accepted, and assisted with the additions, revisions, refinements, and selections of upwards of two million excerpts from almost five million submissions. It was a massive work that had been going on since 1878, and required the maximum skills of philologists and other scholars. To be appointed to such a responsible position—especially for one as young as Tolkien, who was still in his twenties—was a singular honor and attested to the high reputation he had obtained as an undergraduate.

Apparently Tolkien greatly enjoyed contributing to the *Oxford English Dictionary*. He was probably responsible for checking many of the entries that had their origins in Anglo-Saxon. As a philologist, he had to carefully construct the definitions and double check that the etymologies were, as far as could be discerned, correct. Sometimes this scholarly exercise became a spirited guessing game, and in many instances scholarship had to give way to speculation. Years later, Tolkien wrote a delightful tale called *Farmer Giles of Ham* that poked gentle fun at philologists in general, and all those (including himself) who worked on the dictionary in particular. For example, while *Farmer Giles of Ham* is set in a time and place not unlike pre-Arthurian England, Tolkien uses a seventeenth century blunderbuss (an obvious anachronism), and then refers those readers who might inquire what a blunderbuss is to the "Four Wise Clerks of Oxenford," a reference, of course, to Craigie, Murray, Bradley, and Onions, the Dictionary's editors. The definition that the "Four Wise Clerks" give is, incidentally, a word-for-word quotation from the *Oxford English Dictionary*; it may well be some inside joke among Tolkien and his friends, or just as likely this could have been one of the many definitions that Tolkien himself wrote.

Another example of Tolkien's satirization of those who worked on the dictionary—as well as some of the more speculative scholars who are wont to stretch a point to justify their theories—is in the forward to *Farmer Giles of Ham*. There he promises to illuminate "the origin of some difficult place-names" in the text. One such name was the river Thames. Tolkien explained that one of Farmer Giles's titles was *"Dominus de Domite Serpente,* which is the vulgar Lord of the Tame Worm, or shortly of Tame."* Giles was also known as the Lord of Ham. Therefore, the "natural confusion" between Ham and Tame gave rise to *Thame,* "for Thame with an *h* is a folly without warrant." As author, Tolkien disclaims responsibility in the matter, saying that he received the etymology of such words from those "learned in such matters."*[5]

In 1919, Tolkien was elected an M.A. of the university. Unlike the master of arts or master of science degrees at American colleges and universities, the Oxbridge M.A. degree is honorary, and is usually bestowed upon graduates of the colleges who remain in residence for a total of five years. It is also awarded—again, on an honorary basis—to faithful employees of the university, as well as to professors and fellows resident at Oxford who have taken their degrees at other universities. The Oxbridge M.A. usually signifies that the person to whom the degree is granted has been elevated from a junior to a senior member of the university. Prior to 1926, M.A.'s had considerable voting power, and therefore authority over the policies of the university. The only real authority vested in Oxford M.A.'s today has to do with the nomination and election of a candidate to the poetry chair.

Since Tolkien was not attached to any college, he was granted the M.A. degree by the University of Oxford (known in that context as Oxon). The M.A. Oxon added a certain legitimacy to the work he had been doing as a mere junior member of the university; such responsibilities were usually only granted to those with M.A.'s or above. Incidentally, Tolkien never applied for acceptance to a Ph.D. program, possibly because he realized that with a wife and baby he could never meet his family responsibilities on the modest grant he would have been allowed. Therefore he never received a Ph.D., and for many years could not be properly addressed as Dr. Tolkien. It wasn't until after his first honorary doctorate in 1954 that he could have used the title, although he never did. He preferred being called professor instead.

Tolkien continued to work with Craigie on the dictionary project for many months. He seems to have abandoned writing at the time, but pursued his own studies on Midlands literature, especially *Beowulf*, which is generally acknowledged as the oldest existing nonecclesiastical work in English. By that time he could read, write, or speak most of the Romance languages, Anglo-Saxon, Welsh, Finnish, Icelandic, German, Old German, Gothic, and several other obsolete tongues, and had begun to build a reputation as a linguist as well as a philologist.

In October, 1920, the Tolkiens' second son was born. They named him Michael Hilary Reuel Tolkien, the middle name in honor of Tolkien's younger brother Hilary, who had become an apple farmer in the Midlands shortly after the war. By 1921, with work on the dictionary almost completed, Tolkien began to inquire about vacant fellowships and other academic posts. Around that time, a tragic summer accident in the industrial city of Leeds was to have a profound effect on Tolkien's future. F. W. Moorman, the popular Professor of English Lanuage at the University of Leeds, accidentally drowned while on holiday. This left a gap in the English language department of the university, one that could only be filled by a philologist who was also a scholar of Anglo-Saxon literature. In 1921, Tolkien was offered a post as Reader of the English Language at the University of Leeds, which he accepted.

Leeds, along with Sheffield, Birmingham, Nottingham, and Manchester, came to prominence during the Industrial Revolution and mushroomed to international importance during the nineteenth century. Leeds became known primarily for its textile manufacturing—it was the first city in England to install the new spinning jennies in the early nineteenth century—but it was also noted for iron, coal, metal foundries, tool manufacturing, and steam engines. The city is located in Yorkshire, on the edge of the moorlands, about 185 miles north of London. Like Yorkshire, it is landlocked, and almost equidistant between the Atlantic Ocean and the English Channel.

At first Tolkien lived in a small bedsitter and commuted to Oxford on the weekends. Later, he, his wife, and two small sons took a small Victorian terrace house in a cul-de-sac at 11 St. Mark's Terrace near the university, from which he was able to walk to his classes.

The university was relatively new, one of the "redbrick" universities established during the nineteenth and twentieth centuries throughout England. It had grown out of the old Yorkshire College, which was founded in 1875 to provide instruction in arts and sciences that were applicable to manufacturing, engineering, and mining. In 1887, Yorkshire College became one of the constituent colleges of the new Victoria University in Manchester, which had large endowments from the factories and industries in Leeds and surrounding towns. In 1904, the University of Leeds was incorporated, absorbing Yorkshire College and creating nontechnical departments for the humanities and the classics.

When Tolkien joined the faculty as Reader of the English Language in autumn, 1921, the English department was heavily oriented towards literature rather than language. Tolkien set out to correct this imbalance. During his four years at the University of Leeds, he was responsible for establishing an interest in philology and languages within the English department and a dialogue of cooperation with other departments teaching foreign languages and literature. He was an innovator rather than an administrator, but the ideas he put into practice set the tenor for the teaching of English language and literature at the university for the next few decades.

During Tolkien's tenure at Leeds, the Ph.D. program was established for the first time. As reader and later professor, he was responsible for planning the advanced degree program. This was, of course, ironic, since he did not have a doctor of philosophy degree himself. In addition, he was one of the youngest readers—and later, the youngest professor[6]—in the entire university. In the early 1920s, the English department at Leeds was small and close-knit. The Tolkiens were on social terms with most members of the faculty and a few became life-long friends.

After 1924, there were two professors: Tolkien and G. S. Gordon. Gordon was the professor of English literature, but he later accepted a chair at Oxford and ultimately was elected Vice-Chancellor of the University of Oxford. Another fellow reader was Bruce Dickins, who became the professor of English language after the tragic death of Tolkien's successor, E. V. Gordon; ultimately, he was elected to a chair at the University of Cambridge. A close friend in the department was Lascelles Abercrombie, with whom Tolkien collaborated until Abercrombie's death in 1938. Others at the university with whom Tolkien was friendly included F. P. Wilson and W. R. Childe of the English department, Dr. Gunnell and Professor Paul Barbier of the French department, and the Vice-Chancellor, J. B. Baillie.

Tolkien's tenure at Leeds was remarkable in many respects, but especially for the quality of his pupils. Quite a number of his honors students were invited to join the Leeds faculty after graduation or completion of their Ph.D.'s, and most later went on to become professors or tutors at Leeds and other universities throughout the world. Those students and later colleagues included T.V. Benn, J.I.M. Stewart,[7] Ida Pickles, Geoffrey Woledge, Brian Woledge, Albery Hugh Smith, and Tolkien's star pupil, protégé, and later collaborator, E.V. Gordon. Gordon, a brilliant research student[8] who received his Ph.D. while Tolkien was still a reader, was also a philologist and a scholar of medieval texts. Even as a student he was an acknowledged authority on medieval Welsh, and Tolkien was part of a small informal group that studied the subject under Gordon. He joined the faculty as an assistant lecturer, but a measure of his genius is that when Tolkien stepped down and left for Oxford in 1925, Gordon was promoted over the heads of the older lecturers to the chair in English language. Gordon married one of his fellow students, Ida Pickles, shortly after they both received their Ph.D.'s.

It was in collaboration with Gordon that Tolkien achieved his first international recognition as a philologist. Several years before accepting the academic post at Leeds, Tolkien had collaborated with one of his former Oxford tutors, Kenneth Sisam. Sisam had been preparing a book entitled *Fourteenth Century Verse and Prose* and, remembering Tolkien's extensive knowledge of Anglo-Saxon vocabulary, as well as his work on the *Oxford English Dictionary,* he asked Tolkien if he would write a paper that would provide a basic Middle English vocabulary for use with his own book. Tolkien enthusiastically agreed, and published *A Middle English Vocabulary* in 1922.[9] Both Sisam's and Tolkien's works were successful in academic communities, and Tolkien achieved a fine reputation among English scholars for his brilliance and extensive knowledge. But the work that established him internationally was that done in collaboration with Gordon, *Sir Gawain and the Green Knight.*

Arthurian legend and the myth of the Holy Grail had always fascinated Tolkien. As a child, he had devoured Sir Thomas Malory's *Morte d'Arthur,*[10] and later he attempted to write—but did not finish—an epic poem of his own on the Arthurian legends. The myth and legend surrounding Sir Gawain, knight of King Arthur's Round Table at Camelot, apparently stretches back to Celtic times, and has surfaced in varying forms through the centuries in France, Italy, and even Scandinavia. Gawain was also transformed in some versions into Galahad or Perceval (who became the hero in Richard Wagner's opera *Parsifal*). Chaucer spoke of the Gawain legend as coming ''again out of faërie,'' which coincided with Tolkien's own opinions on the subject.

The most famous Gawain work in the English language is the fourteenth century romance, *Sir Gawain and the Green Knight.* The romance is by an anonymous Midlands writer, a contemporary of Chaucer, who was evidently highly educated and quite literate. The same manuscript containing *Gawain* also includes two alliterative poems, *Patience and Purity* and *Pearl*,[11] which are believed to have been written by the same author. *Gawain* is an extraordinarily rich and sophisticated work, colored with many foreign and English dialects, and utilizing an extensive vocabulary. There are elements in the text that reflect both Irish and Welsh mythic influence as well. The original manuscript (which was probably a copy) that Tolkien and Gordon worked from had a difficult text and required extensive deciphering and editing. The result of this fruitful collaboration was the production of the definitive text of *Sir Gawain and the Green Knight,* published by the Oxford University Press in 1925. Their Middle English text of *Gawain* became the standard version of the famous poem, and it is still used in most American and British universities. Tolkien and Gordon made an indelible mark on the academic world with the publication of *Gawain,* and it probably played a major part in both men's subsequent rapid professional advances. Many years later, Tolkien himself translated his own edition of *Sir Gawain and the Green Knight* into modern English.[12]

At Leeds, the English department, joined by members of other faculties who taught languages, met regularly to discuss methodology, staff problems, and plans for progress. But after work, the language specialists—and their more advanced students—held periodic informal dinner parties, replete with poetry recitations, songs, and general merrymaking. Tolkien's humor and scholarship dominated these delightful parties, both at Leeds and later at Oxford. On one occasion, he handed out mimeographed sheets with songs he had written in Gothic, Icelandic, Middle Scots, Anglo-Saxon, and of course English. One was written in delightfully atrocious doggerel and began ''A troll sat alone, on his seat of stone, and munched a bare old bone. . . .'' Tolkien persuaded his colleagues to join him in singing these songs, a practice that pleased him so much that he continued to compose songs for his friends throughout his entire academic career. At another party, Tolkien wrote a song jeering the students and lecturers of ''Scheme A,'' the honors group that elected to concentrate on Old French rather than Old English (which was ''Scheme B''). Eventually these songs were collected into a departmental song sheet, which unfortunately was never published.[13] Geoffrey Woledge, one of Tolkien's students who later joined the Leeds faculty, remembers one departmental dinner in which ''it fell to me to propose the health of the staff, and I based my speech on an imaginary Latin manuscript which I said I had found. Tolk (as we always called him)[14] was called on for reply and began '*I was going to find a manuscript, but Mr. Woledge has found one, so I must have had a dream.*'' At still another dinner, Tolkien composed and read a long, rambling poem that consisted of a series of puns on the names of his colleagues.

As a lecturer, Tolkien was both popular and effective—although he was often inarticulate and incomprehensible. At Leeds, the English department was entirely too small to be able to give private one-to-one tutorials (the backbone of the Oxbridge system), but this deficiency in individual instruction was in part compensated by the small, intimate, and often informal lectures and seminars. Tolkien's classes sometimes had as few as two students, although the average seems to have been about twelve. As reader and later professor, Tolkien took charge of the ''Scheme B'' honors program in Anglo-Saxon, but his classes also included students from ''Scheme A.'' Perhaps his most important and memorable seminars were those at which he read, translated, and interpreted Old English texts, especially *Beowulf*. While at Leeds, Tolkien gave two-year honors courses in *Beowulf* to both ''Scheme A'' and ''Scheme B'' students for one hour each week; he later continued the same seminars at Oxford.[15]

According to T.V. Benn, one of Tolkien's early students and later a professor at Leeds himself, ''if you have listened to his lectures, and forgotten them, but not him, you cannot talk of a Tolkien freed from his *Beowulf*.'' ''It was mostly a line-by-line commentary—sometimes barely audible,'' recalls Geoffrey Woledge, another student who later joined the Leeds faculty. ''It was generally found very wearisome; I generally sat at the back, talked in whispers to my neighbors, or wrote poetry or letters. Nevertheless, in after years I have come to think that the most valuable thing I owe to my university teachers was his teaching, not indeed of the texts he was lecturing on, but of the way in which antiquarian scholarship can be used to illuminate literature.''

''Tolk'' was well liked by his students. His manner might be described as humorously informal rather than academically aloof. J.I.M. Stewart said that ''he could turn a lecture room into a mead hall in which he was the bard and we were the feasting, listening guests.'' According to David Abercrombie, ''with his striking good looks, his elegance, his wit and his charm he was, of course, an influential figure as far as his students were concerned.'' Typical of Tolkien in those days—indeed, during his tenure at Oxford as well—was his friendly, almost puckish attitude toward his students. ''Once, he had not arrived at the lecture room five minutes after the lecture should have started,''[16] recalled Geoffrey Woledge, ''and I and two friends decided to spend an hour in a neighboring pub; as we were nearing the end of the corridor leading from the lecture room, he suddenly appeared around the corner. We stopped in some confusion, but he waved his class register cheerily, said 'Shall I mark you absent?' and passed on, leaving us to pursue our quest for refreshment.''

''Tolkien was liked as a lecturer,'' commented T.V. Benn. ''He was not eloquent, but quiet and factual and kindly. Fewer than a dozen of us, in 1920 to 1923, taking the three-year course at the University of Leeds (''Double Honors'') in English and French, joined the weekly English honors group for *Beowulf. Beowulf* was, as we saw at a glance, a menace and a challenge; the bloodthirsty text was rather an occasion for patient comment, but more than a philological problem. My reaction was to buy a translation of the *Beowulf* and concoct my own literal translation with its help. Our standard was low, but we never feared that Tolkien would mark us down.'' Benn's experience was common among Tolkien's students; he would be as patient as possible, sharing his scholarship with anyone who asked for his assistance. Through the years, Tolkien helped his students and junior colleagues write and rewrite papers, theses, and books, and gave them advice and encouragement—yet he never claimed credit for himself. It was an unusual practice in the competitive environment of academia. One student praised Tolkien because he ''took endless pains with his students, helped them so much that work they published . . . was really his own. Yet he never took credit for this, only pleasure for his pupils.''

Tolkien had probably been aware of, but not overly concerned by his noticeable weaknesses as a lecturer. Years after he retired, Tolkien explained that part of his speech problems came from an injured tongue he had received while playing rugby at the King Edward School. But since his contemporaries recall that he was difficult to understand even before he was hurt, it seems likely that he was searching for an excuse rather than an explanation. In any case, he did little in the following years to improve his delivery, but he constantly introduced new and challenging ways to make scholarship more interesting to his students. For example, crossword puzzles were just coming into vogue in England during the early 1920s, and Tolkien appropriated the popular format for his own purposes. He amused his students by giving them assignments to complete Anglo-Saxon crossword puzzles he had invented. (Tolkien tried to write crossword puzzles in Gothic, but abandoned the project when he decided that there wasn't enough vocabulary to make it worthwhile.) He even had his students *sing* their lessons on occasion, to everyone's enjoyment. Often, the lecture was abandoned in favor of a spirited debate on any subject that happened to strike his fancy.

At Leeds, Tolkien was apparently more open and informal than he was in later life at Oxford; he and his wife enjoyed an active social life that intertwined with the younger readers and instructors of the university. After the Tolkiens returned to Oxford, Edith Mary declined to become socially involved with her husband's colleagues. Apparently she was acutely aware of her academic and intellectual deficiencies, and did not share any of her husband's enthusiasm for scholarship or culture. But at Leeds she was open and friendly.

Tolkien was a keen sportsman, and enjoyed playing tennis and fives[17] with his colleagues. Lunchtime for his crowd was an enjoyable ritual, during which they would retire to a local pub for sandwiches and beer. According to several students who were privileged to be invited to lunch with Tolkien and his friends, the young reader greatly enjoyed imbibing prodigious amounts of beer, telling jokes, and puffing away on his pipe. He often invited students to his house, where they were likely to catch sight of him working away, sitting in an armchair by the fireplace with books and papers spread over a large tray propped on his knees. More often than not, while Tolkien worked his two small boys would be playing on the floor. The commotion apparently did not bother him in the least.

In those years Tolkien amused his sons by telling them fairy stories; not fairy stories read from a book, but tales Tolkien made up himself. Actually, inventing fairy stories for one's children was a favorite Victorian pastime among upper-middle-class men. A banker named Kenneth Grahame told his son animal stories, one of which later became *The Wind in the Willows*. A Scottish playwright named James Barrie amused his children by telling them tales about Peter Pan and a never-never land where people could fly. And a shy, bachelor Oxford don named Charles Dodgson entertained the three children of a married friend with stories as they poled up the Cherwell towards the village of Godstow. One of the children was Alice, and she became immortalized in *Alice in Wonderland*.[18] Some of the tales Tolkien told were undoubtedly variations of the sagas, epics, tales, and fairy stories that his years of reading and professional interests had produced. On the other hand, it appears that some of them were wholly original, since Tolkien mentioned many years later that ''stories seem to germinate like snowflakes around a piece of dust.'' One critic has confidently announced that a number of these early fairy stories had been written down and still exist. If this is so, they may well be published at some time in the future.

Tolkien did publish several poems, stories, and papers in a university weekly named *Poetry and Audience,* and later, in a book entitled *A Northern Venture* (1923). In the latter, he contributed a total of six pages of poetry, bearing such titles as ''The Eadigan Saelidan,'' ''Why the Man in the Moon came down too soon,''[19] and ''Enigmata Saxonica nuper inventa duo.''

In 1924, at the age of 32, Tolkien was appointed professor of English language, a position created especially for him. The Leeds University Vice Chancellor, Michael Chandler, promised to create a brand-new chair of English Language especially for Tolkien. This move was not only to reward Tolkien's great contribution to the English Department, but apparently to also give him an incentive to remain at Leeds. (It was known that Tolkien had been deeply disappointed when his colleague Lascelles Abercrombie had been appointed Professor of English Language in 1922, succeeding George Gordon; Tolkien had hoped to be the new Professor of English Language. Chandler knew that Tolkien had been searching for a new academic position in England or South Africa.) Tolkien thus became the youngest professor in the entire university.

He also became a father for the third time when another son, Christopher Reuel Tolkien, was born in November. Tolkien was a very loving and attentive father, and considered himself lucky to have been at home every night to see his children and tell them stories at bedtime. Tolkien spent a great deal of time at home playing with his sons, or watching them play as he worked. An intimate account of Tolkien at home is given by his son Michael, who at present is headmaster at a Jesuit boarding school in Lancashire.

''My earliest memories of him—I am his second son, and was born in Oxford in 1920—was of a unique adult, the only grown-up who appeared to take my childish comments and questions with complete seriousness. Whatever interested me seemed invariably to interest him more, even my earliest efforts to talk. Not many years ago he showed me a battered notebook in which he had carefully set down the words I applied to every object I saw. As a philologist he was fascinated by the fact that all words I used ended in -ng: for example, lalang (light), gong (lampshade), papang (pipe), this last uttered as I removed his pipe from his mouth and inserted it in my own.

''His bedtime stories seemed exceptional. Unlike other people, he did not read them from a book, but simply told them, and they were infinitely more exciting and much funnier than anything read from the children's books at the time. That quality of reality, of being inside a story and so being a part of it, which has been, I believe, at least an important factor contributing to the world-wide success of his imaginative works, was already apparent to a small, though already critical and fairly imaginative boy.

''Inevitably, he was not a super-human father, and often he found his children insufferably irritating, self-opinionated, foolish and even occasionally totally incomprehensible. But he never lost his ability to talk *to* and not *at* or *down* to his children. In my own case he always made me feel that what *I* was doing and what *I* was thinking in my youth were of far more immediate importance than anything *he* was doing or thinking.''

In 1925, Professor W.A. Craigie at Oxford was offered a newly-created chair of English language at the University of Chicago, which he accepted. However, the new post required that Craigie begin during the autumn semester that year. This change of universities left Craigie's Oxford chair vacant, and a candidate to succeed him had to be found almost immediately. *Sir Gawain and the Green Knight* had just been published by the Oxford University Press, and made Tolkien one of the prime candidates (the other being Kenneth Sisam). That he was a graduate of Exeter College, that Craigie had been one of his tutors, that he had published *A Middle English Vocabulary* in conjunction with Kenneth Sisam's book, and that his work on the *Oxford English Dictionary* was well known all helped to enhance his qualifications for the chair. Moreover, the year before he had been appointed to the Leeds professorship.

In spring, 1925, Tolkien was first informed that he was being considered for election to the chair of Bosworth and Rawlinson Professor of Anglo-Saxon, and he accepted the candidacy with enthusiasm. Not long afterward, he was officially informed that the professorship was his, and he immediately told J.B. Baillie, the University of Leeds vice-chancellor, of his decision to accept the Oxford chair at the beginning of the 1925 Michaelmas term. Such short notice upset Baillie, who apparently thought of Tolkien as a professional opportunist. Tolkien finished out the spring semester, moved to Oxford during the summer, and assumed the position as Bosworth and Rawlinson Professor of Anglo-Saxon on October 1, 1925.

The Tolkiens had been quite happy at Leeds and left many friends behind when they returned to Oxford. It had been a productive period for Tolkien as both a teacher and a philologist, although his creative talents apparently did not have much of an opportunity to become manifest. Tolkien had fully recovered from the effects of the war, although the following years at Oxford were marked by an increasing withdrawal from all but the academic world.

Tolkien briefly returned to Leeds in 1926 to attend the official dinner held on June 29 for departing senior members of the faculty (he had resigned too late to be honored at the 1925 dinner). Geoffrey Woledge, who had received his B.A. and joined the staff in 1925, recalled the occasion. "The Vice-Chancellor, J.B. Baillie, in proposing the health of the retiring members, praised them all, but Tolk only for his good looks, and he implied that he had deserted his post for personal advancement. In replying, Tolk, who was evidently rather annoyed, said that he loved the university more than any other institution he had ever known, but that man has a higher loyalty than to institutions—his loyalty being to his subject."

E.V. Gordon was advanced over the heads of others from assistant lecturer to professor, aided by the publication of *Sir Gawain and the Green Knight* and Tolkien's personal recommendation. (Gordon and his wife Ida later moved to the University of Manchester, where both became professors.) Through Tolkien's efforts, the English department at Leeds had been expanded and strengthened. He was shortly to apply those same talents to healing the rift that had developed in the English School at Oxford between the linguists and the literati.

THE PROFESSOR
1925-1937

THE OXFORD to which Ronald Tolkien returned in autumn, 1925, as the Bosworth and Rawlinson Professor of Anglo-Saxon was already markedly different from the Oxford of 1911 and 1921. The process of change stimulated by such post-Victorian moves as the Reform Bill and the ascendancy of the university over the colleges had been accelerated by the war and intensified by rapid industrialization, social upheaval, and economic uncertainty. Wherever one looked, change was apparent. Woods were cleared, open fields became villages, and villages suburbs; and the suburbs were incorporated into cities. Colleges, factories, industrial plants, and housing estates were being built. Thousands of workers, technicians, and professionals moved their families from depressed areas to find work in booming Oxford. The ratio of university members to city residents not connected with the educational system was increasingly distended. For the first time in its history, the university was beginning to become secondary to the town.

By 1925, the motorcar had arrived in England and, despite the great depression of 1921, the postwar devaluation of the pound, and the abolition of the gold standard, it began to sell by the hundreds of thousands and then by the millions. As once the great oak forests had been cut down to build British sailing ships, so the open English countryside became increasingly fenced in, developed, subdivided, and criss-crossed with motor roads. Petrol stations sprang up, and houses and shops joined the stations to form villages. With new roads and better communications came industry, increased population, and more buildings. Every day, the countryside and open farmland shrunk a bit more. Such changes in Oxford and throughout the United Kingdom apparently disturbed Tolkien far more than the great political issues of the day. His response to change was to withdraw increasingly from the outside world and into himself.

In the first great confrontation at Oxford between tradition and progress, Tolkien had been on the side resisting change and what it portended in England. At that time, in 1913, auto manufacturer William Morris wanted to replace the horse-drawn street trams in Oxford with motorized omnibuses, which were more efficient and less expensive. The university bitterly fought Morris's efforts to bring the twentieth century to Oxford, just as they had resisted the construction of the canal, the railway, and the advent of electricity. After months of debate, underhanded political maneuvering, and Draconian tactics, Morris succeeded both in introducing his omnibuses and in driving the horse-pulled trams out of business. In the '20s, Morris—by now, Sir William—was well on his way to becoming the British equivalent of Henry Ford, and Oxford was about to become the English Detroit.

The university itself was also changing. Since 1877, all official university proceedings had been held in English rather than Latin. By 1925, the power of the M.A.'s had been all but broken. By 1926 the university had achieved permanent dominance over the colleges, and people like Tolkien helped make the transition from the traditional tutorial system to the university schools. The colleges were becoming democratized—against their will—by adopting altered admissions policies, which allowed more working and middle-class students to attend. Women were now accepted as members of the university. Greek was abolished as compulsory for matriculation.

The student population grew greatly after the war, partly because of government programs giving grants to qualified veterans and Oxbridge's decision to offer school-funded scholarships to former officers. Also responsible were dynamic social changes that allowed, encouraged, and assisted many working-class students to continue their education.

Postwar Oxford during the '20s was part of the age of Hemingway, T.S. Eliot, and James Joyce: adventurous, cynical, and brilliant. The students were self-indulgent, and their parties wild; few had concerns deeper than daily pleasures. Many were trying to forget the war and the destruction and mutilation it had inflicted.

The world that Tolkien had loved so much as a child and a young man was quickly passing, and its disappearance greatly disturbed him. The lines of demarcation between the classes had been stretched to the breaking point, and the generation-long struggle for women's rights had finally been won. Workers had given power to the growing trade unions and the Labor Party, and strikes were becoming endemic as capitalism crumbled in the Depression. Both the land and the people were changing, leaving behind persons like Tolkien, who looked to the past for inspiration and enlightenment.

And yet parts of Oxford were calm. The Oxford of Matthew Arnold could still be discovered in the '20s in long, rambling walks through unspoiled parts of the countryside, in village churches and country inns, in comfortable college rooms and in quiet commons and parks. To the south and east of the city, progress had yet to catch up with the rustic farmlands and open fields; motorcars rarely travelled the rutted country roads and common right-of-way footpaths. In Oxford itself, despite the presence of motorcars and omnibuses, the bicycle was still king of the ancient, narrow city streets, which at certain times of the day were flooded with black two-wheelers.

Tradition and ritual were still alive at the university. Bulldogs and proctors still wandered the town and "progged" errant students. Academic robes had to be worn outside college, and even mature undergraduates were fined anywhere from a penny to a shilling for staying out late at night. Dances were tolerated, but only by invitation, and heavily chaperoned. Women were forbidden to visit male students without an approved chaperone, and no male was permitted to call upon a female student in college without at least two other women and an approved chaperone present. Latin was still a mandatory subject, and although the "Grand Compounder" category had been eliminated, lazy students could still scrape by with a lowly fourth- class degree.

Tolkien returned to Oxford in the midst of this confusion and change, and it affected him profoundly. According to Professor Roger Sale, "he withdrew more completely from the modern world than any other maker of the Myth of Lost Unity, and in his more dogmatic pronouncements Tolkien had always spoken as though only madmen or fools would contemplate the twentieth century without horror." For the next decade, Tolkien devoted himself to his work, his family, and his close friends, accepting only responsibilities of his own choosing, avoiding the path of international recognition that could have been his, and refusing to follow the established academic dictum, "publish or perish." At Oxford, he was well-known and influential, and by virtue of his *Sir Gawain* text and *A Middle English Vocabulary,* respected by the small community of English philologists around the world. He never sought, however, the popularity that his professorship could have brought him. He did not want the celebrity status that C.S. Lewis, Hugo Dyson, and others achieved through popular books, radio, and television appearances and contributions to leading newspapers and magazines. He could easily have become a public favorite, for at age thirty-three, Ronald Tolkien looked far more like a matinee idol or an up-and-coming young politician than an Oxford professor. He cut a dashing figure—tall, fair-haired, and muscular, always fashionably dressed.

His wife Edith was a great beauty; one would never have thought, to look at her then, that she was already a mother three times over. She is said to have been somewhat aristocratic and aloof. *Proper* would have been a more accurate word, since she successfully conformed to the accepted standards of behavior for a young don's wife: genteel, modest, submissive, charming, intelligent, and literate. Together, they were well-liked, but became increasingly inaccessible except to close friends, neighbors, and favored students. (Mrs. Tolkien was never happy at Oxford, however, and frequently suffered migraine headaches that became a convenient excuse for avoiding unwanted social contact. Privately, the Tolkiens were at odds with each other over the question of religion, and it has been said that Edith Mary was jealous of her husband's male friends and all-consuming work. In later years they maintained separate bedrooms, not because of any estrangement, but because Tolkien worked far into the night and disturbed his wife with his loud snoring.)

The Tolkiens quickly acquired a comfortable and relatively new house at 22 Northmoor Road, one of many homes built on a field in north Oxford, one of the most pleasant parts of the city. It is likely that their house was rented to them by one of the colleges.[1] The Tolkiens moved next door to a larger house at 20 Northmoor Road in 1929, about the time their only daughter, Priscilla Anne Reuel Tolkien, was born. Most of *The Hobbit* and *The Lord of the Rings* were written in this rambling red stone house. It was so large that Mrs. Tolkien needed part-time day help to assist with cleaning and other housework. Apparently Tolkien was occasionally intimidated by the size and expense of the house, dubbing it ''the mansion,'' nor was he particularly unhappy when the house was sold nearly twenty years later and he and his wife moved into a much more modest college-owned house.

Northmoor Road was within easy commuting by bicycle to the Examination Halls, where Tolkien lectured; the English School, where he worked on administrative matters; and Pembroke College, where he held tutorials. Tolkien had been elected a fellow of Pembroke College in 1926, the year in which university reform had definitively established its supremacy over the colleges. This meant that teaching at Oxford would be more uniform, that there wouldn't be such wide disparities in academic standards, and that the centuries-old conflict between the tutorial and professorial systems would finally be settled. Until the latter part of the nineteenth century, tutors—who were also fellows of the colleges—tended to look down their noses at professors. The tutors and the colleges wanted to preserve the ancient but increasingly impractical one-to-one educational system that had been the backbone of Oxbridge for centuries. However, the steady growth of the student population meant that each tutor had to double, triple, and even quadruple the number of private tutorials given each week, thus diminishing their effectiveness. On the other hand, professors associated with the university through the various schools felt that the only effective modern way to give an education to such large numbers was to have lectures, seminars, and uniform examinations supersede tutorials as the academic mainstay of an Oxford education. Most professors were not fellows of the colleges, so intercourse between the tutors and professors really was limited.

The university's plan for shifting emphasis from the tutorial to the professorial system involved coercing the colleges to elect professors as fellows. It was hoped that by placing tutors and professors side by side at high table, the closer association would help break down the headstrong professional resistance to change and reform. The tutors, supported by the colleges and many M.A.'s, struggled for decades to retain their status. The university's plan to make professors fellows of the colleges was sound, and so all the more resented by the colleges, which were reluctant to surrender any of their prerogatives. It took more than forty years to implement the plan, and so it was in 1926 that Tolkien, as well as all the other professors not already fellows, were given that position by the various colleges. The university pressured Pembroke to "elect" Tolkien a fellow, which it did with no great enthusiasm. During his twenty years as a Pembroke Fellow, Tolkien never felt comfortable at the college or at ease with other college fellows. Therefore he was pleased when Merton College elected him a fellow in 1945, and he could move to more congenial surroundings.

The English professor usually enjoys more prestige and authority than his American counterpart. This is because there are far fewer professors at English universities; only one person, the principal public teacher of a particular faculty or subject, is given the title. For example, there would only be one professor for medieval French literature or Anglo-Saxon at a university. Also, there are no associate or assistant professors; other instructors who "profess" a subject are usually called lecturers. Another difference is that professorships at Oxbridge are usually endowed—established by a benefactor (frequently a wealthy scholar) who sets up a fund from which the salary of the professor is paid. This endowment is known as a professorial "chair," and often the chair is named after the benefactor. Tolkien had been elected to the chair of Bosworth and Rawlinson Professor of Anglo-Saxon, administered by the English School at Oxford. The chair had been established in 1755 with an endowment in the will of Richard Rawlinson, an eighteenth century antiquarian and collector. This endowment was added to in the 1860s by Joseph Bosworth, an Anglo-Saxon scholar who had been elected to the Rawlinson chair himself in 1858. Bosworth also attached his name to the chair.[2]

Although Tolkien was a junior professor of the English School when he joined the faculty in 1925, he quickly established himself as one of the more influential and innovative. He was a philologist in a faculty long dominated by specialists in literature; certainly Tolkien's predecessors had not been distinguished for their philological scholarship. Tolkien assumed the responsibility of re-establishing the respectability and importance of English philology in the faculty. This he did by being as helpful as possible to any of the other members of the English School, by preparing lectures and syllabi, by assisting in researching and editing scholarly papers and publications, and by using every possible opening to demonstrate the importance of language as the cornerstone of literature. Another invaluable contribution was Tolkien's fantastic ability to train and recruit new members for the faculty from his best students. It has been said that after *The Lord of the Rings*, Tolkien is best remembered for the large number of first-rate philologists he nurtured.

Nevill Coghill was not a student of Tolkien's, but Tolkien "adopted" the younger man when he joined the faculty after graduation. Tolkien saw that the newest member of the faculty was apprehensive about his first course of lectures to be delivered in the Michaelmas term and volunteered to help Coghill "find himself." He did this by showing him how to develop a style of delivery and by teaching him how to organize his notes and outlines. But Tolkien went beyond this generous assistance by actually *writing* some pages of lecture notes for Coghill to give as his own, as an example and as a vote of confidence in Coghill's ability. In later years, Tolkien and Coghill became friendly competitors as they vied for student allegiance by extemporaneously improvising stories from the sagas and relating interesting incidents and anecdotes from literature, as well as snatches of personal poems.

From all accounts, Coghill as a speaker was as brilliant as Tolkien was dull. But Tolkien's lifelong speech affectations never seemed to alter his enthusiasm for his subject or his concern for imparting knowledge to his students. Unlike his small, almost intimate classes at the University of Leeds, Tolkien's lectures were frequently packed not only with his own students, but with other students and dons anxious to hear him. It is a tribute to Tolkien's formidable reputation as a scholar that he had such a wide following in the years before he became a celebrity, and despite his difficulty in communicating. According to Nevill Coghill, Tolkien "was a very good lecturer himself—if you were on the front row, because if you were any further back than that, you wouldn't be able to keep up with it, this rapid machine gun fire of his lecturing." Elaine Griffiths, one of many Tolkien students who stayed in academia (she is now a fellow and tutor at St. Anne's College, Oxford), has similar memories. "I was a devoted, hard-working, simple-minded undergraduate, and I went to his lectures, and, contrary to popular opinion . . . he was really in many ways an appalling lecturer. When he came to the main point, he would turn around and address the blackboard." Another student thought that "he had his faults. He would ruffle through his notes rapidly, speaking in a quick, almost stuttering monotone until he struck something that interested him. Then he would light up, expand, expound.''

Perhaps the most perceptive assessment of Tolkien's rhetorical affectations is that of a non-native speaker of English, Przemyslaw Mroczkowski, a Polish scholar who became friends with Tolkien shortly after World War II, and is at present a professor of English philology at the Jagiellonian University in Cracow, Poland. ''Tolkien's speech was extremely difficult to follow, since it was all but inarticulate. I personally believe that the supreme test of a foreign English scholar was trying to understand Tolkien. If he did, perhaps he deserved an extra Ph.D. or the like. Tolkien didn't care to articulate; he simply expected and assumed that you could follow him with ease.

''Tolkien's lectures had a keen following, but they weren't, in my opinion, especially popular—at least, not popular in the sense that Nevill Coghill's were. He didn't specialize in his subject, but would occasionally speak extemporaneously on whatever interested him at the moment. Sometimes he would spend the entire lecture period reading a translation of a Norse saga or a Middle English poem instead of concentrating on the work at hand. Like his conversation, his lectures were very often difficult to understand.''

But those able to cope with his difficult speech and rambling lectures were deeply impressed by his scholarship and his devotion to his faithful students. He had little time for lazy or disinterested students (though he never punished those he failed to inspire with low marks), but no effort was too much for him when it came to helping those who exhibited either talent or enthusiasm for language or mythology. According to John Layerle, a former student of Tolkien's, and now director of the Center for Medieval Studies at the University of Toronto, Tolkien managed to create between himself and his favored students a special bond which went far beyond the ordinary student-tutor relationship. He gave of his time and knowledge, and strove to impart a love of language and lore to those who previously had only a slight appreciation. To argue that Tolkien helped train an entire generation of English philologists seems scarcely an exaggeration when one considers the number and the quality of his students who chose philology as their profession.

In the years following his return to Oxford, Tolkien was fortunate in making a number of intense, lifelong friends who undoubtedly influenced and encouraged him as a writer. There was Coghill, of course, and his boyhood acquaintance, Gervase Mathew, who had just become a don at Balliol College and would later take Catholic Holy Orders with the Blackfriars on St. Giles in Oxford. There were other associates at the English School who became friends:

Professor Dawkins and Helen MacMillan Buckhurst, who were Icelandic scholars and lovers of Norse sagas; Hugo Dyson, the brilliant scholar, severely wounded in the war, who survived to establish himself in the academic world; and Professor George Gordon, who had also left a chair at the University of Leeds to accept one at Oxford.

Coghill, Buckhurst, Dyson, Dawkins, Gordon, and Tolkien had many interests in common, not the least of which was Old Icelandic, the language of the great Norse sagas and the fountainhead of most nothern European legend and mythology. Their conversations at the English School led to further discussions at nearby pubs and in the best Oxford tradition, such get-togethers eventually became an institutionalized ritual—a club. They called themselves the Coalbiters, an Anglicized version of the Icelandic word *Kolbítar,* meaning people who huddle around a warm fire in winter and bite pieces of coal in order to get as near as possible to the warmth. According to Nevill Coghill, it was Tolkien who suggested both the idea for the club and its name. During the winter the group met weekly over dinner at the Eastgate Hotel, in John Bryson's rooms in Balliol College, or in back rooms of local pubs. "So we joined together and met once a week, sat around the fire in winter, each having a passage from one of the sagas to translate for the others," recalls Coghill. "I was allowed to do a paragraph. Professor Dawkins, who had a little experience of this sort of thing, was allowed to do a page. Tolkien did twenty pages. He was completely fluent in this difficult language and translated easily in appropriate style, at speed."

The Coalbiters suffered the fate of hundreds of other ad hoc clubs at Oxford and died so quietly that no one is quite certain when it ceased to function. Coghill seems to think that the later literary club, the Inklings, grew out of the Coalbiters, since many of the Coalbiters became Inklings. According to Tolkien's recollection, however, this was not the case. The Inklings were created at a much later time under quite different circumstances.

The most important friendship that Tolkien developed was with a tutor at Magdalen College, Clive Staples Lewis. C.S. Lewis, the son of a Belfast solicitor, was born in Ulster in 1898, attended University College, Oxford in 1916 for one semester in order to qualify for a commission in the army, was wounded on the Western Front, and then returned to complete his studies. He was a brilliant student, taking three firsts, but was unable to obtain a fellowship in philosophy at any of the Oxford colleges after receiving his degree. Failing that, he decided to prepare for a position in the English School, having read Anglo-Saxon with his tutor, Elizabeth Wardale. In 1923, he attended Professor Gordon's lectures on Spenser, and this led to a substitute position as a tutor of English philology at University College in 1924 when the regular tutor, E.F. Carritt, was away in America on sabbatical. Lewis continued to apply for fellowships with the various colleges, still hoping that he would receive one in philosophy rather than language. But when Magdalen College offered him a fellowship in English language and literature in 1925, he accepted—and he held the position until his election to a newly endowed professorial chair at Magdalen College, Cambridge, in 1954.

If Tolkien ever encountered a kindred spirit at Oxford, it was Lewis. Lewis also loved Oxford with an intensity that turned to the past rather than the present and, indeed, when he reluctantly accepted the Cambridge chair (after failing to be appointed Merton Professor of English Literature at Oxford), it was only on the condition that he could continue to live and commute from Oxford. In 1919, Lewis expressed some of these feelings about the city in a poem:

> We are not wholly brute. To us remains
> A clean, sweet city lulled by ancient streams,
> A place of vision and of loosening chains,
> A refuge of the elect, a town of dreams.

To Lewis, as to Tolkien, Oxford was ''a refuge of the elect'' after the horrors of war, and he also deplored the systematic encroachment of industrialization that the '20s and '30s brought. He was a Christian—in a distinctly un-Christian age—a poet, a writer of fantasy, and a lover of mythology. He liked ''sitting up till the small hours talking nonsense, poetry, theology, metaphysics over beer, tea and pipes.'' His memory was astonishing (he was able to recite long poems without a mistake), his interests wide (literature, philosophy, theology), and his published output prolific (more than forty books during his lifetime, including poetry, literary history, fiction and essays). Lewis cherished his privacy, even when he became famous. Though he did not waste time, he once shot back to an interviewer, who suggested that his seemingly hermitically sealed life tended to be a bit stuffy, ''I *like* boredom.'' Alan Watts noted that Lewis had ''a certain ill-concealed glee in adopting an old-fashioned and unpopular position.'' The same could have been said of Tolkien. Also applicable is Jocelyn Hill's description of Lewis as a man with an excellent sense of humor, great self-confidence, and ''above all, an unshakable deep sense of truth.''

Lewis, as well as Tolkien, was one of the so-called ''Oxford Christians.'' He was devoutly religious—an Anglican—and wrote a number of books on Christian theology. His faith was acquired and cultivated rather than inborn; to use his words, a "purely philosophical" conversion. "I gave up Christianity at about fourteen. Came back to it when getting on for thirty. Not an emotional conversion; almost purely philosophical. I didn't *want* to. I'm not in the least the religious type. I want to be left alone, to feel I'm my own master; but since the facts seemed to be just the opposite I had to give in." Although Lewis makes no mention of Tolkien's role in his return to Christianity, Tolkien once told his friend Przemyslaw Mroczkowski (a devout Roman Catholic, like Tolkien) sometime in the 1950s that he had had a definite hand in the affair. "I got him as far as the Church of England from atheism," Tolkien boasted, implying he would have liked to bring Lewis around to Catholicism. In any event, Lewis called himself a "theist" around 1930, and openly professed his Christianity at the end of that decade.

In later years, Lewis came to resemble Tolkien's hobbits: balding, rotund, with a large double chin, dressed in baggy, conservative clothing. Like Tolkien, he hated being interrupted or contradicted and could be quite cross when irritated. He was a inveterate letter writer—Tolkien was decidedly *not*—and a faithful friend. Lewis married only late in life, and like Tolkien he preferred the company of men, and the fellowship of scholars and writers. He became a popular figure throughout Britain because of his weekly radio programs, children's books, and contributions to periodicals. Together, Lewis and Tolkien were formidable, brilliant conversationalists who could speak authoritatively on almost any subject.

There is a story—apocryphal, according to Tolkien—that the two of them were having an animated dialogue at a pub one day, and an interested eavesdropper strolled over to ask them what they were so enthusiastically discussing. Lewis is supposed to have replied, "Tolkien and I were talking about dragons,"[3] and then continued his conversation without breaking stride. The probable source of that story, according to a letter that Tolkien later wrote Lewis's biographer and literary executor, Reverend Walter Hooper of Oxford (also a friend of Tolkien's), was as follows: "I remember Jack [as Lewis was called by his close friends] telling me a story of Brightman, the distinguished ecclesiastical scholar, who used to sit quietly in a Common Room saying nothing except on rare occasions. Jack said that there was a discussion on dragons one night and at the end Brightman's voice was heard to say, 'I have seen a dragon.' Silence. 'Where was that?' he was asked. 'On the Mount of Olives,' he said. He lapsed into silence and never before his death explained what he meant." Lewis apparently used that incident as inspiration for creating an example of the alliterative meter in poetry. In an essay published during the mid-1930s in a short-lived literary magazine titled *Lysistrata*, Lewis wrote:

We were *TALKING* of *DRAGONS*,
Tolkien and I
In a *BERK*shire *BAR*.
The *BIG WORK*man
Who had *SAT SIL*ent
and *SUCKED* his *PIPE*
ALL the *EVE*ning,
from his *EMPTY MUG*
With *GLEAMING EYE*
*GLANCED to*WARDS us;
'I seen 'em myself,'
he said *FIERCE*ly.

Lewis introduced Tolkien to Owen Barfield, whom Lewis had known as an undergraduate. Barfield was a lawyer by profession, but had already published several books, among them *Poetic Diction*. Lewis once said, "Barfield cannot talk on any subject without illuminating it." Some time around 1930, Barfield was at Oxford for a weekend, and Lewis invited him to dinner at the Eastgate to meet Professor Tolkien. "Tolkien was extraordinarily aggressive that evening," recalled Barfield, "and he contradicted everything I said. In fact, he contradicted some of my remarks with which I thought he would agree. Finally, I said to him 'Look, we haven't even got to the points on which we might *dis*agree.' " Lewis then apologized for Tolkien's behavior, salvaging the evening. Barfield later would invite Tolkien on days-long springtime walking tours around the Oxfordshire countryside along with A.C. Harwood, W.E. (later Sir Eric) Beckett, Leo Baker, Walter Field, and Colonel Hanbury Sparrow. This annual ramble continued through the '30s right up until the Second World War.

Like others in Tolkien's circle, Barfield perceived Tolkien as a typical Oxford don, but with a somewhat contradictory nature. Although a friendly person, Tolkien was often withdrawn and remote. He could comment on many subjects far removed from his principal areas of interest, but had a habit of automatically assuming that others knew what he was talking about when he spoke on some arcane subject or intricate point. This could either be maddening or charming to Tolkien's audiences or interviewers. He would rarely stop to explain, assuming that his listeners always knew what he was saying, and shared the same interest and enthusiasm for the subject he did. He once gave a public lecture at the University of Leeds about the Celts and Teutons in Europe during the Dark Ages. According to Geoffrey Woledge, "It was very learned and very informal, rambling, and charming. He said that only one thing was certain about the original Teutons—that they were completely wiped out at some date in the Dark Ages; and only one thing was probable—that they were Celts. Quoting some source about a certain individual, he said 'He is in fact our old friend Vortigern, of Hangist and Horsa fame,' a characteristically informal way of putting it."

Tolkien lived in the world of the intellect, of the university. His work was scholarship, his tools, words. He was completely at ease in an academic environment, especially when surrounded by friends and cronies, but somewhat less adequate once outside his own sphere. "I could never see him outside the university," recalled Barfield. "He was never practical or handy, but a typical scholar. I would think that to call him a man of the world would be the very last thing."

Finance was almost the only element in Tolkien's personal life that ever came up in conversation. He was always strapped for money. No matter how much he had—even after *The Lord of the Rings* made him wealthy—it never seemed quite enough to make him feel comfortable. At Oxford, professors received salaries that were relatively higher than most Englishmen earned, but substantially less than those of their American counterparts. Tolkien was not a materialist, but his financial obligations were heavy: a large house with day servants, four young children, the expense of sending them to the "right" schools, and the necessity of keeping up appearances. After his first year back at Oxford, Tolkien correctly concluded that he couldn't make ends meet on his salary alone, and since he didn't supplement his income, as did so many other Oxford dons by publishing books and magazine articles, he decided to find a way to make up the difference. This he did by working summers for the university, reading school certificates (examinations given secondary school students seeking acceptance by one of the colleges). Tolkien also worked as an examiner for other universities as well, and this often necessitated traveling throughout England. Later, after the Second World War, he gave up most of his examination work in England, although he did visit the Catholic University in Ireland from time to time almost until his retirement in 1959. "One of the tragedies of the underpaid professor is that he has to do menial jobs," Tolkien once complained. "I was reading exam papers to earn a bit of money. That was agony . . . ." Such work was boring, but Tolkien continued marking the papers well into the '30s.

In the summer of 1928,[4] while marking an especially boring lot of examination papers, Tolkien came across one with a blank page in it. "One of the candidates mercifully left one of the pages with no writing on it—which is possibly the best thing that can happen to an examiner—and I wrote on it 'In a hole in the ground lived a hobbit.' Names always generate a story in my mind and eventually I thought I should find out what hobbits were like. But that was only the beginning; I spun the elements out of my head; I didn't do any organizing at all."

Tolkien was never certain how he came to invent the word "hobbit." It was more spontaneous generation than calculation; certainly, not the combination of "rabbit" and (Thomas) "Hobbes," as the eminent American critic Edmund Wilson speculated.[5] "I don't know where the word came from," admitted Tolkien. "You can't catch your mind out. It might have been associated with Sinclair Lewis' *Babbit*.[6] Certainly not rabbit, as some people think. Babbit has the same bourgeois smugness that hobbits do. His world is the same limited place." Another theory on the origin of the word hobbit is advanced by Paul Kocher, author of *Master of Middle Earth*. According to Kocher, the Oxford English Dictionary defines the Middle English word "hob" (or "hobbe") as a rustic or a clown, a sort of Robin Goodfellow (the English equivalent of the "little people" of Celtic mythology). Since hobbits seem to display many of the characteristics of hobs—small size, simple nature, love of countryside,—then perhaps Tolkien unconsciously transformed a word with which he was undoubtedly familiar into a new creature. In any event, the word "hobbit" is uniquely Tolkien's invention, like "pandemonium" in Milton's *Paradise Lost* and "chortle" in Carroll's *Alice in Wonderland*.

For Tolkien, stories germinated from words, and the word "hobbit" stimulated the beginning of a tale following in the best tradition of the old Norse sagas. In those days, Tolkien had no idea of his story's plot or probable ending; his method was improvisational, and the story grew in the telling. He said later that *The Hobbit* was really a distillation of several ideas that had occupied his professional mind for some years and that he merely adapted those ideas to children. But he emphasized that *The Hobbit* was *not* simply a children's book. When an interviewer asked him if he had only written *The Hobbit* to amuse his children at bedtime, Tolkien replied, "That's all sob stuff. No, of course, I didn't. If you're a youngish man and you don't want to be made fun of, you say you're writing for children. At any rate, children are your immediate audience and you write or tell them stories for which they are mildly grateful: long, rambling stories at bedtime." When confronted with the suggestion that *The Hobbit* reads like a children's tale with a somewhat paternalistic narrator who uses the simplest language, Tolkien admitted that "*The Hobbit* was written in what I should now regard as bad style, as if one were talking to children. There's nothing my children loathed more. They taught me a lesson. Anything that in any way marked out *The Hobbit* as for children instead of just people, they disliked—instinctively. I did too, now that I think about it. All this 'I won't tell you any more, you think about it' stuff. Oh no, they loathe it; it's awful.''

Since Tolkien denied he wrote *The Hobbit* solely to amuse children, then precisely why did he write it? At one time, Nevill Coghill thought he had done it for the money. After all, Tolkien frequently complained about his uncomfortable financial position, and everyone knew he was always in need of money. For that reason, when the book was published in 1938, Coghill refused to read it, and only picked it up years later when he discovered it at a friend's house on a bedroom bookshelf. He read the book through, quickly changed his mind, and declared it a wonderful tale with elements—like the riddle game with Gollum and the dialogue with the dragon Smaug—right out of the Norse sagas.

But the real reason Tolkien wrote *The Hobbit* can be found in a statement he made about *The Lord of the Rings*, which applies equally to his earlier work: ''In *The Lord of the Rings*, I have tried to modernize the myths and make them credible.'' Both as mythmaker and as philologist, Tolkien knew the importance of mythology to language and culture. Myths develop a link with the past, a continuity that helps people weather the present and look forward to the future. In an era of unprecedented change, the links to the past are stretched to the breaking point, and a people without roots are likely to become, analogously, a people without branches or flowers. The roots of the past —mythology— are no longer acceptable in their traditional form[7] and have to be recast in a more contemporary, relevant mode. *The Hobbit*, *The Silmarillion*, and *The Lord of the Rings* are Tolkien's contributions to modern mythology. Tolkien once commented that it was unfortunate there were virtually no native English fairy stories (with the exception of *Jack and the Beanstalk*), and that he had written *The Hobbit* in order to help fill this vacuum.

As chronicler of a modern myth, Tolkien borrowed heavily from the myths and sagas of the past, with which he was intimately familiar. He never claimed originality for either his names or plots. Only his most devoted readers later disputed and denied any attempts to establish wellsprings from which many of his ideas flowed. The names of the dwarfs in *The Hobbit*, for example, were not invented by Tolkien, but lifted intact from *The Elder Edda*, a series of old Norse poems taken from a thirteenth century Icelandic text.[8] In that work, the dwarfs' names were Durin, Dwalin, Dain, Bifur, Bofur, Bombur, Nori, Thrain, Thorin, Thror, Fili, Kili, Fundin, Gloin, Dori, and Ori (there was even a Gandalf)—the same as those of the dwarfs with whom the hobbit Bilbo and the wizard Gandalf went on their adventure to recover the dragon's gold. "This particular lot of dwarfs are very secretive," Tolkien once explained, and since in the book they came from the extreme north, "I gave the dwarfs actual Norse names which are in Norse books. Not that my dwarfs are really like the dwarfs of Norse imagination, but there is a whole list of attractive dwarf names in one of the old epic poems." The name for the forest of Mirkwood also appears in an Icelandic saga, *King Heidrek the Wise*, which Christopher Tolkien translated in 1960. Gandalf is mentioned in the saga of *Halfdan the Black*, and the term Middle-earth comes from an obsolete phrase describing our own world. Each name Tolkien used was carefully constructed or selected to describe the individual bearing it. His fantastic ability to give attractive, descriptive, and unusual names is one of the most appealing aspects of his works. Being a philologist and knowing the importance of words and titles meant that this name-giving ability was important to Tolkien. He said, "In the writing, I always begin with a name. Give me a name and I'll produce a story— not the other way about."

In writing *The Hobbit* and *The Lord of the Rings*, Tolkien applied his talents as a professor of language and a lover of mythology. "I used what I knew" he said. "Every human being has an individual character, just as everyone has an individual face. I think people have linguistic predilections, but like one's physical characteristics, they shift as you grow, also as you have more experience. In language, I've tried to fit my actual personal predilection or pleasure."

Tolkien probably produced a handwritten draft of *The Hobbit* in the early 1930s. It was written late at night in an attic at 20 Northmoor Road. He worked sitting on the edge of a camp bed, writing on a late nineteenth century English oak keyhole desk that his wife Edith had given him in 1927. This handwritten manuscript of *The Hobbit* was never intended for publication, but was circulated privately among friends and students. C.S. Lewis encouraged Tolkien to submit it to a publisher, but he refused. Nor would he listen to other friends who suggested he seek publication. Why Tolkien was uninterested in having the book published is not clear. There are a few possible explanations, though they are not particularly convincing. One is that he feared the ridicule the public might have heaped upon an Oxford professor writing a children's book, or the disapproval of his colleagues for writing such a frivolous, time-wasting work when he could have been engaged in much more serious scholarship. Another possibility is that as a truly modest man who sought privacy and anonymity, he feared that publication might inadvertently bring popularity, and put him in the limelight. Still another explanation may be the fear of rejection. Tolkien apparently never recovered from the humiliation he suffered when some of his poems were rejected by Sidgwick & Jackson in 1916. Several of his early stories, later incorporated into *The Silmarillion,* were similarly rejected.

There is one more possibility that may explain why *The Hobbit* was not offered to a publisher before 1936. In 1934, Tolkien was awarded a Leverhulme Fellowship, which enabled him to pursue a scholarly subject of his own choosing. The Leverhulme Foundation awarded annual grants to graduate students, scholars, and professors living in the British Isles. The grant to professors—which lasted up to two years and sometimes amounted to the equivalent of a year's salary—was designed to enable professors not on sabbatical, and therefore prevented from taking a paid leave of absence, to undertake original research in their spare time by underwriting reasonable expenses for hiring secretaries, research assistants, or consulting with foreign colleagues. The topics selected were left to the professors' discretion, but were supposed to relate to European themes. Tolkien received a Leverhulme for the years 1934 through 1936; in all probability, he used the grant to do research on *Beowulf.*

An acknowledged authority on *Beowulf,* Tolkien had long been concerned over how the work was usually approached by scholars and critics. He felt the critics had lost sight of the work itself and become more involved with its supposed meaning than with its story. In 1936, Professor Tolkien was invited to present the annual Israel Gollancz lecture at the British Academy. He chose to entitle his lecture *Beowulf: The Monsters and the Critics.*

That lecture is still considered by scholars to be the finest exposition on Anglo-Saxon literature in this century. In brilliant, witty, and poetic language, Tolkien chided those critics who had become so muddled in scholarship that they did everything but read what the works they were writing about said. He began by gently poking fun at one of his predecessors as Rawlinson Professor, Dr. John Bosworth. Tolkien continued his attack. "For it is of their nature that the jabberwocks of historical and antiquarian research burble in the tulgy wood of conjecture, flitting from one tum-tum tree to another. Noble animals, whose burbling is on occasion good to hear; but though their eyes of flame may sometimes prove searchlights, their range is short." Tolkien proceeded from the critics to the monsters. "It is the strength of the northern mythological imagination that . . . put the monsters in the center, gave them victory but no honor, and found a potent but terrible solution in naked will and courage. . . . So potent is it, that while the older southern imagination has faded forever into literary ornament, the northern has power, as it were, to revive its spirit even in our own times." That Tolkien himself used monsters in both *The Hobbit* and *The Lord of the Rings* apparently was in keeping with the tradition of *Beowulf,* since the "impression of depth is an effect and a justification of the uses of episodes and allusions to old tales, mostly darker, more pagan, and desperate than the foreground.'' The existence of monsters portends still more evil creatures and histories not revealed.

Beowulf: The Monsters and the Critics was published by the Oxford University Press and was later included in *An Anthology of Beowulf Criticism,* published by Notre Dame Press in 1963, and still later in a Folcroft book. It established Tolkien as one of the foremost philologists of the century.

The story of how *The Hobbit* came to be published is interesting because it reveals Tolkien's reliance upon others to recognize and support his genius. The manuscript was known to a small but select circle of friends and colleagues. One of these was Elaine Griffiths. She tried to persuade Tolkien to let a publisher look at the manuscript, but he preferred to leave it in his desk drawer. Shortly afterwards, Griffiths happened to meet an old friend and fellow undergraduate, Susan Dagnell, who had taken a position at a small but distinguished London publishing house, George Allen & Unwin. She mentioned that her former professor had a wonderful children's story in manuscript that would make a smashing book—if only he could be persuaded to part with it. "Susan had a delightful voice,'' recalled Griffiths, ''And if anyone could get it out of him, it was her.'' Apparently, Susan Dagnell succeeded, for in autumn, 1936, he first allowed *The Hobbit* to be considered for publication.

Susan Dagnell gave the manuscript to Sir Stanley Unwin, chairman of George Allen & Unwin. Sir Stanley, judging himself incompetent to evaluate children's books, turned it over to his ten-year-old son Raynor. Young Unwin had an arrangement with his father in which he was paid between one shilling and a half crown for reading and reporting on each children's book given him for consideration. Of *The Hobbit,* Raynor Unwin wrote to his father on October 30, 1936:

> Bilbo Baggins was a hobbit who lived in his hobbit-hole and *never* went for adventures, at last Gandalf the wizard and his dwarves persuaded him to go. He had a very exciting time fighting goblins and wargs. At last they got to the lonely mountain; Smaug, the dragon who guards it is killed and after a terrific battle with the goblins he returned home—rich!
>
> This book, with the help of maps, does not need any illustrations. It is good and should appeal to all children between the ages of 5 and 9.
>
> *Raynor Unwin*

Many years later, Raynor Unwin said, ''Some publishers get their lucky break at a very tender age. At the age of ten I was handed the manuscript of a children's book called *The Hobbit,* and promised the fee of one shilling for my report on it. My father, Sir Stanley Unwin, reckoned children the best judges of juvenile books, and I think he was right. I earned that shilling. I wouldn't say my report was the best critique of *The Hobbit* that has been written, but it was good enough to ensure that it was published."

Despite Raynor Unwin's advice that the map Tolkien had drawn to go with the manuscript made illustrations unnecessary, Tolkien wanted the book to include his own drawings (he was an inveterate doodler and enjoyed painting water colors). The map, however, was absolutely vital to the story, and it is likely that, as with *The Lord of the Rings,* it had been drawn up long before the book was written. Tolkien once advised that in an adventure story it is essential for the author to draw a map first; otherwise, he is likely to encounter great discrepancies.

The Hobbit was published in autumn 1937, and for the most part received excellent reviews. The *Times*'s review read:

> All who love that kind of children's book which can be read and re-read by adults should note that a new star has appeared in this constellation. If you like the adventures of Ratty and Mole you will like *The Hobbit* by J.R.R. Tolkien (Allen & Unwin 7s7d [about $1.90]). If, in those adventures, you prized the solidarity of the social and geographical context in which your small friends moved, you will like *The Hobbit* even better. . . .
>
> The truth is that in this book a number of good things, never before united, have come together: a fund of humor, an understanding of children, and a happy fusion of the scholar's with the poet's grasp of mythology. On the edge of a valley one of Professor Tolkien's characters can pause and say: "It smells like elves." It may be years before we produce another author with such a nose for an elf. The professor has an air of inventing nothing. He has studied trolls and dragons at first hand and describes them with the fidelity which is worth oceans of glib "originality." The maps (with runes) are excellent, and will be found thoroughly reliable by young travelers in the same region.

The London *Observer*'s reviewer spoke of "Professor Tolkien's finely written saga of dwarves (sic) and elves, fearsome goblins and trolls, in a spacious country of far-off and long ago . . . a full length tale of traditional magic beings . . . an exciting epic of travel, magical adventures . . . working up to a devastating climax." And *The New Statesman & Nation* concluded that "his wholly original story of adventure among goblins, elves and dragons . . . gives . . . the impression of a well-informed glimpse into the life of a wide other-world; a world wholly real, and with a quite matter-of-fact, supernatural natural history of its own.'' W. H. Auden (who was a friend, colleague, and former student of Tolkien's) called it ''the best children's story written in the last fifty years,'' and when *The Hobbit* was published in America by Houghton Mifflin the following year, it won the prestigious New York *Herald Tribune* prize as the best children's book of 1938. After World War II, *The Hobbit* was placed on many approved reading lists in elementary schools, and was (and still is) a highly recommended children's classic in thousands of libraries in both England and America.

Curiously enough, despite the reviews, the book did not sell well initially. It barely went through one edition; a second edition was destroyed in 1942 in the London Blitz. Tolkien did not realize any significant financial rewards from his book until much later, but he lived to see the day when well over a million copies of *The Hobbit* would be sold in the United States alone. But then, Tolkien once admitted, ''I never expected a money success.''

By 1937, J.R.R. Tolkien had just begun to emerge from a long period of self-imposed hibernation. He had sought, obtained, and accepted fame and recognition as a scholar and writer, something that he had steadfastly refused to do in earlier years. Professor Roger Sale notes Tolkien's position prior to 1936: ''As a lecturer, Tolkien's great virtue was as an enunciator of *Beowulf;* as a tutor his strength lay in giving his students ideas he never claimed title to himself; as a scholar his only serious work before 1936 is as editor of *Sir Gawain and the Green Knight.* He seems, thus, to have been devising ways of living such that he could carry on his relations with the outside world at one remove. What he was, or knew, or cared for, could not be discerned directly, and no one except friends and close admirers need have had any sense of him other than as the figure he obviously offered, of a diffident and learned professor.'' But 1936 appears to have been a turning point in his life, marked by the *Beowulf* lecture and by having his first full-length fairy story accepted for publication. It is probably not a coincidence that the hobbit, Bilbo Baggins, happened to have been just about the same age as his creator, Professor Tolkien, when he embarked on his great adventure with Gandalf and the dwarfs. Perhaps it might even be said that they were traveling in roughly the same direction.

THE MYTHMAKER
1937-1953

N HIS AUTOBIOGRAPHY, *Surprised By Joy*, C.S. Lewis wrote, "At my first coming into the world I had been (implicitly) warned never to trust a Papist, and at my first coming into the English Faculty (explicitly) never to trust a philologist. Tolkien was both." Happily, Lewis proved indifferent to his religious prejudices and the English School rivalries, for the two became fast friends. They had a symbiotic relationship in which Tolkien offered criticism and Lewis encouragement. Lewis acknowledged his debt by dedicating his best-known book, *The Screwtape Letters,* to Tolkien; Tolkien reciprocated when he dedicated the original edition of *The Lord of the Rings* to his friends, the Inklings, of whom Lewis was the most prominent member.

The Inklings, which existed between the mid-1930s and 1962, were a highly informal group of Oxford writers and poets who met regularly in college rooms and local pubs to read their works in progress to each other. According to Lewis, they discussed everything "from beer to *Beowulf,* to torture, Tertullian, bores, the contractual theory of medieval kingship, and odd place names." The group included several influential thinkers, but unlike, say, the Bloomsbury crowd of an earlier decade, they were avowedly Christian, conservative, and romantic. They were shamelessly self-indulgent, unserious individuals who enjoyed sharing their love of literature, borrowing ideas from one another, and reading excerpts from manuscripts that later were counted among the more memorable books written in England during that time.

Neither Tolkien nor Lewis was responsible for creating the Inklings, though it is possible that Lewis gave the club its name. Nor did it grow out of the earlier Icelandic club, the Coalbiters, or the University College Martlets Society. According to Tolkien, the Inklings were first suggested as a sort of literary joke by an undergraduate at University College named Tangye-Lean. Of Tangye-Lean, Tolkien said, ''He was, I think, more aware than most undergraduates of the impermanence of their clubs and fashions, and had an ambition to found a club that would prove more lasting. Anyway, he asked some 'dons' to become members. C.S.L. [Lewis] was an obvious choice, and he was probably at that time Tangye-Lean's tutor . . . . The club met in T.-L.'s rooms in University College; its procedure was that at each meeting members should read aloud unpublished compositions. These were supposed to be open to immediate criticism. Also, if the club thought fit, a contribution might be voted to be worthy of entry in a Record Book. (I was scribe and keeper of the book.)

''Tangye-Lean proved quite right. The club soon died: The Record Book had very few entries: but C.S.L. and I at least survived. Its name was then transferred (by C.S.L.) to the undetermined and unelected circle of friends who gathered around C.S.L., and met in his rooms in Magdalen. Although our habit was to read aloud compositions of various kinds (and lengths!), this association and its habit would in fact have come into being at that time [around 1933 or 1934], whether the original short-lived club had ever existed or not.''

Strictly speaking, the Inklings did not constitute a traditional Oxford society or club. The group had no officers or rules, no elections or agendas. Members were not nominated or formally inducted. They became Inklings only with the tacit approval of the others, who permitted them to find their way back to the meetings as often as they wished. There were no dues, budgets, or prizes, and though no formal regulations against female members existed, no woman ever became an Inkling.[1] True to its tradition as an Oxford nonclub, the Inklings did not have any set hour of meeting and in earlier years would meet on Fridays almost as often as Thursdays. Nor did they have any formally designated meeting place; the favorite spots were Lewis's spacious rooms at Magdalen, the Eagle and Child (known affectionately as the Bird and Baby), the Burning Babe, and the Lamb and Flag. Those pubs had private back rooms behind the saloon bars where members could meet and drink without interruption. On such occasions, the publicans would set rooms aside for their use; gradually, it became a matter of pride to them that the Inklings graced their establishments with their presence. Generally, the Inklings met around 8 o'clock and broke up around 10:30, but this was about as close to a set routine as they had.

The opening ritual centered around Lewis, who was the fountainhead of the Inklings, and it scarcely varied a single word for many years. According to Lewis's brother, W.H. (Warnie), ''When half a dozen or so had arrived, tea would be produced, and then when pipes were alight Jack [C.S. Lewis] would say, ''Well, has nobody got anything to read us?' ''

Lewis and Tolkien (and later Charles Williams) are the best-known of the Inklings, and but for their prestige and wide readership, it is doubtful whether the famous nonclub would have ever become so well-known outside Oxford. This is not to say that the others were not distinguished in their own right, for most of them were, or later became, published authors. Over the years, some members came and went, a few died, but the nucleus remained. Nevill Coghill was one of the original members. He was a distingusihed Chaucer scholar who later succeeded Tolkien as Merton Professor of English Language and Litera-ture. Hugo (H.V.D.) Dyson was a seventeenth century schoiar who left Ox-ford shortly after Tolkien returned there to become a professor at the Universi-ty of Reading. He loved Oxford so much that he retained a summer position at the Oxford English School that kept him in contact with his friends and col-leagues, and later he returned to Oxford full-time to become a Merton fellow. He had been severely wounded in the leg during World War I, and walked with a cane. Dyson, Lewis said, ''was a most fastidious bookman . . . but as far away from being a dilettante as anyone can be; a burly man, both in mind and body, with a stamp of war on him . . . . He is a Christian and a lover of cats.'' Dyson later became well-known through his BBC lectures on Shakespeare. Oddly enough, he is best remembered as an actor, having played the university pro-fessor in the Julie Christie movie, *Darling.*

Lewis invited his close friend Owen Barfield to become an Inkling. Bar-field attended infrequently because he lived and worked in London. He came up to Oxford only at the beginning of each term to dine with Lewis in Hall, spend the weekend in town, and attend a meeting of the Inklings on Thursday evening. On one occasion Barfield began to read a short play that he had writ-ten about Medea, but abandoned his reading in considerable embarrassment when Tolkien interrupted him to say that everyone else in the room—Tolkien included—had tried to write a play about Medea at one time or another. On a later occasion, Barfield made the mistake of presuming to bring a friend along unannounced—a serious *faux pas* that almost broke up the group when some members approved and others disapproved of the new candidate. The man was never invited back. Barfield learned his lesson, and when he later ''sponsored'' his friend John Wain, an Oxford don and poet, for membership, he won the group's interest and approval by first reading some of Wain's poetry to them.

Another member of the Inklings was Gervase Mathew, one of Tolkien's childhood acquaintences, and later a close friend and fellow academic at Ox-ford. Mathew, who was a Roman Catholic priest, was also a fellow of Balliol

College. He had a tendency to become involved in helping others—so much so that he was nicknamed ''everybody's aunt'' by the Inklings. He later lived up to that reputation by helping to persuade Tolkien to publish *The Lord of the Rings* after Tolkien himself feared that it was unpublishable. Another Catholic member was Tolkien's physician, Dr. Humphrey Havard. The Tolkiens were close friends of the Havards, and Tolkien even consented to become godfather to Havard's son, David. Lewis's brother, Major W.H. Lewis, remained an Inkling for many years. He was not able to attend many of the meetings, so C.S. Lewis kept him informed and up-to-date by letter of the proceedings. W.H. Lewis, although having a military background and being a graduate of Sandhurst, was also an eighteenth century French scholar and an author himself. Other regular Inklings included Charles (C.L.) Wrenn, a Pembroke Fellow and Professor of Anglo-Saxon, and Aleistar (Roy) Campbell, who succeeded Wrenn when he retired. Later, Tolkien's own son Christopher was invited to join the Inklings during the Second World War.

And then there was Charles Williams. Williams was unlike the other Inklings in that he came from a lower-middle-class background, and not only had not attended an Oxford college, but never earned a degree anywhere else. He was of Welsh ancestry, six years older than Tolkien, the son of a poor, unsuccessful London poet and translator. He never went to public school, and the extent of his education was several semesters at the University of London. When he ran out of money, he dropped out and started taking night courses at the Workingman's College. Nevertheless, he managed to work his way up from assistant clerk in a small publishing house to become the head of the Oxford University Press. Williams was creative and talented, and wrote prodigiously in his spare time—novels, poetry, biography, theology, literary criticism, and essays—in addition to editing books and writing introductions for the books of other writers. Though a devout member of the Church of England, he also expressed a deep interest and involvement in mysticism, the occult, and even witchcraft. Williams's personality was multifaceted: a realist with the soul of a poet and the heart of a believer. T.S. Eliot described him as ''a man who was always able to live in the material and spiritual world at once, a man to whom the worlds were equally real because they are one world. So while his novels are constantly flashing with religious insight, his religious books communicate a good deal of the excitement of a sensational novel.'' This is remarkably similar to Geoffrey Parson's perception: ''Williams lived and breathed in a world that knew no sharp dividing line between natural events and spiritual events.''

Williams was, according to Eliot, ''a plain, spectacled man of rather frail physique, who made no attempt to impress anybody.'' Lewis was more generous in his description. "He is an ugly man with a rather Cockney voice. But no one ever thinks of this for five minutes after he has begun speaking. His face becomes angelic. But in public and in private he is of nearly all the men I have met, the one whose address most overflows with *love*." Lewis first met Williams through Nevill Coghill, who had probably known Williams through his position at the press. Coghill was sufficiently impressed to read at least one of Williams's novels (he wrote more than thirty-eight books), *The Place of the Lion,* which he gave Lewis to read. The book also impressed Lewis, who then dispatched a letter to Williams inviting him to dinner. At that time, the Oxford University Press was based in London rather than Oxford, and Williams was therefore not a resident of the town. When the two met, Lewis's first reaction was negative—Williams's Cockney accent was quite removed from the lilt of Oxbridge scholars—but this was quickly forgotten and the two became fast friends. Years later, when Williams moved with the press to Oxford and gave lectures at the university, he was said to have rivalled Lewis himself in eloquence and audience appeal.

Lewis invited Charles Williams to a Thursday night meeting of the Inklings to read part of an unfinished sequence of poems titled *Taliessin Through Logres,* which was later published in 1938[2]. By unanimous acclaim, he was made welcome and invited to join the Inklings as a regular member. Every one of the Inklings happened to be avowedly Christian, but Tolkien, Lewis, and Williams stood out as torchbearers of their faiths. Still, religion was rarely discussed at the Inklings' meetings.

Tolkien's treatment and incorporation of religious themes into *The Lord of the Rings,* however, is nothing less than extraordinary. Middle-earth is a pre-Christian world without Original Sin, and therefore without a need for a Christ. There are no gods or saints, no religious ritual. And yet the "benevolent" races (hobbits, humans, wizards, ents, fairies, dwarfs, and even Tom Bombadil) are motivated and guided by a system of ethics that is Christian in everything but name. It is my opinion that Tolkien attempted to recreate the world as God had first created it, and since Middle-earth was part of God's handiwork, it was ruled by natural order.[3] Natural order implies Christian order, with or without a Christ. In other words, any world created by God would naturally reflect its Creator, and therefore its delineation and definition of good and evil would be absolute, unchangeable, and inviolate, since God never changes. Tolkien perceived a Manaechean theological cosmology where natural order meant Christian order, and he peopled that world with races who recognized and respected a universal ethical system. This syllogistic substitute of natural order for Christianity is borne out by Tolkien's extensive use of Christian elements in *The Lord of the Rings,* not in an allegorical manner, but more as familiar points of reference that would mark Middle-earth as God's world for any Christian traveling through it.

Tolkien told his friend Professor Mroczkowski, a fellow Catholic, that the waybread, or lembas, that the elves gave to the hobbits to eat on their journey was really the Eucharist. Mroczkowski speculated that if the waybread was the Eucharist, then Lady Galadriel must represent the Virgin Mary. Tolkien declined to confirm Mroczkowski's conclusion, but neither did he deny it. Nor did he vigorously deny that Frodo *could* be interpreted by some readers as Christ. This curious language of disaffirmation could lead one to conclude that there are Christ-like attributes and parallels about Frodo. The name of God is not used in *The Lord of the Rings,* but Tolkien made it quite clear in later interviews that "the one," or Eru, was really God, and that the Valar were angels. As to the identity of Gandalf the Grey, Tolkien privately admitted to critic Edmond Fuller in 1962 that "Gandalf is an angel."

There are inherent theological problems in accepting Middle-earth as a Christian world without Christ, but Tolkien apparently realized them. A perfect world would be one without evil—which obviously exists in Middle-earth—and this would therefore imply both a fall and the need for redemption. Tolkien gives no specific details of The Fall in his mythology, but he does emphasize that although no creatures in Middle-earth were created evil, they made themselves evil through ambition. This, of course, parallels the defection of the Devil from heaven. Without a spiritual being in Tolkien's mythology who closely conforms to the Biblical archetype of the Devil (Sauron was a flesh-and-blood creature), without this creature to deceive and lead the faithful astray, there is no necessity for redemption in the Christian sense of the word.

Middle-earth is a dynamic world; at least it does not remain static. The Third Age passes on to the Fourth Age, and Gandalf perceives that although Sauron's power has been forever broken, evil has not been permanently exorcised from the world. Thus, the Hegelian cycle of history would continue *ad infinitum.* Tolkien could not allow so existential a phenomenon to go on forever and therefore deny God's mercy, so he introduced into his cosmology the concept of eucatastrophe. "Eucatastrophe" is a word Tolkien made up (it means that good will overturn evil, according to Tolkien's use of the Greek *eu*—good, and *katastrophe*—to overturn), and in context, it means "The Fall with a good ending." Eucatastrophe is implicit in *The Lord of the Rings;* the destruction of the one ring of power prefigures the ultimate end of evil, and the "Scouring of the Shire" parallels both Jesus's cleansing of the Temple and the war in heaven in Revelation. Although Tolkien does not specifically discuss how or when eucatastrophe would take place in Middle-earth, I believe everything in Tolkien's own life and religious beliefs indicates that such would ultimately happen in any world created by God. And Tolkien, as the mere "sub-creator"[4] of Middle-earth, was naturally bound by the established theological parameters of the Original Creator.

It may be argued that this kind of critical analysis is precisely what Tolkien objected to, since it searches for "meaning" in a work that he adamantly claimed contained none. On the other hand, Tolkien admitted that "an author cannot of course remain wholly unaffected by his experience," and that must be construed to mean religious experience as well. Mythology is built on established cultural or historical points of reference, and reflects both the ethics of the storyteller or mythmaker and the values of society. It would therefore be both difficult and dishonest for Tolkien's mythology *not* to reflect his own serious involvement with Christianity. An example of this synthesis of personal belief and imagination can be found in one of Tolkien's lesser-known works, a long narrative poem called *The Lay of Aotrou,* first published in the *Welsh Review,* in December, 1945. The poem is about a knight who visits a witch in order to receive a forbidden potion that will help his barren wife bear children. The temptation proves too much, and the knight's desire proves greater than his resistance. The interplay of good and evil, in the Christian sense of those words, is central to the poem. After all is lost, Tolkien introduces a very moving prayer as an act of contrition:

> *God help us all in hope and prayer*
> *from evil rede and from despair,*
> *by waters blest of Christendom*
> *to dwell, until at last we come*
> *to joy of Heaven where is queen*
> *the maiden Mary pure and clean.*

Even within the all-Christian Inklings, Tolkien, Lewis, and Williams came to be recognized as intense advocates of Christian morals and theology—so much so that they eventually became known as the "Oxford Christians." The three were "unabashedly" romantic in an age of realism (to use a phrase coined by Marjorie Wright of the University of Illinois), and primarily concerned with metaphysics, theology, and the ultimate structure of the universe. According to Dr. Clyde Kilby of Wheaton College,[5] Tolkien, Lewis, and Williams had found a system of cosmic order and "created a myth to contain it." And that system was Christian in outlook, though not necessarily in form.

Both Lewis and Williams acted as lay spokesmen for their faith and the Anglican church. In contrast, Tolkien never publicly defended Catholicism or took to lecturing about theology, as did Lewis and Williams; nor did he write religious books or essays as such.

The Inklings existed for a quarter century; during that time Lewis and Tolkien remained prominent members (Charles Williams died in May, 1945). Lewis freely acknowledged the positive influence they had on him, both as a writer and a Christian. In dedicating *The Problem of Pain* to the Inklings, to whom he had read the work aloud before publication, he said, ''What I owe to them is incalcuable . . . . Is there any pleasure on earth as great as the circle of Christian friends by a good fire?'' Lewis even ''borrowed'' from Tolkien's writings[6] in his *Silent Planet* trilogy. In one instance, he writes about Numinor, ''a misspelling of Númenor which . . . is a fragment from a vast private mythology invented by Professor J.R.R. Tolkien.''[7]

On the other hand, although Tolkien received encouragement, he was influenced by neither Lewis nor the other Inklings. He was outwardly oblivious to specific criticism of any kind, and did not easily admit to mistakes or passages of bad writing. When Charles Moorman approached Lewis hoping to gather information for a book about how the Inklings had influenced each other, Lewis replied, ''No one ever influenced Tolkien—you might as well try to influence a bandersnatch.'' Furthermore, ''he has two reactions to criticism; either he begins the whole thing over again from the beginning or else he takes no notice at all.'' Tolkien partially agreed with his friend's assessment. ''He [Lewis] used to insist on my reading passages aloud as I finished them, and then he made suggestions. He was furious when I didn't accept them. Once he said 'It's no use trying to influence you. You're *uninfluenceable*!' But that wasn't quite true. Whenever he said 'You can do better than that. Better, Tolkien, please,' I used to try.''

A sterling example of how oblivious Tolkien was to criticism and correction can be found in his most glaring mistake throughout both *The Hobbit* and *The Lord of the Rings*—the use of the word ''dwarves'' in place of ''dwarfs'' and ''elves'' for ''elfs.'' Most devout Tolkien fans are convinced that Tolkien's mistake was both intentional and desirable, and that the common usage rather than Tolkien's variation should be corrected and changed. Tolkien himself took this attitude some years ago when the first paperback edition of *The Hobbit* was scheduled to be issued in England. The publisher noted Tolkien's use of ''dwarves'' for ''dwarfs'' and ''elves'' for ''elfs'', and indicated that he would like to change it for the paperback edition. To reinforce his request, he cited the *Oxford English Dictionary's* declension of the word. In response, Tolkien used all his academic authority to insist that dwarves was precise; ''After all, I *wrote* the *Oxford English Dictionary*!'' Years later, Tolkien reluctantly admitted that ''of course, dwarves is originally a mistake in grammar, and I tried to cover it up; but it's purely the fact that I have a tendency to increase the number of these vestigial approvals—that is, a change of

consonant—like leaf/leaves. I tend to make more of them than are now standard. I thought that it was dwarf/dwarves, wharf/wharves. Why not?'' But he
said this only in retrospect. ''There are mistakes. Also, although it amuses me
to say, because I suppose that I am in a position in which it doesn't matter what
people say of me now, some vital mistakes in grammar, from a professor of
English language. It's rather shocking, isn't it? There's one in which I use
bestrode as the past participle of bestride.''[8]

Although oblivious to others' criticism, Tolkien was an excellent critic of
his fellow Inklings' works. Tolkien and Lewis together provided many evenings of fine-spirited dialogue concerning a favorite literary controversy between the two: allegory.

Lewis believed in allegory—especially Christian allegory—and his novels
(even his *Narnia* stories for children) are in large part allegorical. Diametrically
opposed to Lewis's appreciation and use of allegory was Tolkien, who said, ''I
dislike allegory whenever I *smell* it!'' In the introduction to the Ballantine edition of *The Lord of the Rings,* he wrote, ''I cordially dislike allegory in all its
manifestations, and always have done so since I grew old and wary enough to
detect its presence. I much prefer history, true or feigned, with its varied applicability to the thought and experience of readers. I think that many confuse
applicability with allegory; but the one resides in the freedom of the reader, and
the other in the purported domination of the author.'' He reinforced his statement that the trilogy was not allegorical when he told an interviewer that ''it
has *no* allegorical intentions, general, particular or topical, moral, religious or
political.'' And when asked if the ''Scouring of the Shire'' did not in fact refer
to postwar Britain, he replied with some exasperation, ''It does not. It is an
essential part of the plot . . . without, I need say, any allegorical significance or
contemporary reference whatsoever.''

Lewis and Tolkien argued about the merits and pitfalls of using allegory at
the Inklings' meetings, and also when they met in private. For many years,
Tolkien and Lewis met every Tuesday for lunch at the Eagle and Child pub on
St. Giles. Their lunchtime get-togethers became so well known that in a detective novel written in that period a character says, ''It must be Tuesday—
there's Lewis going into the Bird.'' They also saw each other in Lewis's rooms
every Monday morning, ''a regular custom that Tolkien should drop in on me
. . . and drink a glass. This is one of the pleasantest spots in the week.
Sometimes we talk English School politics; sometimes we criticize one
another's poems; other days we drift into theology or 'the state of the nation';
rarely we fly no higher than bawdy or puns.'' With Lewis, Tolkien felt free to
discuss his orthodox—and therefore unfashionable—views on religion, his disdain for both fascism and socialism, and the problems and success that he had

in strengthening the English faculty at Oxford. Lewis occasionally visited Tolkien at his home, but because Tolkien's wife apparently was jealous of Tolkien's easy friendship with him, most of their meetings took place elsewhere.

Some time in 1937 Tolkien and Lewis met together alone "because the usual Thursday party did not meet," recalled Lewis. "So I went up to Tolkien's [on Northmoor Road]. We had a very pleasant evening drinking gin and lime juice and reading our recent chapters to each other—his from the new *Hobbit* and mine from *The Problem of Pain.*" This recollection was the earliest written record of Tolkien's work on *The Lord of the Rings.*

Tolkien's publisher, Allen & Unwin, had asked him for a new hobbit story. Instead he sent them the manuscript of *The Silmarillion* that he had completed many years earlier. Privately, he suspected that *The Silmarillion* was quite unpublishable, an opinion with which Stanley Unwin agreed. It was rejected, but Unwin again encouraged Tolkien for another book similar to *The Hobbit.* The new book that Tolkien began was known to the Inklings for at least nine years afterwards as the "new *Hobbit*" book, which leads to the critical speculation that the final title was not selected, or at least applied, until sometime in the mid-1940s. Tolkien read excerpts from *The Lord of the Rings* to the Inklings for many years (at least from 1937 on, and possibly as early as autumn, 1936, to as late as 1948), and though the Inklings probably had little to do with the final shape of the story, it appears unlikely that Tolkien would have persisted in the writing for fourteen years unless he had their attention and encouragement.

It is not possible to talk about the conception and development of *The Lord of the Rings* without first discussing Tolkien's most famous lecture, "On Fairy-Stories," first presented on March 8, 1939, at the University of St. Andrew in Scotland.[9] On that occasion, Tolkien expressed his most serious and far-reaching thoughts regarding both fantasy and mythology. Not only did he establish the origin of—as well as the need and the desire for—fantasy literature, he also gave specific information about the technique for creating and constructing successful mythology, knowledge that he directly applied to his own great novel. To Tolkien, the modern need for fantasy is directly related to the increasingly oppressive and intolerable conditions in this, the real world. Because our world is a place punctuated with wars, poverty, and disease, and because we would rather live in a time and place when life was simpler and safer, we turn to fantasy. Tolkien compared this longing for "far away and a long time ago" to what a prisoner feels when he finds that jail is too boring and confining, and attempts to escape. Such an escape makes more sense than staying in prison; similarly, escape through fantasy literature is not a childish whim for evading daily responsibilities in the real world, but a desire for finding a better world than the one we live in. When the present is unacceptable and the future frightening, people naturally turn to the past, or to other places, real or imagined, for comfort and inspiration. In fantasy—the world of Faerie—dragons, wizards, and enchanted forests often are more appealing and far less evil than our own world with its bombs and machine guns.

In contrast, the world of Faerie is where good and evil are well defined (and the latter, therefore, is avoidable), where the rules of behavior are known instinctively, and where virtue rather than vice is rewarded in the end. Danger may be ever present, but it can always be repulsed—albeit with difficulty—by a pure heart and a stout sword.

After establishing the need for and the appeal of fantasy in our society, Tolkien proceeded to analyze in detail just how successful fantasy allows the reader to voluntarily suspend disbelief (to paraphrase Coleridge's formula) and thereby accept fantasy as something ''real.'' Tolkien knew that an important rule in the creation of fantasy is that a writer should use those things in the real world with which he is most familiar.[10] In fact, fantasy is made from components of the real world, and must therefore be consistent with itself and in agreement with natural law (and, by deduction, God's world). Such a world or universe cannot make a mockery of our senses and sensibilities, and though it may introduce such obviously impossible ideas as one-eyed giants or invisible elves, there must be logic and consistency even in the absurd.

When a fantasy world is consistent with the real world—with variations and differences, of course—the storyteller or mythmaker is less a creator than a *sub*-creator. He *discovers* rather than *invents* a never-never land that is at once similar to and unlike our own. Tolkien developed the concept of the sub-creator to encompass one who professes to recount old tales or neglected histories—such as a professor discovering and translating the *Red Book of Westmarch*. Therefore, a sub-creator is not so much an inventive writer as the professed *discoverer* of other worlds, not unlike our own, which are credible and can be reified by imagination.

Later, in *The Lord of the Rings*, Tolkien placed himself in the role of sub-creator (as he had in *The Hobbit*), and the world of Middle-earth is consistent enough with our own world to make it believable. True, it is an impossible world in which dragons talk, wizards perform magic, evil creatures lose their flesh-and-blood forms, and magic rings of power both rule and corrupt. But even seemingly impossible events are made consistent with the natural laws of Middle-earth, laws that usually became manifest through the limitations of application (such as Gandalf being unable to fly, or to see the future in detail).

Tolkien's successful role as the sub-creator of Middle-earth was probably one of the prime reasons his book was beloved and widely read.[11]

The years between 1936 and 1939 were happy and creative ones for Tolkien. He had reached the top of his profession, and enjoyed an international reputation as a philologist. Moreoever, he could take great satisfaction in seeing the innovations he had introduced in the English School bear fruit. His health was excellent (although the Apollo image of his youth had sagged somewhat in middle age), his marriage was relatively strong, his wife was still in reasonably good health, and his children showed signs of talent and intelligence. Tolkien had sent his three boys to expensive boarding schools, a heavy drain on his already overtaxed salary, but it was a move that successfully prepared them for Oxford. Eldest son John went up to Exeter College—Tolkien's *alma mater*—in 1938 to read English; Michael matriculated into Trinity College the following year to read modern history; and Christopher briefly went up to Trinity College in 1942 in order to obtain a commission in the Royal Air Force.

Besides giving the Andrew Lang Lecture and publishing *The Hobbit*, Tolkien also found time to write a delightful fairy story called *Leaf by Niggle*. The inspiration came from a neighbor's tree, which Tolkien often admired from his bedroom window. One day, Tolkien looked out the window towards Lady Agnew's garden and noticed with great horror that the poplar tree had been ''lopped off and mutilated by its owner, I know not why. It is cut down now, a less barbarous punishment for any crimes it may have been accused of, such as being large and alive. I do not think it had any friends, or any mourners, except myself and a pair of owls.'' Tolkien probably completed *Leaf by Niggle* just as Germany invaded Poland in September, 1939, a time when the first nine chapters of *The Lord of the Rings* had been written. The subject, or moral, of the fairy story probably reflects Tolkien's apprehension over the coming war, and the possible end of Western civilization. In *Leaf by Niggle,* an unsuccessful artist named Niggle becomes obsessed by one of his paintings: a leaf that had become a tree. He drops all his other works and tries to finish his tree, but falls ill. On his deathbed, his canvases—including the tree—are taken away by an official to help patch houses that had been damaged during a flood. The artist dies, and his tree is used to repair a roof. Some time later, the village schoolmaster rescues a single scrap from Niggle's painting and hangs it in the town museum. Few see it before the museum is burnt to the ground and the fragment destroyed. On the other hand, Niggle, who lives on in the afterworld, is given time to finish his painting there before moving on to the Ultimate.

Leaf by Niggle is a rich and complex work presented with deceptive simplicity; possibly, it reflects Tolkien's deep concern over the destruction of art and beauty that war would bring. Of *Leaf by Niggle,* Paul Kocher writes: ''Tolkien had fought through to a meaning for his work. Unheeded except by a few it may be, perish in the end with all man's other artifacts it certainly will, but it is a glimpse of ultimate reality, and there is a safe and continuing usefulness for it somewhere beyond 'the walls of the world.' ''

During this period, Tolkien was appointed coeditor (along with C.S. Lewis and D. Nichol Smith) of the Oxford English Monograph series. They were responsible for selecting and issuing edited texts of Nordic and Anglo-Saxon literature for publication by the Oxford University Press. Years later, Tolkien and Lewis decided to collaborate on a book, but Tolkien procrastinated so much and deferred the starting date so often that Lewis finally wrote to a lady friend that the book was dated to appear on the Greek Calends (in other words, never). The two, in fact, never did collaborate.

In 1936, shortly after Allen & Unwin informed Tolkien of their decision to publish *The Hobbit,* and several years before he submitted *The Silmarillion,* Tolkien began preparing a sequel. His publisher encouraged him, possibly hoping for a *Hobbit* series. Tolkien was enthusiastic. ''I now wanted to try my hand at writing a really, stupendously long narrative and see whether I had sufficient art, cunning or material to make a really long narrative that would hold the average reader right through. One of the best forms for a long narrative is the adage found in *The Hobbit,* though in a much more elaborate form, of a pilgrimage and journey with an object. So that was inevitably the form I adopted.'' Tolkien looked for some object or event that would provide continuity between *The Hobbit* and the new work. The link he used was the magic ring that Bilbo had found during the riddle match with Gollum. Once decided, Tolkien ''felt it's got to be *the* ring, not *a* magic ring.''[12]

The ring was an attractive link because it would bind Bilbo (and hobbits) together with Gandalf, but it also meant that Gollum had to be included as well. ''You couldn't get Gollum out, could you? When you think of Gollum's relation to the ring, if the ring is going to be important, then the Gollum business must be important.'' Soon after, Tolkien composed the opening poem:

> Three Rings for the Elven-kings under the sky,
> Seven for the Dwarf-lords in their halls of stone,
> Nine for Mortal Men doomed to die,
> One for the Dark Lord on his dark throne
> In the Land of Mordor where the Shadows lie.
> One Ring to rule them all, One Ring to find them,
> One Ring to bring them all and in the darkness bind them
> In the Land of Mordor where the Shadows lie.

The poem, incidentally, was composed while Tolkien was taking a bath. "I still recall kicking the sponge out of the bath when I got to the last line, and I knew it all and jumped out."

There is no ultimate answer as to *why* Tolkien wanted to write *The Lord of the Rings.* Certainly one reason must have been to exercise his abilities as a storyteller and mythmaker, as he stated in public, but not in the same manner, nor with the same motivation, he had for writing *The Hobbit. The Hobbit* had been composed as a bedtime tale for his young children, a private amusement that made use of his imagination and scholarship. Only after repeated urgings from his friends did he seek to have it published. But by the time Tolkien had begun writing *The Lord of the Rings,* his sons had passed beyond the stage of demanding nocturnal fairy stories, and his young daughter was just at an age when she could appreciate the simplicity of *The Hobbit.* That the story was not written for children is evident in that Tolkien chose to read it to the Inklings— grown, mature, literate men. Nor did he simply tell a story he had worked out in his head and wanted to put down on paper. "It grew without control, except a major one that the ring had to be destroyed, which came out quite early through Gandalf. Several times I tried to write that last scene ahead of time, but it didn't come out, never worked."

Perhaps Tolkien wanted a literary *tour de force* for his linguistic experiments in Elvish, and also wanted to construct, as sub-creator, an entire cosmology to encompass the mythology he had been working on for so many years. Tolkien himself said that "the invention of language is the foundation. The stories were made rather to provide a world for the language than the reverse. To me a name comes first and the story follows. But, of course, such a work as *The Lord of the Rings* has been edited and only as much language has been left in as I thought would be stomached by readers. I now find that many would have liked much more." Tolkien confessed, as a matter of fact, that he had thought of writing the entire trilogy in Elvish. On the other hand, Tolkien also said that "the problem is to get across a whole mythology which I've invented before you get down to the stories." But if one accepts Tolkien's premise that language presupposes mythology, then perhaps it may be speculated that he wrote *The Lord of the Rings* as his personal contribution to understanding the link between language and mythology. This, coupled with his own understanding of the dynamics of the sub-creator, could possibly give him the key as to how and why truth becomes myth, and how myth in turn becomes a point of reference for the real world. The only way he could synthesize his theories on myth, language, and the sub-creator was to write a credible myth of his own. If this is so, then the only way to establish and make known the process was to allow others to discover it for themselves in his work. This is a possible explanation for his insistent denials that there was no meaning to be found in *The Lord of the Rings.* Such would be true in a sense, since the plot would have become irrelevant; it would be the form that was significant for those perceptive enough to discern it. Moreover, if it were not discerned, he would have failed in his task, but no one would ever be the wiser.

As to the story itself, Tolkien said that he "wanted people simply to get *inside* this story and take it in a sense of actual history." He wanted his readers to voluntarily "suspend" their disbelief and accept his fantasy as part of the real world. According to Tolkien, moreover, the principle theme of his work is the inevitability of death. "If you really come down to any really large story that interests people and holds their attention for a considerable time, it is practically always a human story, and it is practically [always] about one thing all the time: *death.* The inevitability of death. Simone de Beauvoir once said that there is no such thing as a 'natural' death. Nothing that ever happens to man is ever natural. And his presence calls the whole world into question. All men must die, but for every man his death is an accident, and even if he knows it . . . an unjustifiable violation. You may agree with those words or not, but those are the keyspring of *The Lord of the Rings.*"

In constructing his lengthy saga, Tolkien freely borrowed from both experience and scholarship. "Most people have made the mistake that Middle-earth is another kind of earth or planet, in science fiction or this sort; but it's simply an old-fashioned word for this world we live in, as imagined and surrounded by the ocean . . . at a different stage of imagination." However, Tolkien never tried to establish an historical time frame. "It would be impossible, because it was completely interfered with and trampled by the free invention of history and incidents of one's own story. It wouldn't really work out paleontologically or archeologically at all, actually. You can't relate the land masses as I've described them satisfactorily to the land masses as we know now. Nor can you really have a mixed culture as I've described, which includes tobacco, umbrellas, and things little known to archeological history." Middle-earth, however, "resembles some of the history of Greece and Rome as against the perpetual infiltration of people from the East."

According to Lin Carter's *A Look Behind The Lord of the Rings,* Tolkien drew inspiration for his work from *The Elder Edda.* "*The Elder Edda* is the original source, the fountainhead, of Norse mythology. Every Norse myth in modern literature, in every verse and form, from L. Sprague de Camp . . . all the way to Richard Wagner's *Ring* cycle of operas, springs from this one work." Carter, who was Ballantine's fantasy editor when that publishing house first issued Tolkien's books, points out a number of similarities between

Wagner and Tolkien: a dragon guarding a treasure; a magic ring of power involving a curse; a talisman of invisibility; the slaying of a dragon through one unprotected spot; a broken sword made whole again; a quarrel between two beings over a ring that ends with one slaying the other; a creature that the ring maddens, perverts, and ultimately leads to death; and, a curse that brings corruption and death to all who would possess it. Carter points to possible name sources, such as the dwarf names from *The Elder Edda,* Mirkwood from *King Heidrek the Wise,* Orc from both *Paradise Lost* and *Beowulf,* and Frodo (Frode) from the saga of *Halfdan the Black* (or *Beowulf* or *Gesta Danorum*).

There are certain similarities between Wagner and Tolkien, but they appear to be coincidental. What Carter fails to consider is that many of the components in *The Elder Edda* are found also in earlier, unrelated mythologies, especially the works of Homer. In any event, Tolkien considered it quite unimportant that he borrowed from the things he knew, and made no secret that he incorporated his love of rural England and his knowledge of Norse mythology into *The Lord of the Rings.*

A large number of personal experiences and private jokes found their way into the trilogy: for example, Treebeard and the ents. In an interview Tolkien said, ''I knew there was going to be some trouble with tree-like creatures at one point or another'' because they were totally his own invention, like the hobbits, and seemed to violate natural law by being able to think, move, and speak. But when he was asked if the trees were symbolic of anything, he said no. ''I don't work in symbols. Other people may find that they are symbolic. . . . An emblem, yes, but what are the leopards of England symbolic of?'' The true explanation for the invention of ents, however, is that Tolkien's son Michael asked that they be put in the story. ''From my father I inherited an almost obsessive love of trees: as a small boy I witnessed mass tree-felling for the convenience of the internal-combustion engine. I regarded this as the wanton murder of living beings for very shoddy ends. My father listened seriously to my angry comments and when I asked him to make up a tale in which the trees took a terrible revenge on the machine-lovers, he said, 'I will write you one.'''[13] Another family contribution to the story was the character of Tom Bombadil, who was originally a jointed wooden doll that belonged to Priscilla. She demanded that Tom be written in somewhere, and he was. That hobbits have hairy feet and wear no shoes can be traced to Tolkien's American friend at Exeter College, Allen Barnett. Barnett was from Kentucky, and Tolkien loved to hear his stories about country boys and their down home names, contempt for shoes, and insatiable urge to steal tobacco out of curing casks.

Tolkien used technical points of reference from our world and applied them to Middle-earth. For example, the cycles of the moon in *The Lord of the*

Rings are from the 1942 calender. And when Tolkien had his characters walk or travel over any great distance, he actually used a British Army ordnance survey manual to find out precisely how far soldiers could move on forced marches.

It is possible that the lacy golden trees of Lothlórien came out of Tolkien's memories of South African desert scenes, just as the hobbit-carrying eagles may have been appropriated from a painted sign over the Eagle and Child pub in Oxford. The spiders of Mirkwood and Shelob came from Tolkien's own youthful traumatic encounter with a tarantula, and Éowyn was probably introduced in deference to his teenage daughter Priscilla's interest in romance and the fairer sex.

Tolkien began writing *The Lord of the Rings* in 1936, shortly after *The Hobbit* was first submitted to its publisher. Parts of the book, such as the "History of the Elvish Languages," had undoubtedly been written earlier, and the mythology was a continuation of *The Silmarillion,* written almost two decades before. At first, Tolkien wanted to continue with the hobbits, but "the story was drawn irresistibly towards the older world, and became an account, as it were, of its end and passing away before its beginning and middle [*The Silmarillion*] had been told. The process had begun in the writing of *The Hobbit,* in which there were already some references to the older matter: Elrond, Gondolin, the High-elves, and the orcs, as well as glimpses that had arisen unbidden of things higher or deeper than its surface: Durin, Moria, Gandalf, the Necromancer, the Ring."

The newly begun manuscript was almost the mystery adventure to Tolkien that it later became to his readers. He had no idea what was to happen, save that the ring was to be destroyed in the end. He was right when he said that "this tale grew in the telling." At first, he attempted to block out an outline, but "all the things I tried to write ahead of time just to direct myself proved to be no good when I got there. The story was written backwards as well as forward."

Tolkien began to read his new work to the Inklings around 1937, and continued to do so for almost eleven more years until the first draft was completed. Lewis occasionally mentioned the "new *Hobbit*" (as it was then called) in his letters over the next decade. In 1939, he wrote his brother that the Inklings had dined at the Eastgate Hotel one night and heard a "roaring cataract of nonsense" from Hugo Dyson, an original Christmas play by Charles Williams; excerpts from Lewis's own book, *The Problem of Pain;* and, of course, a chapter from Tolkien's "new *Hobbit.*" Of course really meant of course: Tolkien read a chapter, or parts of a chapter, at virtually every meeting he attended. Some of the Inklings would even let out groans whenever Tolkien would take portions of his work out of his pocket, for its length made it difficult to appreciate the continuity of its genius over the span of years. In addition, unlike his fellow Inklings, Tolkien was outwardly oblivious to criticism. It was as if he were giving a lecture or a professional reading instead of putting his work on display for comment and criticism. It is therefore doubtful that the Inklings had any significant effect on the style or content, although their patience gave him moral support and encouragement to complete the manuscript (he seriously considered abandoning the work on at least two occasions). Tolkien later acknowledged his debt when he dedicated the first edition of *The Lord of the Rings* to "all admirers of Bilbo, but especially to my sons and my daughter, and to my friends the Inklings. To the Inklings, because they have already listened to it with a patience, and indeed with an interest, that almost leads me to suspect that they have hobbit-blood in their venerable ancestry."

The first chapter, "The Shadow of the Past," had been the earliest part Tolkien had read to the Inklings, and in it he established that the ring Bilbo had found was significant, perhaps *the* ring. Bilbo uses the ring at his eleventy-first birthday party to take leave of his friends and neighbors. Before departing from Hobbiton for many years, Gandalf persuades the wary, reluctant Bilbo to leave the ring for his nephew, Frodo. Eighteen years later, Frodo must flee from dark horsemen who are searching the Shire for him, since it is now known that Frodo has the ring. Gandalf was to have appeared by a certain date to escort Frodo, and when he fails to arrive, Frodo, Samwise, Merry, and Pippin flee the Shire without him. At the time he wrote this passage (about 1937), Tolkien did not really know what had become of Gandalf, but continued the tale without him, waiting for an opportunity and an explanation as to why he had been unable to meet Frodo. Several chapters later, at the Prancing Pony in Bree, the frightened hobbits meet a mysterious character named Strider, who appears to know much about their business with the ring. As with Gandalf's disappearance, Tolkien introduced Strider without knowing who he was or what role he would ultimately play, and despaired of ever finding out.

Some critics have speculated that Mordor was modeled either upon Nazi Germany or Stalin's Russia. However, Tolkien himself said that "the real war does not resemble the legendary war in its process or its conclusion." As to "The Shadow of the Past" being Tolkien's premonition of the coming war, as many readers have felt it to be, Tolkien replied, "It was written long before the foreshadow of 1939 had become a threat of inevitable disaster, and from that point the story would have developed along essentially the same lines if that disaster had been averted. Its sources are things long before in mind, or in some cases already written, and little or nothing in it was modified by the war that began in 1939 or its sequels."

By the end of 1939, Tolkien had almost completed Book I. Progress beyond that point was painfully slow for him, and the writing came in intervals and spurts rather than in methodical advances. After the initial shock of the war, Tolkien picked up the temporarily halted work and started adding to it. ''In spite of the darkness of the next five years,'' Tolkien wrote in the Ballantine introduction to *The Lord of the Rings,* ''I found that the story could not now be wholly abandoned, and I plodded on, mostly at night, till I stood by Balin's tomb in Moria. There I halted for a long while. It was almost a year later when I went on and so came to Lothlorien and the Great River late in 1941. In the next year I wrote the first drafts of the matter that now stands as Book III, and the beginnings of Chapters 1 and 3 of Book V; and there, as the beacons flared in Anorien and Theoden came to Harrowdale, I stopped. Foresight had failed and there was no time for thought.''

For Tolkien the war years proved especially taxing, both physically and psychologically. Rationing became a bitter way of life, and Tolkien, used to liberal amounts of beer, food, and especially tobacco, experienced great anguish and deprivation. His wife Edith suffered greatly from arthritis and migraine headaches, and Tolkien himself was frequently plagued by severe ulcers and bouts of depression. His long-term pessimism had until then been countered only by his religious faith; now there was something else to offset it: America. To many Britons the effect of the United States' entrance into the war on the side of the Allies was as great as that of General Pershing's American Expeditionary Force when it landed in France a generation earlier. Tolkien expressed his new-found hope and enthusiasm to Allen Barnett, who was now a schoolmaster in Woodbury Forest, Virginia. He wrote:

''May 1942 be a year of at least good hope for all of us—and bring a Victorious peace within sight. In spite of disaster and anxieties, we have held to our belief in the ultimate victory of the Democratic Powers—and now that you people are in the War, up to the hilt, that belief is only the more sure. And I hope at this time, our cooperation will extend beyond the War, into the Peace.'' Tolkien also reported that he and his family were well, and added that Oxford hadn't yet been bombed. (It never was.) At that time John was studying for the priesthood (he had been in Rome when the war broke out in 1939), Michael had just transferred from the army to the RAF, where he would become a tail-gunner,[14] and Christopher was about to come up to Oxford before receiving a commission in the RAF.

By the time war broke out, Oxford was already a city of more than one hundred thousand, with an all-time high of five thousand students. The war seriously depleted the university ranks, but not as thoroughly as when Tolkien had been a student. Tolkien was too old for military service—in any event, he had a stomach ulcer—so he remained at his post at the English School. Unlike many other academics, Tolkien did not work for the War Office, although he did serve as a volunteer air raid warden and prepared a ''hurry-up'' method of teaching English to naval cadets. The attrition of retirement, death, and transfers had thrust Tolkien to the position of senior professor of the English faculty. This added responsibility, along with the war and the unavailability of paper, helps explain why Tolkien published nothing during those years, and why progress on *The Lord of the Rings* was so painfully slow.

The Inklings continued to meet—not as often as before, and with a reduced membership, though they still managed to remain productive during this time of adversity. The Oxford University Press had moved to Oxford because of the Blitz, so Charles Williams became a regular rather than an occasional member. Tolkien went through a relatively unproductive period in which he had to content himself with listening to the works of others; he did not resume work on his epic until 1944, about the time the Allies invaded Normandy. His youngest son, Christopher, had left Oxford and joined the RAF, and had been promptly shipped to the Union of South Africa for flight training. This apparently gave Tolkien incentive to continue, and he derived great satisfaction from sending Christopher newly-completed chapters.

''Nevertheless,'' Tolkien wrote in the introduction to *The Lord of the Rings*, ''it took another five years before the tale was brought to its present end.'' This delay was in part due to two great changes in Tolkien's life that occurred between 1945 and 1948. The first was his resignation as Bosworth and Rawlinson Professor of Anglo-Saxon at the English School, a position he had held for twenty years. In that time, Tolkien's own work and professional reputation had shifted slightly. Whereas he had once been known primarily as a philologist or a technician of language, such academic credits as the lectures on *Beowulf* and ''On Fairy-Stories'' had established him as an interpreter of literature as well. At war's end, Tolkien was offered the distinguished chair of Merton Professor of English Language and Literature, which he accepted. The Merton chair was associated with Merton College—one of the oldest and most prestigious of all the Oxford colleges—so he resigned his fellowship at Pembroke College as well.

The second major change was the sale of the house at 20 Northmoor Road and the move to a smaller rented house in the city's center. At that time, Priscilla was the only child still living at home (even she was to leave for college rooms at Lady Margaret Hall when Tolkien and his wife Edith moved to 3 Manor Road in 1947), and the house was too large and expensive for their reduced needs and modest means. In a letter to Allen Barnett dated October

20, 1946, Tolkien wrote, "I can no longer afford this 'mansion,' nor can we cope with it without help any longer. It's only 11 rooms, this home, but that is very large for present-day shortened dons, and I am going to sell and move into a minute house (I hope) belonging to my college. You may remember Manor Road that existed in your time (whereas Northmoor Road did not, and was still open space). Manor Road turns left out of Cross Road, just beyond the opening to the Holywell Tennis Courts (where our Exeter group rented a court in those days)."

Until the mid-1950s, England was almost as difficult to live in as it had been during the war. Rationing continued for years, and such staples as sugar, fats, meat, and tobacco were unavailable. When Tolkien's son Christopher was with the RAF in South Africa, he sent sugar and other difficult-to-get delicacies to his family in England. The Tolkien had a victory garden when they lived on Northmoor Road, but they could not have a sizeable garden when they moved to the small, ugly, post-Victorian twin on Manor Road. One welcome mainstay was the food packages from America that Tolkien's old friend Allen Barnett sent them periodically. The Barnetts' generosity deeply moved Tolkien, and he wrote on December 21, 1947, "we can now report that the noble parcel (which caused you so much trouble) has arrived—two or three days ago—in perfect condition. It is difficult to thank you warmly enough, not only for the great kindness of thought and wish inspiring it (which we find so deeply moving), but for the practical sagacity of your selection. Only because you so firmly insist would I dare to look so splendid a gift-horse in the mouth or say which of his teeth I preferred. If pressed, I would say that above all sugar (which you so generously included) and cooking fat also are among the most welcome of all things. Or anything containing meat; as any small tin of luncheon meat or the like cost us more than one person's ration of points in a month. But do not be distressed. We are not starving ourselves—but the spectre of suffering far worse than ours is not far away. We cannot alleviate it by private endeavor (except in the matter of clothes) since we are not allowed to send anything except what comes out of our personal rations. I may send my chocolate ration, or part of it, but as a father I cannot spare much when one can see one's own children insufficiently fed to support the strain of giving and sharing—let alone providing. Where we previously were rather bored with monotony and poor quality and the penance of never having what you feel like but only what was available, we are now definitely a little hungry. And rich gifts as yours do wonders! God bless you." After receiving another food parcel, Tolkien wrote, "Americans really are the warmest-hearted people in the world. I only hope you are right in imagining we should prove so kind in reversed conditions (as a people, I mean, and apart from ourselves personally).

Perhaps we should, for beneath the surface frictions, and the less kind and more ill-mannered scribblings, there endures a deep sense of kinship.''

Tolkien was now entering the most mature and creative period of his life. The war's end revitalized the Inklings[15], and according to most critics, 1946 was an especially noteworthy year for the quality and quantity of the works read and eventually published. Although Tolkien's health was not good at the time, it seems not to have affected his work on *The Lord of the Rings*. Tolkien again began to publish. In 1945, several of his poems appeared in obscure journals (he never wrote for popular, large circulation periodicals). Around that time, he also tried—unsuccessfully at first—to have Allen & Unwin bring out another edition of *The Hobbit* to replace the one destroyed in the war. When it was published the following year, Allen & Unwin had to delete the color plates of Tolkien's illustrations. This caused some ill feeling, since Tolkien erroneously believed that his publisher could have used them. Actually, the only paper then available was a poor grade quite unsuited for color reproduction, and, rather than wait, Stanley Unwin cut the color illustrations.

Apparently Tolkien also offered Allen & Unwin the opportunity to publish a fairy story, *Farmer Giles of Ham*, which he had written earlier, but they were unable to issue it because they couldn't find a paper allotment.[16] It was eventually published in a small Irish Catholic journal in 1947, and brought out by Allen & Unwin two years later. In 1947, his essay, ''On Fairy-Stories,'' was published in an Oxford University Press memorial edition, *Essays Presented to Charles Williams*.

The Tolkien family survived the war. John, the eldest son, had been ordained, and his first parish was a bombed-out working-class district in the industrial city of Coventry. Michael was demobilized in 1945 and returned to Trinity College. Youngest son Christopher, who had transferred from the RAF to the Fleet Air Arm in order to avoid becoming a physical equipment training officer, was also demobilized in 1945 and returned to Trinity College at the end of that year. Priscilla was still in high school at Oxford, but went up to Lady Margaret Hall, Oxford, in 1948 as one of only a handful of students who had passed the stiff competitive examination for a place. (She just missed winning a scholarship, and Tolkien had to pay for her room, board, and tuition.)

Meanwhile, Edith Tolkien's health grew poorer yet, and her failure to improve in the years immediately following the war was the primary reason Tolkien reluctantly declined a visiting professorship—with full salary and traveling expenses—at the Catholic University in Washington. Of this, he wrote to Allen Barnett, ''I thought a long while before I finally refused with regret. It would have been a grand way of visiting your country, and the vacations would have offered chances of travel and visits. But I cannot shut up my home yet [this was written at the end of 1946, when they were still living on Northmoor Road] in my daughter's last year at school, 1947-8. And the money offered could not have allowed me to keep it open as well as go abroad with my wife. Also at this critical time for universities (which will certainly last to 1948) I can hardly afford so long a time away, as I am now—odd though it seems to me—the senior professor of the Oxford English School. If I get any such offer later (say 1948-9), I shall think of taking it. Or if I can find any way of financing a shorter visit. I very much desire to see you [they had not seen one another since 1914, and were never to meet ever again]; and a change after a sabbathless 21 years 'professing' would be a refreshment. As you say, professing has many acres of boredom—but yet now and again some crops.'' Unfortunately, Tolkien received no other offer of a visiting professorship in America; nor did he ever receive a sabbatical leave from Oxford to travel abroad.[17]

Tolkien worked on *The Lord of the Rings*, and indications are that the first draft was nearly completed by the end of 1947. He then wrote Barnett that, in addition to a new edition of *The Hobbit* and a Swedish version that ''I trust will acquire a few Kroner,'' he had ''another large book nearly written.''

Tolkien completed the remainder of Book VI, ''The Scouring of the Shire,'' some time in 1948. According to one story, he sat down and wept when he finally completed the first draft of *The Lord of the Rings*. According to another, he immediately submitted the completed manuscript to Allen & Unwin, had it rejected, and put it in a drawer for almost five years until persuaded to revise it. Still another story has Father Gervase Mathew wrenching the manuscript out of Tolkien's hands and visiting various London publishing houses trying to get the work accepted. What most likely happened (consistent with Tolkien's own estimate that his work took fourteen years[18]), is that once Tolkien finished the first draft, he almost immediately began revising and retyping, a labor that took about a year and a half. That was necessary because, as he explained later, ''When the 'end' had at last been reached, the whole story had to be revised, and indeed largely rewritten backwards. And it had to be typed, and retyped;[19] the cost of professional typing by the ten-fingered was beyond my means.''

The final draft of *The Lord of the Rings* was completed near the end of 1949, and was submitted to his publisher, George Allen & Unwin, early the following year. Allen & Unwin had been expecting a sequel to *The Hobbit* for many years, and had almost given up hope of ever seeing one. Not that they were unaware of the work in progress—young Raynor Unwin had gone up to Oxford in 1944, and Tolkien had periodically permitted him to read parts of his draft. On his first visit to Tolkien's house Raynor Unwin saw bits of the

Ring manuscript stuffed away in cupboards, filing cabinets, and desk drawers (Tolkien was quite unmethodical and casual about his manuscripts, and wrote on any odd pieces or scraps of paper that happened to be around when the creative urge hit him). On that and subsequent visits, Tolkien grabbed sections of his manuscript and thrust them into Raynor Unwin's hands, muttering something like "take this away and let me know what you think of it." Of course Tolkien didn't want—and never received—Raynor Unwin's opinion. Whenever he brought pages back, he would say something noncommittal like "that's awfully interesting."

When Tolkien completed the revised draft and submitted it to Allen & Unwin, probably in 1950, it arrived while Raynor Unwin was away. Sir Stanley's son had joined the publishing firm after receiving his degree, and had been looking forward to reading the entire manuscript as soon as Tolkien finished it. He didn't see it then, however, and it was many months before he even knew it had arrived. Someone else not familiar with Tolkien had read—and rejected—the manuscript, and returned it to the author with no encouragement to revise and resubmit.

As with a similar rejection of *The Simarillion* in 1937, Tolkien was deeply hurt and humiliated over the unexpected turn of events—so much so that he initially refused to submit the manuscript elsewhere.[20] Despite the encouragement of his friends, he declined to pursue the matter further. This period of limbo lasted at least through 1952, because C.S. Lewis told Charles Moorman that "at the time we all hoped that a good deal of that mythology would soon become public through a romance which the Professor was then contemplating. Since then the hope has receded." During this period of "receded" hope, Tolkien wrote his own version, in poetic style, of the ancient battle of Maldon, fought between the English and the Danes almost one thousand years ago. In the Anglo-Saxon saga, *The Battle of Maldon*, the English commander, Beorhnoth, foolishly allows his honor to overcome his good sense and his responsibility as leader when he permits the Danes to cross a footbridge in order to have a "fair" fight. Boerhnoth and all his men are needlessly killed as a consequence, and a battle that could have been won is lost. Tolkien's small epic concerns itself with the aftermath of the battle, when the Christian monks of Ely send men to recover the headless body of the slain hero. A minstrel named Torthelm accompanies the party on its sad mission. He sees at first only the epic glory and the splendid heroism of battle, but subsequent events and a full realization of the foolish slaughter of brave men gradually help Torthelm see the wanton wastefulness of war. Instead of a heroic ballad, he ends up singing a threnody: *Dirige, Domine, in conspectu tuo viam meam* (here at last after courage shines hope). The poem *The Homecoming of Boerhnoth, Boer-*

thelm's Son was first published in the 1953 edition of *Essays and Studies of the English Association*, and printed by Ballantine in *The Tolkien Reader* thirteen years later. Tolkien was quite proud of this small work, and later wrote a verse play based on it; that work is expected to be published sometime in the near future. Also written in this period was an epic poem, *Imran*, a narrative account of the voyage of the famous Irish ecclesiastic St. Brendan to lands west of Europe. According to Paul Kocher, this poem (yet to appear in a popular edition) has many elements in common with the final voyage to the Undying Lands that ends *The Lord of the Rings*.

After many months, Tolkien's friends finally persuaded him to try once again to find a publisher. Apparently Gervase Mathew acted as Tolkien's personal agent, introducing Tolkien to Milton Waldman of the London firm of William Collins and Sons. Waldman was interested in publishing *The Lord of the Rings*, but considered it far too long and asked that it be cut nearly in half. At another publishing house he was flatly told that *The Lord of the Rings* was unsaleable. Mathew related Collins' offer to Tolkien, who seriously considered radical surgery to his manuscript. Why he considered making such a major compromise at that time is unclear, but the most probable explanation is that Tolkien had just passed his sixtieth birthday and was fast approaching the mandatory retirement age for Oxford professors. He had just moved once more, to a rented house in Holywell Street (adjacent to New College), and expressed a desire to live out his life in a house of his own without financial fears. It is likely that he looked at the prospect of a professor's pension with great alarm, concluded he could not live comfortably on it, and wished to have some sort of supplementary income.

Tolkien was undoubtedly weighing these factors and about to make the necessary changes when he was contacted by Raynor Unwin. The young publisher had just heard that *The Lord of the Rings* had been in the house some time before, and had been rejected without his knowledge or approval. He wanted the opportunity to read the work himself in its entirety, and urged Tolkien, who proved stubbornly reluctant, to resubmit the manuscript.

Perhaps it is only coincidental that John Ronald Reuel Tolkien happened to be fifty-seven when he finished writing *The Lord of the Rings* in 1949. That was the exact age of the hero of a delightful little fairy story that Tolkien wrote titled *Smith of Wootten Major* when he could no longer enter the world of Faërie. It may be mere coincidence that Tolkien had almost reached Bilbo's age when *The Hobbit* was first published. But if Tolkien identified himself with his own creations—and there is evidence he did—then the completion of *The Lord of the Rings* represented some sort of milestone in his life. Perhaps he felt a loss of innocence, but more likely he experienced a realization that innocence is transient and increasingly desirable, but infinitely rare, in the modern world. Like Thomas Wolfe, Tolkien may have felt that the world he had known had passed him by, although his allegiances were still wedded to it. He wanted the world of Faërie to exist—as indeed it did in his imagination—because it was markedly superior in his own mind to our world, with its war, hunger, and violation of the environment. But he never deluded himself: the two worlds were universes apart. Perhaps writing *The Lord of the Rings* expressed his loyalties, but *Smith of Wootten Major* recognized the sad realities. Tolkien had not grown too old; the world had grown old around him.

THE AUTHOR
1953–1965

FTER READING *The Lord of the Rings* manuscript in its entirety for the first time, Raynor Unwin had no doubt that it was a work of absolute genius. He also had no doubt that Allen & Unwin would publish the book, and furthermore, no doubt that the firm would probably lose £1,000 ($2,800) on it. As William Cater aptly pointed out in the London *Sunday Times* magazine, "What is remarkable is that *The Lord of the Rings*, on which Tolkien's fame depends, had all the earmarks of a publishing disaster. A book for the adult market, at an adult price, it continued the story of *The Hobbit*, which was a children's book; it ran to three volumes, longer than *War and Peace*; it contained stretches of verse, five learned appendices [not all in the original edition, however], and samples of imaginary languages in imaginary alphabets; but only the most slender 'romantic interest.' It was concerned with good and evil, honor, endurance and heroism, in an imaginery age of our world, and was described by its author as 'largely an essay in linguistic aesthetics.'"

Raynor Unwin did not have the authority to commit the firm to what seemed an inevitable financial loss; the only person who could make such a decision was his father, Sir Stanley Unwin, and he was away on business in Japan and the Far East. Raynor Unwin sent a cable to his father asking authority to publish the book, stating that in his opinion it was a work of genius, but that it would probably cost the firm £1,000 in losses. Sir Stanley cabled back to his son: IF YOU THINK IT A WORK OF GENIUS THEN YOU MAY LOSE £1000.

Many publishing firms exercise to some degree a policy of patronage for well-written or important works that would bring the firm prestige, if not profits. Most of the poetry printed in the United States by major publishing houses does not even pay its own way, let alone make a profit, but it continues to be

117

published because it is, in part, "subsidized" by best-sellers and money-making works of lesser talent. Many publishing houses have an unoffical annual allotment of books that they publish strictly on merit and not on profit potential. To Allen & Unwin, Tolkien's book fit into this category. By American standards, the loss of £1,000, or $2,800, seems negligible, even for the early '50s. After all, a large publishing house like Doubleday or Random House may issue an average of a book a day and deal with annual budgets in the tens of millions. But English publishers, for the most part, do not enjoy the mass circulation or the advantageous financial arrangements of their American counterparts. In 1953, their total budgets were measured in thousands of pounds, not millions of dollars. This difference meant that a "subsidy" of £1,000 was, relatively speaking, a large amount and therefore a major commitment, in return for which Allen & Unwin hoped to gain favorable reviews, good will, perhaps a literary prize, a well-rounded seasonal list, and other less tangible benefits. Playing patron to works of art was not pure altruism on Sir Stanley Unwin's part; he expected, and usually got, something back for his money.

Once the decision to go ahead was made, Raynor Unwin began applying his skills as a publisher to help minimize the projected loss. The text could not be edited or cut down. (Apparently, very little was ever done by Allen & Unwin to change Tolkien's own version, possibly on the premise that one should not tamper with great literature, but more likely out of the realization that such a task would require an editor with the skills of a philologist and a mythologist.) So the book's length made necessary a substantial investment in paper, ink, typesetting, and binding. Raynor Unwin wanted to minimize the risk that a single large volume would not sell out even a modest first printing. He decided to split Tolkien's single large work into *three* smaller books: *The Fellowship of the Ring, The Two Towers*, and *The Return of the King.* (Raynor Unwin selected the titles himself.) In addition, publication dates of the three books would be staggered over a three-year period so that a large loss would not be incurred at one time. Futhermore, working on the usually accurate premise that each subsequent volume would have diminished sales, Raynor Unwin scheduled a progressively smaller print run for each book. *The Fellowship of the Ring* was to be issued in an edition of 3,500 in 1954; *The Two Towers* in an edition of 3,250 in 1955, and *The Return of the King* in an edition of 3,000 the following year. To further minimize investment risks, Unwin insisted on reverting to the kind of contract used a century earlier in which the writer and publisher equally split all profits after the initial investment is recovered. If the book made little money Tolkien would receive nothing, but if it turned out to be a best-seller (which it did), Tolkien stood to make a fortune. In retrospect,

Raynor Unwin's cautious approach cost his firm hundreds of thousands of dollars, while Tolkien made far more money than he would have under a standard publishing contract.

In English publishing, printings above the 3,000 mark reflect an average, and not a small edition. The initial runs were to be high relative to the projected modest sale because Tolkien's American publisher, Houghton Mifflin, had agreed to issue the trilogy in the United States, but did not wish to risk investing money in printing its own edition. Instead they followed a practice common to publishers on both sides of the Atlantic, importing unbound sheets (sections of a book) already printed abroad and binding them under their own imprint. This saved Houghton Mifflin the cost of book design, typesetting, and printing. In doing this, they were making a wise business move, but it was to cost everyone involved dearly a decade later.

Initially, Tolkien opposed issuing *The Lord of the Rings* in three parts. He argued that it was a single, unified work, and should be published as such. But Allen & Unwin reminded Tolkien of the hard economic realities of the publishing industry, that it was their money being risked, and that they ought to have a measure of control over the form the book was to take. Tolkien acquiesced to their decision. (The nearest to a complaint Tolkien voiced was to an American interviewer. "But of course it's not a trilogy. That was just a publisher's device.") So his book was published in its entirety and Allen & Unwin even encouraged him to prepare an appendix to and an index for the work.

Preparing *The Lord of the Rings* for publication was not an easy task: the typesetting required extra keys for accents, Elvish script, and other symbols. Mistakes were unusually easy to make, given the large number of proper names and references, and both copyeditors and proofreaders had to be especially meticulous in their work. Then there was the question of the dust jacket. Allen & Unwin felt it inappropriate to write a self-congratulatory blurb extolling the artistry of the work or the brilliance of the writing, and thought it inadvisable as well to write a glowing biography of the author. Yet it was almost impossible to write a short synopsis of the story. Ultimately, Allen & Unwin commissioned three prominent English literary figures, C.S. Lewis, Richard Hughes, and Naomi Mitchison, to write their own perspectives on the work, with one individual's review appearing on each of the three volumes.[1] This unusual procedure was an excellent way of introducing *The Lord of the Rings* to the most knowledgeable section of the reading public, and of insuring that it would be reviewed in the major English dailies. It also suggested with a certain stamp of authority that the work was *not* a mere fairy story, but a mature work reflecting great imagination and brilliant writing.

119

Allen & Unwin released the first volume, *The Fellowship of the Ring,* with some fanfare in 1954. It received a few passing notices in the press, but most reviewers seemed to hold back until the complete work was issued. One review, by Lewis himself, appeared in *Time and Tide.* ''Here are beauties which pierce like swords or burn like cold iron; here is a book that will break your heart . . . good beyond hope.'' The *Guardian* said that Tolkien was a ''born story-teller,'' and the *New Statesman & Nation* (now the *New Statesman*) declared, ''It is a story magnificently told, with every kind of color, movement, and greatness.''

At first, *The Fellowship of the Ring* had steady but unexciting sales. Allen & Unwin, as well as Houghton Mifflin, were gratified that the book was doing better than expected and that the entire first printing would probably be sold. Meanwhile, some academics in England and America discovered the work and spread their interest and enthusiasm to their colleagues. An example of this underground excitement over the book is revealed in a eulogy to Tolkien published four days after his death by the Oxford *Mail.* It was written by an Oxford don who had been a research student when *The Fellowship of the Ring* had first been published.

''Towards the end of my last long vacation when a postgraduate student at Oxford,'' wrote Dr. John Grassi, ''another book about another imaginary land written by another Oxford scholar had been published. By happy accident I happened to buy the book almost on the day of publication. The discovery of that book and the world to which it gave entrance was as profoundly exciting and as joyous an experience as had been the discovery of the world of Alice. The book, of course, was *The Fellowship of the Ring,* the first volume of the trilogy which has made the name of J.R.R. Tolkien as immediately recognizable throughout the world as that of Lewis Carroll.

''I read that first volume three times before the publication some months later of the second volume of the trilogy and was, indeed, lucky to be able to do so for the book was scarcely ever in my own possession. It passed from hand to hand among my fellow postgraduate students and for the whole of that academic year our conversation was as much about Middle-earth as about our maturing theses and job prospects.

''For there was a price to be paid for the privilege of being the first generation of Tolkienians which millions who have joined our ranks since can scarcely appreciate. That price was the protracted and intolerable suspense in which we lived in the period before the publication of the second and third volumes, not knowing what the final outcome was to be.

''I never knew him,'' concluded Dr. Grassi, ''but then I never knew Lewis Carroll.''

Reports of similar experiences came from other English and American campuses, primarily among graduate students and staff who were most likely and best able to recognize and appreciate the scholarship that went into the work. Those libraries that had been fortunate enough to possess copies of the books found them permanently disappearing from the shelves, and when they were put on reserve shelves, long waiting lists developed. Both Allen & Unwin and Houghton Mifflin sold out the first printing many months before they expected.

But the first inkling Allen & Unwin had that *The Lord of the Rings* was likely to turn a profit occurred when people began writing to them to demand that they speed up publication of the remaining volumes. In the publishing industry, it is highly unusual for any book to elicit so popular a response; normally such requests are the result of a calculated campaign by friends of the author. Students, scholars, professional people, teachers, and many others wrote to Allen & Unwin in England and to Houghton Mifflin in America to express their enthusiasm. At that point, Tolkien's publisher realized for the first time that the book had a universal appeal, and not just a narrow following among academics. The trickle of letters became a steady stream, whereupon Sir Stanley Unwin decided to accelerate the publication schedule of the two remaining books. Instead of dropping to 3,250 printed copies for *The Two Towers* and 3,000 for *The Return of the King,* Sir Stanley inverted the pyramid policy and *increased* the number. He then concluded that two years was too long a time to wait for the release of the complete work, and published *The Two Towers* six months, and not a year, after *The Fellowship of the Ring.* *The Two Towers* appeared in early 1955, and Tolkien was pressed to complete his expanded appendices and index as soon as possible for the early release of *The Return of the King.* Instead of having two years in which to complete work on the addenda, Tolkien suddenly had only six months. The amount of time was woefully insufficient for the monumental task of indexing and completing the appendix, especially since Tolkien still had his professorial responsibilities and had been, for the most part, working alone on the book. When Allen & Unwin released the last volume in the autumn of 1955, they had to include a publisher's note regretting that "it has not been possible to include as an appendix to this edition the index of names announced in the Preface of *The Fellowship of the Ring.*"

Once the entire work was published, many important magazines and newspapers in both England and America assigned it for review. In the main, these notices were enthusiastically favorable, praising the Professor's originality, imaginative style, epic narration, and sensitive descriptions of nature. One critic said that *The Lord of the Rings* was "an onomasthologist's [someone who studies the origin and history of proper names] delight,'' and another thought it ''super science fiction.'' Others compared it to Mallory and Ariosto, and a couple went so far as to say that Tolkien was superior to them. In America, the New York *Herald Tribune* reviewer called it ''an extraordinary, a distinguished piece of work.'' The Boston *Herald Traveler* described it as ''one of the best wonder-tales ever written—and one of the best-written.'' W.H. Auden wrote in the *New York Times* that Tolkien ''succeeded more completely than any previous writer in this genre in using the traditional properties of the Quest, the heroic journey, the Numinous Object . . . . satisfying our sense of historical and social reality.'' Auden concluded that Tolkien ''has succeeded where Milton failed.'' Michael Straight wrote in the *New Republic* that ''Tolkien's trilogy is fantasy, but it stems of course from Tolkien's own experiences and beliefs. There are scenes of devastation that recall his memories of the Western Front where he fought in the First World War. The description of a snowstorm in a high pass is drawn from a mountain-climbing trip in Switzerland. And through the descriptions of life in Hobbiton and Bywater runs his own bemused love of the English and his scorn for the ugliness of the industrial surroundings in which they live. But Tolkien shuns satire as frivolous and allegory as tendentious. His preparation is immersion in Welsh, Norse, Gaelic, Scandinavian and German folklore . . . . There are very few works of genius in recent literature. This is one.''

But the longest and most important review given to *The Lord of the Rings* was decidedly negative. Edmund Wilson, America's protean literary critic, wrote a review entitled ''Oo, Those Awful Orcs!'' in the April 14, 1956 issue of *The Nation* in which he said that *The Lord of the Rings* ''is essentially a children's book, which has somehow gotten out of hand. . . . The Author has indulged himself in developing the fantasy for its own sake.'' After berating Tolkien for his pretentious introduction, Wilson continued that the ''prose and verse are on the same level of professional amateurishness. . . . What we get is a simple confrontation—in more or less the traditional terms of British melodrama—of the forces of Evil with the Forces of Good, the remote and alien villain with the plucky little home-grown hero. . . . Dr. Tolkien has little skill at narrative and no instinct for literary form. The characters talk a story-book language that might have come out of Howard Pyle,[2] and as personalities they do not impose themselves. At the end of this long romance, I still had no conception of the wizard Gandalph [sic], who is a cardinal figure, and had never been able to visualize him at all. For the most part such characterizations as Dr. Tolkien is able to contrive are perfectly stereotyped: Frodo the good little Englishman. Samwise, his doglike servant, who talks lower-class and respectful, and never deserts his master. These characters who

122

are no characters are involved in interminable adventures the poverty of invention displayed in which is, it seems to me, almost pathetic. . . . An impotence of imagination seems to me to sap the whole story. The wars are never dynamic; the ordeals give no sense of strain; the fair ladies would not stir a heartbeat; the horrors would not hurt a fly.'' Wilson continued in such a vein right to the end of the review, finding no particular merit whatever in the work.

Tolkien was unexpectedly sensitive to the negative reviews. He was depressed that in Great Britain none of the Catholic publications reviewed it favorably (many declined to review it at all), and that the country's most important Catholic journal, *The Tablet,* gave it a lukewarm reception. (He was later mollified when two Catholic publications in the United States and New Zealand gave glowing reviews.) When an interviewer once suggested that *The Lord of the Rings* seemed to have been written for boys rather than for girls, Tolkien took issue and explained that it was necessarily masculine because of the nature of the subject matter.[3] ''These are wars and a terrible expedition to the North Pole, so to speak. Surely there is no lack of interest, is there? I know that one interviewer explained it: It is written by a man who has never reached puberty and knows nothing about women but as a schoolboy, and all the good characters come home like happy boys, safe from the war. I thought it was very rude—so far as I know, the man is childless—writing about a man surrounded by children, wife, daughter, granddaughter. Still, that's equally untrue, isn't it, because it *isn't* a happy story. One friend of mine said he only read it at Lent because it was so hard and bitter.''

After another reviewer described his poetry as simply bad, Tolkien replied that ''a lot of the criticism of the verses shows a complete failure to understand the fact that they are all dramatic verses; they were conceived as the kind of things people would say under the circumstances.'' When Ballantine published a revised edition of *The Lord of the Rings* ten years after the original work was first reviewed, Tolkien used that opportunity to state in the introduction that ''Some who have read the book, or at any rate have reviewed it, have found it boring, absurd, or contemptible; and I have no cause to complain, since I have similar opinions of their works, or the kinds of writing that they evidently prefer.''

After being a professor for some thirty years, Tolkien finally began to win both recognition and reward for his academic achievements and scholarly contributions to English philology and literature. In 1954, he was named an honorary Doctor of Letters by both University College in Dublin, Ireland, and the University of Liège in Belgium. The professor of English philology at the

University of Liège was Professor Simonne d'Ardenne, who had once been Tolkien's star student at Oxford. Professor d'Ardenne undoubtedly played no small part in securing the honorary degree for his old friend and colleague.

Although Tolkien was nearing the end of a long and distinguished academic career, and his most important scholastic contributions had been made some years earlier, it was only in the 1950s that he came to be known outside his own field. In 1953, he was invited to deliver the William Paton Ker Memorial Lecture at the University of Glasgow in Scotland. Ker had been a famous medievalist, teacher, and poet; he had held several professorial chairs, including one at Oxford. After he died in 1923, the University of Glasgow established an annual lecture in his name, to be given by a distinguished scholar to an audience comprising scholars. Tolkien was accorded the honor of delivering the lecture on the eve of the publication of *The Fellowship of the Ring*. Another honor bestowed upon Tolkien was honorary membership in the *Hid Islezka bokmennta-félag*, an Icelandic society. And before his retirement, Tolkien was elected vice-president of the Philological Society of Great Britain.

The honors came so late in life because Tolkien published so very little in the way of academic papers, texts, or reference books. It has been said that "Lewis published too much and Tolkien too little." This is borne out by fellow Inkling and Oxford professor C.L. Wrenn, who once told Professor Przemyslaw Mroczkowski, "Tolkien is a genius! If only he wrote accordingly, what wonders could he accomplish." It was gratifying to Tolkien that international recognition as a scholar came *before* his fame as a writer, and not the other way around.

The Tolkiens moved once more in 1954, at the time that *The Fellowship of the Ring* was first published. Their new house was in nearby Headington—a lower-middle-class suburb east of the city—which straddled the busy London road. When Tolkien was an undergraduate, Headington had been a mere village, but like other Oxford suburbs, it had grown to provide housing for workers at the Morris motor works in Cowley. Tolkien purchased a pleasant white house at 76 Sandfield Road, not far from where C.S. Lewis lived, and just down the street from a house in which W.H. Auden later lived. Auden, by the way, did not like Tolkien's house. He told Richard Plotz, president of the Tolkien Society of America, "he lives in a hideous house—I can't tell you how awful it is—with hideous pictures on the walls."

Ironically, the money with which Tolkien purchased the house came not from the advance or royalties from *The Lord of the Rings*, but from the sale of the original manuscript for $5,000 to Marquette University in Milwaukee, Wisconsin. When asked why he did so, Tolkien confessed "I wanted the money very badly to buy this house.''

All the Tolkien children had grown up and branched off on their own. Christopher was a fellow at New College, Oxford, and a member of the English School as a lecturer in Old English. He lived in a rented house on Holywell Street near the house his parents had lived in. Incidentally, when John and Edith Tolkien moved to Headington, Christopher and his family took over Tolkien's rented house at 99 Holywell Street. Michael Tolkien had left Oxford and become a teacher and later a schoolmaster at the Benedictine School in Ampleforth, Yorkshire. Priscilla Tolkien became a teacher at a technical college in Oxford (not associated with the university), and later a probation officer. She lived in the northernmost part of the city. The eldest, Father John Tolkien, was the Catholic chaplain at Keele University in Staffordshire, and also had a small parish in the district. John and Priscilla remained single; Christopher and Michael married and had families.

Tolkien greatly enjoyed having young children in his house once again. He delighted in playing with his grandchildren (who called him Grand*fellow*) whenever they came to Headington. Once, when one of his grandsons was busy being overly rambunctious during a walk, Tolkien threatened the child that if he wasn't good, something black and terrible would come from the sky. At that instant, a truck driver lost control of his vehicle and swerved through a nearby hedge before crashing to a stop. The child was astonished and awe-struck at his grandfather's supposed magical powers, and while the story does not recount what happened afterwards, the lad probably mended his ways for a brief time.

Tolkien's was a happy household, and when the children came visiting, he amused them as he had his own a generation earlier by making up stories. He was a conventional grandfather, extremely proud of his sons' children, slightly doting, mildly indulgent, and always respectful of them as human beings. Tolkien once said that ''children aren't a class. They are merely human beings at different stages of maturity. All of them have a human intelligence which even at its lowest is a pretty wonderful thing, and the entire world in front of them.'' He was especially proud of his grandson, Michael George David Reuel Tolkien, a ''demon chess player,'' who later studied English philology at Merton College.

Tolkien's grandchildren visited him more often than he visited them; his wife Edith was still in poor health and not up to casual social visits. In later years they became rather reclusive, staying at home for weeks at a time. Tolkien wished to travel now that he had the money, but with his wife's ill health and the high demands of his position at the English School, he found he had to stay at home. Thus, he was unable to accept an invitation to visit the

United States in the autumn of 1957, when both Harvard University and Marquette University wished to confer honorary degrees upon him. In response to the latter invitation, Tolkien wrote rather belatedly in May, 1957, "I have ill repaid the gererosity of Marquette by my discourtesy of silence. Without going into long details this has been due not to lack of pleasure (indeed excitement and delight) in the generous invitation, but to overwork, difficult domestic and academic circumstances, and the necessity of coping (or trying to cope) with a now very large mail, as well as heavy professional work and duties, without *any secretary*!" Later that year, he wrote that both health and an overloaded schedule were still plaguing him. "I will not bother you with a long wail, but June and July are usually crowded months academically, and I have been much harassed. Also, I have not been well recently, and arthritic trouble with the right hand has been a hinderance. Fortunately the hand does not object to tapping keys as much as to a pen; but I prefer a pen."

The Inklings continued to meet, but rather sporadically after C.S. Lewis accepted the new chair in Medieval and Renaissance History at the University of Cambridge in 1954, as well as a fellowship at Magdalen College, Cambridge. Lewis continued to live much of the time in Oxford, even after his marriage to Joy Davidman in 1957. He surrendered his life-long bachelorhood in a Christian act of charity, marrying a woman who was terminally ill with cancer; she lived on for three more years. Lewis himself was in poor health, and was about to relinquish his Cambridge chair when he died in 1963. His death ended what was left of the Inklings, and Tolkien lost his closest companion and most valued colleague as well.

The first edition of *The Lord of the Rings* not only sold out, but became an instant collector's item. Allen & Unwin issued another printing, and has continued to do so on a regular basis. Over the years, they have published limited editions, editions on India paper, paperback editions, one volume editions, boxed editions, and four-volume editions that include *The Hobbit.* By 1957, *The Lord of the Rings* had settled down to steady sales, and became a strong staple in both Allen & Unwin's and Houghton Mifflin's catalogs.

Early on, the book had attracted the attention of the British Broadcasting Corporation, which had once dramatized *The Hobbit* on radio. In September, 1955, the BBC serialized *The Lord of the Rings* in ten parts for use in school broadcasts in the "Adventures in English" series. The BBC broadcast the programs to 27,697 schools throughout the British Isles, reaching upwards of five million children. Six years later, a thirteen-part dramatization of *The Lord of the Rings* was broadcast over BBC radio to the entire country; the cast included one of England's most popular radio actors, Bob Arnold, who regularly played the part of Tom Forrest in the long-running series *The Archers*. (Tolkien expressed interest in reading *The Lord of the Rings* himself over the air, a suggestion wisely vetoed by the BBC.)

In 1957, Tolkien received, at the World Science Fiction convention held in London, the first of many awards for his trilogy. *The Lord of the Rings* was voted the best fantasy of 1956, and Tolkien was given his "Hugo" silver starship on September 10, 1957, by Miss Clemence Dame. During her presentation speech, Miss Dame said "there is nothing in literature to rival it," and then ribbed the professor who "should be doing learned works" but instead wrote fantasy sagas. "But of course my answer is that it is a learned work," she hastily amended. To Tolkien, the World Science Fiction award was something of a mixed blessing, since, as he said in his acceptance speech, "I have never written any science fiction." Ten years later, when a *New York Times* writer asked what he had done with the stainless steel sharp-finned rocket, he replied vaguely, "it's upstairs somewhere. It has fins. Quite different from what was required, as it turned out."

Tolkien found himself deluged with requests to speak, lecture, or attend luncheons, dedications, and club meetings of all sorts. Most of the requests and invitations he turned down, claiming the excuses of work and age; he also declined to be interviewed by journalists for some years, and only relented after *The Lord of the Rings* became a best seller. One of the few invitations he was happy to accept was the dedication of the new Oxfordshire County Library on December 14, 1956. Books had always been important to his life, and he used the opportunity to reaffirm his belief in their increasing relevance to our society. "Books are besieged by a great many embattled enemies," he said, "but from them comes the food of the mind. It is not good for the stomach to be without food for a long period, and it is very much worse for the mind."

Tolkien's long and distinguished academic career was approaching its end; in 1958 he reached the mandatory retirement age. On the day before his sixty-sixth birthday, Merton College announced that they would bestow upon Tolkien an honorary fellowship, not because of his writings, but for service to the college, the university, and the many students whom Tolkien had influenced. Later, Exeter College followed suit. A year and a half later, the Merton College Hall was packed for Tolkien's valedictory lecture. It was a strictly academic farewell in which Tolkien repeated some of the thoughts that he had voiced in his famous *Beowulf: The Monsters and the Critics* lecture twenty-three years earlier. He denounced the "old errors" and "deflating asides" by scholars who sometimes lose sight of their objectives and, rather than concentrate on reading the old sagas and epics, make "melodramatic declamations in Anglo-Saxon." His audience greeted his words with thunderous applause, a fitting climax to a brilliant career.

As Professor Emeritus, Tolkien continued his research in philology and Anglo-Saxon literature. He contributed to the *New Jerusalem Bible*, an interdenominational translation hailed by both scholars and theologians. In 1962, he published the text to the *Ancrene Wisse*, a religious treatise from the late twelfth century; Tolkien probably collaborated with his former student, Professor Simonne d'Ardenne of the University of Liège, in the preparation of the text. Tolkien and d'Ardenne edited the work for the Early English Text Society, and it was published the same year by the Oxford University Press. As late as 1967, Tolkien concerned himself with such matters. At that time he also finished a modern translation of his own edited text of *Sir Gawain and the Green Knight*. With the *Sir Gawain* translation was the translation of a poem called *The Pearl*; both were published by the Oxford University Press.

By 1961, the excitement generated by *The Lord of the Rings* had quietly expanded from academics to science fiction addicts. Since news of the trilogy and mention of Professor Tolkien had all but disappeared from public view, some critics mistakenly concluded that *The Lord of the Rings* had been merely a fad. The English critic Phillip Toynbee wrote in the London *Observer* that "there was a time when the Hobbit fantasies of Professor Tolkien were being taken very seriously indeed by a great many distinguished literary figures. Mr. Auden is even reported to have claimed that these books were as good as *War and Peace*; Edwin Muir and many others were almost equally enthusiastic. I had a sense that one side or the other must be mad, for it seemed to me that these books were dull, ill-written, whimsical and childish. And for me this had a reassuring outcome, for most of his more ardent supporters were soon beginning to sell out their shares in Professor Tolkien, and today those books have passed into merciful oblivion."

Perhaps it is difficult to appreciate now the intense controversy *The Lord of the Rings* at first stimulated. According to the critic R.J. Reilly, Tolkien's trilogy provoked on a modest scale the kind of critical controversy that had accompanied T.S. Eliot's *The Waste Land* and James Joyce's *Ulysses*. Literary critics could not *ignore* Tolkien and felt impelled either to support or condemn his work. Colin Wilson gives an example of such divided loyalties in his essay, "Tree by Tolkien." "A few years ago, I went to have lunch with W.H. Auden in his New York apartment. It was the first time I'd met him, and Norman Mailer had warned me that I might find him difficult to get along with. (Very reserved, very English—but more so than most Englishmen.) I found this true on the whole—he seemed to be very formal, perhaps basically shy. But after we had been eating for ten minutes, he asked me suddenly: 'Do you like *The Lord of the Rings*?' I said I thought it was a masterpiece. Auden smiled, 'I somehow thought you would.' The manner softened noticeably, and the lunch proceeded in a more relaxed atmosphere.

''It is true, as Peter S. Beagle remarked in his introduction to *The Tolkien Reader*, that Tolkien admirers form a sort of club. Donald Swann [who wrote the music for *The Road Goes Ever On* and became a friend of Tolkien's] is another member—but that is understandable, for his temperament is romantic and imaginative. It is harder to understand why someone as 'intellectual' as Auden should love Tolkien, while other highly intelligent people find him somehow revolting. (When I mentioned to a friend—who is an excellent critic—that I intended to write an essay on Tolkien, he said: 'Good, it's about time somebody really exploded that bubble,' taking it completely for granted that it would be an attack.) Angus Wilson told me in 1956 that he thought that *The Lord of the Rings* was a 'don's whimsy' (although he may have changed his mind since then). . . .''

Nevertheless, Tolkien's books continued to sell well, and his publishers encouraged him to prepare a book of poetry from *The Lord of the Rings* for release in 1962. This he did with pleasure, since it promised more money and little exertion. That book became *The Adventures of Tom Bombadil.* Allen & Unwin also encouraged Tolkien to write more about hobbits and Middle-earth, but he was primarily interested in returning to his earlier works in order to prepare them for publication. So it was that after more than thirty years, Tolkien took up again *The Silmarillion*, the ''prequel'' to *The Lord of the Rings*. This task was to continue to the end of his life.

One serious tactical mistake that Allen & Unwin made was in greatly underestimating the audience for *The Lord of the Rings*. The trilogy became an underground classic among science fiction and fantasy readers, many of whom could not afford $15 or more for a three-volume hardbound set. There had been a sizeable paperback market for the work almost immediately after its initial publication in the mid-50s, but no paperback edition was forthcoming. This oversight by both Allen & Unwin and Houghton Mifflin created a vacuum that was filled by a less conservative publishing house, Ace Books.

There is still considerable difference of opinion about the ''great copyright controversy'' over the American edition of *The Lord of the Rings*. The only certainty is that the original edition of the trilogy is *not* copyrighted in the United States, and is therefore in the public domain (which means that any publishing house can issue it without having to pay royalties to Tolkien's heirs). According to Houghton Mifflin, the complicated and confusing American copyright law is really to blame. Before America joined the International Copyright Convention, various subsections of the law were designed to protect the American printing industry. One was known as the "manufacturing clause," and it stated that a publisher would fail to establish American copyright if he imported more than 1,445 printed copies of a book from a foreign country. Houghton Mifflin supposedly imported small numbers of *The Lord of the Rings* at first, but when sales picked up, they ordered more and more until they inadvertantly exceeded the maximum limit by 555. The "restrictive and controversial" law automatically went into force, and copyright was therefore never established.

On the other hand, Donald Wollheim, who was chief editor of Ace Books when Ace brought out an uncopyrighted edition of *The Lord of the Rings*, lays responsibility at Houghton Mifflin's door. "They figured that it would only sell five hundred copies or less in this country, so they imported sheets and didn't *bother* to copyright it. Afterwards, they couldn't sell it to a paperback house under any circumstances because it had no copyright, and if it hadn't been for someone like Ace, *The Lord of the Rings* wouldn't be in paperback to this very day.

"It was very easy to see that the original edition was in the public domain because it carried no copyright; that is the simple situation. English copyright law is quite different from American copyright law. American copyright law requires that a book should carry a statement on the page following the title page: Copyright (the date of publication) by (the name of the copyright owner). In England, this is not required. When an American publisher imports printed sheets from England and binds them here under his own imprint, he must either overprint the copyright, or else take out an *ad interim* copyright that would give him eighteen months in which to print an American edition or lose copyright. But if you place a book on sale without a copyright notice, it falls into the public domain immediately, according to United States copyright law. The original Houghton Mifflin edition is in the public domain, and anyone can print it without asking permission or paying royalties. What they did after we published the Ace edition was to get Professor Tolkien to revise the book, making little changes here and there, and that's what their copyright really covers: only slight revisions."

Ace Books was and still is a major paperback publisher of popular science fiction whose books were distinguished as such for many years because of their usually lurid covers and cheap prices. Wollheim knew about the underground popularity of *The Lord of the Rings* and wanted to get the rights to publish it in paperback. He quickly found out that the trilogy was not copyrighted in the United States and therefore, according to him, began lengthy and frustrating negotiations with Professor Tolkien through Allen & Unwin. Allen & Unwin was unenthusiastic, and Tolkien did not respond at all.[4] When Wollheim finally advised his publisher, A.A. Wyn, of the situation, Wyn told him to go ahead and publish the trilogy. The Ace Books edition (minus the appendices), with suitably sensational covers, went on sale in May, 1965.

Allen & Unwin became aware of the imminent publication of the Ace Books edition, and decided to counter it by bringing out an ''authorized'' paperback edition of their own. Ballantine Books was selected to publish the work in paperback. They persuaded Tolkien to make various changes in the main text, add information to the appendices, and write a completely new introduction. Tolkien wrote the introduction with some enthusiasm, since it gave him an opportunity to make various corrections of unintentional errors that he, and other perceptive readers, had noted.

The Ace edition beat the Ballantine edition into print by almost five months, during which time the initial printing of 50,000 completely sold out. Within a year (during which time it competed against the Ballantine edition) the Ace edition managed to sell an additional 150,000 complete copies of the trilogy, despite the fact that it had neither index nor appendices but, rather, bad publicity and considerable criticism. The Ace edition was also more than a dollar cheaper than the Ballantine edition.

Raynor Unwin condemned Ace's action as ''moral piracy,'' but took no legal action since none was possible. Tolkien himself was publicly indignant, and states in the Ballantine edition, ''I hope that those who have read *The Lord of the Rings* with pleasure will not think me ungrateful: to please readers was my main object, and to be assured of this has been a great reward. Nonetheless, for all its defects of omission and inclusion, it was the product of long labor, and like a simple-minded hobbit I feel that it is, while I am still alive, my property in justice unaffected by copyright laws. It seems to me a grave discourtesy, to say no more, to issue my book without even a polite note informing me of the project: dealings one might expect of Saruman in his decay rather than from the defenders of the West. However that may be, this paperback edition and no other has been published with my consent and cooperation. Those who approve of courtesy (at least) to living authors will purchase it and no other. And if the many kind readers who have encouraged me with their letters will add to their courtesy by referring friends or enquirers to Ballantine Books, I shall be very grateful. To them, and to all who have been pleased by this book, especially those Across the Water for whom it is specially intended, I dedicate this volume.'' But in December, 1965, he relented slightly by admitting, ''There has been a great fuss in the press and on television about this piracy, and it all adds up to rather good advertisement for my work.''

Ace's decision to publish the work in paperback was probably the best thing that ever happened to Tolkien. According to Donald Wollheim's wife, it "took off like a rocket," revealing the unrealized readership potential for an affordable edition of *The Lord of the Rings.* Despite the official acrimony and the charge of moral piracy, Tolkien profited handsomely from the entire affair. Technically, Ace Books was not obliged to give Tolkien a single penny for the rights to his books, but A.A. Wyn decided to set aside all the money that would ordinarily have gone to the author and establish a Tolkien Prize, which would encourage young writers of science fiction and fantasy. When Wollheim wrote to Tolkien of their intention to apply the $11,000 to a literary prize in his name, Tolkien responded and asked for the money himself. Since the agreement was between Ace and Tolkien, the entire $11,000 went directly to the professor. Ordinarily the author and original publisher share equally in any foreign rights; with three publishers—Allen & Unwin, Houghton Mifflin, and Ballantine Books—this meant that Tolkien received only 25 percent of the royalties from the official American edition. Since no other publishers were involved with Ace, Tolkien received 100 percent. It is likely that Tolkien publicly denied any knowledge of Ace's intention prior to publication because he did not wish either to anger or to embarrass his own publishers by going behind their backs in a technically legal but ethically questionable maneuver. On the other hand, Tolkien knew that Houghton Mifflin had muffed the American copyright through negligence. It is possible that he felt little loyalty to them at the time and believed he was justified in taking all the money for himself. After Ace Books paid Professor Tolkien his royalties, they received a letter from him expressing satisfaction with the outcome. Ace, stung from adverse publicity, a boycott of their edition, and continuing acrimony with Tolkien's other publishers, announced that once the current edition went out of print, they would not issue another.

By the end of 1965, *The Lord of the Rings* had become a dramatic bestseller both in England and in America. Tolkien was propelled from relative obscurity to world-wide fame. His works, which had brought him only modest affluence, now promised the comfortable wealth that had eluded him all his life. But the price he was to pay for popular success was one he could not easily afford: the loss of privacy. To a man like Tolkien, celebrity status robbed him of time, peace of mind, and the ability to work unhindered on his remaining life's work, *The Silmarillion.* To Tolkien, success turned out to be a terrible two-edged sword.

THE RECLUSE
1966–1973

THE *LORD OF THE RINGS* burst on the campuses of American colleges and universities like a rainstorm over a parched desert. Since the early '60s, when the American Dream had begun to turn into a nonstop nightmare of presidential assassination, dirty wars in Southeast Asia, black power tirades and white backlashes, urban riots and campus disorders, many younger people began to feel disaffection with and alienation from the mainstream of contemporary life. The vision of perfection that had enchanted a postwar generation—shopping centers, suburban split-levels, two-car garages, and color television sets—failed to satisfy their children; in fact, almost everything about middle-class America became anathema to rebellious youth. At first, the great social issues of the decade attracted their allegiance, spearheaded by an almost fanatical idolization of a youthful, dynamic president. The New Frontier meant the Peace Corps, VISTA, civil rights, the war on poverty, the Nuclear Test Ban Treaty, and a man on the moon by the end of the decade. But after John F. Kennedy was killed in Dallas came the disenchantment of war, civil strife, social upheaval, government wrongdoing, and increasing abuse of the environment. The disenchantment became alienation, the alienation produced a polarity, and one extreme of that polarity became manifest in the hippie movement, drug abuse, and student protest.

Large numbers of intelligent, educated young Americans found no pleasure in the present, no solace in the past, and little hope for the future. ''Be here now'' and ''do your own thing'' reflected the agonizing, hedonistic frenzy of a confused culture. A benign cynicism towards existing institutions inspired a search for new gods: the occult, mysticism, psychedelics, Eastern philosophy, ecology, and back-to-the-land movements. Some found rootless answers and temporary solutions, only to move on in deep dissatisfaction to a new guru, a different movement, another relationship.

In ancient cultures mythology provided continuity from past to present by creating acceptable points of reference, reassurance that acts of hope and heroism were possible. In the West, mythology was in large part superseded by organized religion. Religion provided gods, heroes, and hope for centuries until Darwin, Marx, Freud, and the rise of modern industrial society fatally undercut its foundations. Religion was replaced by nationalism, communism, materialism, and other temporary surrogates. But what was needed were new myths, believable gods, acceptable roots in the past.

Tolkien wrote *The Lord of the Rings* as an attempt to modernize the old myths and make them credible. Apparently he succeeded beyond his own expectations, because his work was so well written and his mythology so well constructed—but perhaps equally because the modern need for a new mythology was so great. Dr. Clyde Kilby, who worked with Tolkien in 1966, asked in the book *Shadows of Imagination:* ''Why is *The Lord of the Rings* so widely read today? At a time when the world was perhaps never more in need of authentic experience, this story seems to provide a pattern of it. A businessman in Oxford told me that when tired or out of sorts he went to *The Lord of the Rings* for restoration. Lewis and various critics believe that no book is more relevant to the human situation. W. H. Auden says it 'holds up the mirror to the only nature we know, our own.' As for myself, I was rereading *The Lord of the Rings* at the time of Winston Churchill's funeral [1965] and I felt a distinct parallel between the two. For a few hours the trivia which normally absorbs us was suspended and people experienced in common the meaning of leadership, greatness, valor, time redolent of timelessness, and common trials. Men became temporarily human and felt the life within them and about. Their corporate life lived for a little and made possible the sign of renewal after a realization such as occurs only once or twice in a lifetime.

''For a century at least the world has been increasingly demythologized. But such a condition is apparently alien to the real nature of men. Now comes a writer such as John Ronald Reuel Tolkien and, as a mythologizer, strangely warms our souls.''

Echoing Dr. Kilby's thoughts is William Cater, an English journalist who came to know Tolkien well in his last years. ''Ours is an increasingly dehumanized age. Just as Malory and his Arthurian legends were needed in Victorian times, I am inclined to feel that Tolkien will go on appealing to young people who are battered by the realization that there are awful people in this world. The longings of all of us are for a world simpler than the one we have got. . . . There is a resemblance between *The Lord of the Rings* and the American Western myth: extremes of good and evil, a world where justice is swift and living is simple.''

Another perspective on why *The Lord of the Rings* had such a fantastic appeal is found in Patricia Spacks's essay in *Tolkien and the Critics:* ''One reason why The Lord of the Rings captivates readers so diverse as W.H. Auden and Edmund Wilson's eight-year-old daughter is that it creates a compellingly detailed and authentic imaginary universe which seems an appealing alternative to our own chaotic world. It is not the never-never land of science fiction or James Bond, but a realm in which moral problems are taken seriously and in which it is possible—not easy, but possible—to make right decisions. Tolkien lavishes such loving detail on his world that he encourages the willing suspension of disbelief; the cultists try to maintain that suspension beyond the limits of the book.'' Writing in more down-to-earth language, Judith Crist explains why her own children became ardent Tolkien readers. ''It's all far from the hot-rod, folk-rock image of the drug-inspired sensations so many are seeking,'' she wrote in the February, 1967, issue of *The Ladies' Home Journal,* ''and yet it isn't, on reflection, surprising. Didn't we—in the midst of song sheets and Big Apples and jitterbugging—retreat into Romance, for that is basically what hobbit history is? True, we pursued it, in our post-fairy-tale days, through the *Aeneid* and the *Odyssey* and the *Idylls of the King* and Scott's novels—and none of these is fashionable and few are required reading any more. Tolkien explains he has 'tried to modernize the myths and make them credible'—as well as readable for a generation used to facile speech.

''More important, no youngster is going to believe in a beautiful knight on a white charger whose strength is as the strength of ten because his heart is pure. He knows too much history and/or sociology, alas, to find knighthood enchanting in the feudal backgrounds and to dream of Greek heroes and of gods who walked on the earth. But give him hobbits—and he can escape to a never-never world that satisfies his twentieth century mind, because the world is meticulously constructed, from alphabet to topography to folk song to political structure to smoking habits.''

But perhaps the most revealing insight about *The Lord of the Rings'* popularity comes from Tolkien's own son Michael, to whom Tolkien once wrote, ''you are one of the few people who really know what *The Lord of the Rings* is *about*.'' ''To me at least,'' Michael Tolkien says, ''there is nothing mysterious behind the scale and extent of the appeal of my father's writing; his genius has simply answered the call of people of any age or temperament most wearied by the ugliness, the speed, the shoddy values, the slick philosophies which have been given them as dreary substitutions for the beauty, the sense of mystery, excitement, adventure, heroism and joy without which the very soul of man begins to wither and die within him.''

For these, and for whatever other reasons a book becomes a best-seller, the paperback edition of *The Lord of the Rings* was on its way to becoming one of the most popular works of fiction in American history almost the moment it was released. By the end of 1968, Tolkien's publishers estimated that more than fifty million people had read his work, not only in America and England, but in those other countries where it had been translated or offered for sale. They based that estimate on the more than five million sets that had already been sold throughout the world, and popular knowledge that the phenomenal work was being passed from hand to hand many times. At the Harvard Coop in Cambridge, Massachusetts, the trilogy was in such demand that stacks of the books were placed at the check-out counter rather than in the book section; the Yale Co-op could barely keep the work in stock. Both stores reported that sales were unprecedented, eclipsing such popular writers as Kurt Vonnegut, William Golding, John Knowles, and even J.D. Salinger. Sales on most college and university campuses were so brisk that Ian Ballantine, president of Ballantine Books, declared, "somehow college kids have managed to get word to each other that this is *the* thing." Even *The Hobbit,* which had always sold well as a children's book, found its way to the adult book section and sold more than a million copies less than eighteen months after Ballantine released the revised version in paperback. When the initial enthusiasm on campus didn't die down, Fred Cody, manager of the college book store at Berkeley, said "this is more than a campus fad; it's like a drug dream."

That *The Lord of the Rings* was much more than simply another best-selling novel is apparent from the fantastic response it generated wherever it was read. Graffiti such as SUPPORT YOUR LOCAL HOBBIT. GANDALF FOR PRESIDENT. FRODO LIVES! and READING TOLKIEN CAN BE HOBBIT FORMING appeared everywhere from subway trains in New York to lapel badges in Shiprock, New Mexico. Kids greeted one another with the hobbit epithet, "May the hair on your toes never grow less," and Tolkien's made-up word "mathom" (meaning an object one saves but does not use) began to enter the language through common usage.

In the early part of this century, a British doctor of medicine named Arthur Conan Doyle became one of the most popular writers in the English-speaking world with the invention of his famous detective, Sherlock Holmes. In time, the number of Holmes addicts became legion, and whenever literary-minded friends got together to talk, conversation inevitably drifted to the great master who lived at 221b Baker Street. The favorite form that such learned and enthusiastic conversation took was to pretend that Sherlock Holmes was a real flesh-and-blood person, and that Doyle's novels were shamelessly stolen from the mythical Dr. Watson's private notebooks. The conversation eventually turned into scholarship, the informal meetings became formal clubs and societies, and thousands of distinguished lawyers, doctors, businessmen, and other professionals became members of Holmes's "Baker Street Irregulars." Even today, hundreds of chapters of the Baker Street Irregulars throughout the world meet to discuss, honor, and even "assist" Sherlock Holmes.

The literary phenomenon generated by Sir Arthur Conan Doyle found its counterpart in what happened after publication of *The Lord of the Rings*. At first, small gatherings of friends or fellow students met to talk about Tolkien. Such literary get-togethers are not uncommon among hard-core science fiction and fantasy readers, although they tend to discuss *types* of science fiction (such as "swords and sorcerers" or time travel) rather than specific authors. Tolkien seems to have been the exception.

In February, 1965, the first formal Tolkien Society came about through the odd medium of subway graffiti. A brilliant fifteen-year-old high school student named Richard Plotz had been attending Saturday morning science classes at Columbia University and happened to see "something written in Elvish on a poster in the station. It had to be Elvish, but I didn't believe it. Who could write things in Elvish? The next week the writing was gone, but someone had written BILBO BAGGINS IS PROBABLY A FAKE on another poster." The running dialogue between unknown Tolkien addicts continued for some weeks until Plotz impulsively scribbled TOLKIEN CLUB MEETS AT ALMA MATER STATUE [on the Columbia campus], 2:00, FEBRUARY FIFTH. A week later, six students—none of whom knew one another—braved the twenty degree weather and met beneath the statue for an hour. Incidentally, "the subway writing still continued; none of those people had been writing it! I realized that Tolkien was a force to be reckoned with, so I put an ad in the *New Republic* that said 'Discuss hobbit lore and learn Elvish,' and signed it Frodo, with my address. My first reply was from a man in Norman, Oklahoma, who was doing his doctoral thesis on the names in Tolkien's books; I got about seventy letters."

Plotz began organizing the Tolkien Club, which later became the Tolkien Society of America. The group met monthly in private homes (at first in New York, where most of the original members lived, and then at various chapters throughout the country) to talk about Middle-earth genealogies, hobbit lore, the religious elements in the *Ring,* and other subjects. Some members would try to speak in Elvish or other Middle-earth tongues, and hobbit food like mushrooms and cider would be served as everyone lit up pipes. "We eat hobbit food," said Plotz, "but basically when we get together it's an ordinary meeting-type setup. Our members are doctors, teachers, lawyers, army officers, housewives and businessmen, as well as students. Until the last time, we've always met at my house, and sat around on the floor talking about the theogony and the geography of Middle-earth and things like that. Of course, every once in awhile, someone may charge someone else with an imaginary sword, crying 'Elbereth Githoniel,' which is the name of a princess of old and a very power-giving thing to say." Each member took a Middle-earth name for himself,[1] such as Gandalf, Druin, Scatha, or even Wormtongue, and was addressed as such at the meetings. Besides amusing and educating each other in Tolkien's mythology, many members also traded Tolkien memorabilia, such as first editions of *The Lord of the Rings,* hand-lettered Elvish scrolls, Middle-earth "mathoms," and even embroidered beanies that read ONE RING TO RULE THEM ALL in Elvish.

Sometimes they managed to persuade a noted critic or even a personal friend of Tolkien's to address the group; W.H. Auden once attended a meeting in Plotz's apartment. Plotz wrote to Tolkien to ask him to join; Tolkien, although flattered, was hesitant for some time, not wanting to be associated with a group wishing to bestow adulation on him. He later relented and joined, and even permitted Plotz to interview him in England for an American magazine.

After the Ballantine edition made Tolkien universally popular, membership in the fledgling Tolkien Society of America grew to more than two thousand persons from every state in the union. Ballantine naturally encouraged the society, since it added favorable publicity and therefore aided sales; it does not appear likely, however, that the society was created by Ballantine merely as a publicity stunt, as Donald Wollheim of Ace Books has implied. It is probable that Ballantine gave the Tolkien Society some material assistance, such as postage and stationery, in soliciting new members.

Once *The Lord of the Rings* achieved widespread popularity, a large number of Middle-earth spinoffs emerged both in America and in England. For example, in Southern California, one hundred and fifty Tolkien fans gathered in a park to celebrate Bilbo's birthday, under the auspices of Diana Paxton, a graduate student at Berkeley who organized "The Elves, Gnomes and Little Men Science Fiction and Fantasy Chowder and Marching Society." Everyone came dressed as a character from Tolkien and honored Bilbo with games, Elvish songs, mock battles, hobbit cookies, and malt cider. The picnic was so successful that those present decided to hold another festival in the spring, ostensibly to celebrate the destruction of the Ring. It too was in costume, and included a mushroom roll contest and a formal ceremony in which a mock ring was burned in a fire. In 1967 a school teacher named Glen GoodKnight decided not only to make Bilbo's birthday and the destruction of the Ring annual events, but to organize a society to discuss the works of Tolkien, C.S. Lewis, and Charles Williams. He called it the Mythopoeic Society[2], and from its initial membership of fifteen, it has grown to one thousand and two hundred members in approximately thirty chapters throughout the country. Besides the picnics, the Mythopoeic Society sponsors an annual convention called "Mythcon" at Scripps College, which begins with a costume parade on campus and includes films, an art show, an auction, and the presentation of an award for the best piece of scholarship on one of the "Oxford Christians."

In 1972, when the current president of the Tolkien Society of America, Ed Meskys, began to lose his eyesight, he approached Glen GoodKnight of the Mythopoeic Society and suggested that the two organizations merge. Although there are many small, scattered Tolkien societies throughout America, the Mythopoeic Society is now the only major national organization devoted to the study, enjoyment, and dissemination of Tolkien's works.

The next major Tolkien society to establish itself was the British Tolkien Society. In 1966, Allen & Unwin finally released *The Lord of the Rings* in a one-volume paperback edition, whereupon it sold an unprecedented 14,000 copies in just three weeks (it continues to sell at a rate of 100,000 copies a year in Great Britain). Tolkien study groups sprung up at several English universities, but the British Tolkien Society became formally established only in 1968 when fantasy writer, Female Mason, and Druid Pendragon Vera Chapman placed an advertisement in the *New Statesman* calling for members. "There has been a Tolkien Society of America for some time, and I joined that. But I used to think that there ought to be a Tolkien Society in Britain, and if nobody else would start it, I'd better do something about it. So I just put an advertisement in the *New Statesman* and all the rest followed that. I got many, many replies, and we finally held a meeting at University College, London, which was well attended; we called it a Hobbit Sock, and many members came from it. Since then, we've lost some of those we first had, but some have persisted, and of course new members are always joining."

Vera Chapman—who was, incidentally, one of the first women to receive an Oxford degree from Lady Margaret Hall back in the 1920s—became the Society's first secretary, rather than its president, since that title was bestowed upon Tolkien himself. (After his father's death in 1973, Michael Tolkien asked that his father be made honorary president in perpetuum, which was immediately done.) Like its American counterpart, the British Tolkien Society meets monthly (at a London pub); they also sponsor an annual "Oxonmoot" (named after the Entmoot, the formal council of Ents held in Fangorn Forest in *The Lord of the Rings*), a weekend in Oxford during which members visit Tolkien's favorite haunts. They also organize a yearly banquet. (At one recent dinner honoring Priscilla Tolkien, members were served "Elvish Boats of Melon," "Soup Ithilien," "Turkey from the Shire with Vegetables from Sam's Garden," "Pudding of Yule for the Man in the Moon, with Brandywine Sauce," "Mints Lembas," and "Gandalf's Brew.")

Another literary phenomenon created by Tolkien's trilogy was the "fanzine," a magazine or printed publication devoted to Tolkien comment, criticism, and scholarship. Since 1965, no less than fifty fanzines—among them *Entmoot, I Palantir, Green Dragon, The Middle Earthworm, The Mallon, The Nazgûl, The Mathom, Mythlore, Mythprint, The Tolkien Journal, Para Eldalamberon*, and *Mythril*—have been published for at least one issue. They have featured articles such as "The Hereditary Pattern of Immortality in Elf-Human Crosses," learned analyses of the Elvish language, limited attempts to write hobbit stories, small biographical squibs on Tolkien, interviews with Tolkien scholars, reports of Tolkien conferences or picnics, original Middle-earth poetry, imaginative illustrations inspired by *The Lord of the Rings,* and articles speculating on the "meaning" of the trilogy. Some of the magazines have been (and still are) quite serious, with well-known literary scholars as contributors; others have been produced with little more than amateur enthusiasm and an available mimeograph machine. Most have circulations of 100 or less and last only one issue; on the other hand, a few have circulations above 1,000 (one has 2,500) and have been publishing regularly for years. No one is quite certain precisely how many Tolkien journals and newsletters have been produced to date, but there is a brisk trade among hardcore Tolkien addicts who try to collect them all.

Serious interest in Tolkien—by both scholars and literate amateur enthusiasts—has led to a relatively large number of contributions to scholarly journals, and academic and popular books of literary criticism. Of several conferences, devoted to discussion of Tolkien's works, the most important were the "Mythcons" held by the Mythopoeic Society and the 1966 Tolkien Conference at Mankato State College in Minnesota. From the latter came several books and anthologies devoted to literary criticism of Tolkien's works. A few of these books, papers, and transcripts of conference proceedings reached Tolkien, and his lack of appreciation was notable. He was puzzled by his popularity, offended at the critics' attempts to analyze his work, and avoided any temptation either to join in or respond to those who wanted to apply literary criticism to *The Lord of the Rings.* About such books and papers, Tolkien said, "They are very bad, most of them; they are all either psychological analyses or they try to go into sources, and I think most of them are rather vain efforts."

During a 1964 radio interview, Tolkien dismissed the possibility that *The Lord of the Rings* might become a classic in his own lifetime, adding that it would somehow not be right if this happened. Tolkien was wrong, of course; the trilogy did become a classic and its author a reluctant literary lion. With fame came popularity, and with popularity came all manner of offers, requests, demands, and infringements. By 1967 Tolkien was besieged by toymakers, soap manufacturers, movie companies, and other business entrepreneurs who wanted to cash in on the hobbit craze. He turned all of them down, and when they refused to go away, he asked that his publisher, Allen & Unwin, insulate him from such intrusions on his privacy. Also, the mail bag began to bulge with an average of more than two hundred letters each week. Devoted readers praised the work; asked questions about the possible significance of certain characters or incidents; criticized him for imagined lapses or stylistic weaknesses; asked for old pipes, locks of hair, discarded pages of manuscripts, or other personal mementoes; pleaded for a personal audience; and even begged that he accept them as students or apprentices. An insight into what this flood of mail was like is given by Joy Hill of Allen & Unwin, who was responsible for opening and sorting the letters and packages sent to Tolkien: ''They came from all over the world, they came in English, French, Spanish, German, Italian and Elvish, they came in conventional and psychedelic envelopes, they came in packets and with gifts, they arrived three times a day six days a week, they have been arriving for years and they are still coming; the trickle has become a stream, a river, a flood. . . . They send questions galore, even parcels of them, some 'to be opened only when the author has completed his next book.' 'Why did you kill. . . ?' 'What was the reason for . . . ?' 'Is there a connection . . . ?' 'What happened to . . . ?' 'I am asking you with tears in my eyes to take me on as a student.' 'Please call me first thing in the morning your time on the 21st.' 'I am crazy about you.' 'I am reading your beautiful story and still weeping.' 'The prose can only be compared to the King James Bible.' 'Admit Middle-earth to the U.N.' ''

The letters came from royalty, composers wishing to set Tolkien's works to music, blind octogenarians, and prisoners. President Johnson's daughter Lynda Bird wrote to ask for an autograph. One of the letters Tolkien received was from a young girl in a mental institution who said that reading *The Lord of the Rings* had given her nightmares. Tolkien asked Joy Hill to investigate, found that it was true, and wrote several letters of encouragement to her. Apparently this significantly helped in her recovery, and she was eventually released. Tolkien felt gratified when he received Christmas cards from her.

In addition to the letters came endless telephone calls. Admirers used to call Oxford at all hours of the day and night to ask questions or make requests;

the calls continued even after Tolkien changed to an unlisted number. The most disturbing calls were those in the middle of the night, invariably from American teenagers who mistakenly thought that British time was six hours *behind,* not ahead, of Eastern Standard Time. Inevitably, a stream of uninvited and unannounced visitors made the pilgrimage to Oxford in an attempt to see and speak to Tolkien. According to a spokesman at Allen & Unwin, ''It was terrible. People were waylaying him on the way to church, microphones were being pushed through the letterbox, fans kept ringing him in the middle of the night, Americans arrived with cameras . . . they made his life hell.''

Tolkien was both surprised and amused at the ''lunatic fringe'' who made *The Lord of the Rings* a cult book, but amusement later turned to anger when his privacy was continually threatened. On the other hand, he was absolutely delighted at the way his mythology had been incorporated into other mythologies. For example, an American Green Beret officer serving in Southeast Asia made an unofficial translation of *The Lord of the Rings* into Vietnamese. General Loc, the commander of the Vietnamese II Corps, was so impressed by it that he chose the lidless eye of Sauron as his battle insignia, thinking it would frighten the superstitious enemy.

Tolkien was also reportedly pleased when he heard that one of his poems from *The Adventures of Tom Bombadil*—''Errantry''—had been published in a school paper, and then had been torn out, recopied, and passed around in many forms until it had become an ''anonymous'' poem. He was also gratified to hear how his mythology had been applied by some American students. ''Many young Americans are involved in the stories in a way that I am not. But they do use this sometimes as a means against some abomination. There was one campus—I forget which—where the council of the university pulled down a very pleasant little grove of trees to make way for what they called a 'culture center' out of some sort of concrete blocks. The students were outraged. They wrote ANOTHER BIT OF MORDOR on it.''

By 1967 *The Lord of the Rings* had been printed in nine languages (that number had grown to twelve by 1977), and total volume sales had passed the 10 million mark. This meant that for the first time in his life, Tolkien had more money than he could possibly spend. But being affluent did little to change the Tolkiens' outward style of living: no mansions, limousines, servants, diamond rings, or round-the-world yacht voyages. Apparently, most of the money was given to the family, or went into a trust fund to be used after Tolkien's death. Whereas before Tolkien frequently complained about the low salaries professors received, he now began to complain about the outrageous taxes wealthy persons had to pay. ''I don't seem to have much more money than I did when I was a professor, but I do pay 18/3 tax in the pound [$2.19

out of every $2.40, the highest tax bracket in England] now.''

Money seems to have been the primary reason Tolkien apparently reversed his earlier decision and permitted *The Lord of the Rings* to be filmed. In 1964 he told an interviewer that he wouldn't like to see the trilogy made into a movie, pointing out that ''you can't cramp narrative into dramatic form. It would be easier to film the *Odyssey;* much less happens in it—only a few storms.'' (A seventeen-year-old American girl once wrote to Tolkien pleading ''don't let them make a movie out of *The Lord of the Rings.* It would be like putting Disneyland in the Grand Canyon.'') Shortly afterwards, in 1966, he sold the BBC the rights to televise a dramatic adaptation of *The Lord of the Rings.* However, it has never been produced.

When the trilogy became world famous, Tolkien was approached by a number of film companies through Allen & Unwin. At that time, Tolkien still had strong reservations about filming his work and attached all sorts of artistic conditions to the rights. In a letter to his Polish friend Professor Mroczkowski, Tolkien recounted his negotiating experience, and proudly said, ''I gave him [the producer] no sparing language.'' Apparently the conditions were more than the producer had bargained for, and the deal was never consummated. But by October 1969, Tolkien had considerably changed his position and sold the rights to United Artists for a ''very high'' price. An animated version of *The Lord of the Rings* was scheduled for release in time for Christmas, 1977, after many years of planning and preparation.

The year 1966 yielded mixed blessings for Tolkien. Success had brought wealth and literary recognition, but also harassment and interruption. The copyright controversy, carried over from 1965, still upset Tolkien, as did his wife Edith's arthritic condition. When an interviewer asked him about the progress of *The Silmarillion,* Tolkien answered, ''As for my new book, heaven knows when I shall finish it. Six months is a long time to lose at my age [supposedly over the copyright acrimony]. I am also delayed because I can get no domestic help and my wife is ill.''

Although nearly crippled, and having great difficulty walking, Edith Tolkien was able to attend a private golden wedding anniversary celebration at the Merton Senior Common Room on March 22, 1966, with Tolkien, the family, and a large number of friends and academic associates. Their marriage had been long, happy, and fruitful, and except for moments of anger and differences over religious matters, the original love they had felt for one another had continued through the years. (When Edith finally died in 1971 at the age of eighty-one, Tolkien mourned her passing with such intensity that he refused to take off his gold wedding ring, still considering himself married.) At the wedding anniversary celebration, a composer of popular musical revues gave the couple a unique present: a series of Tolkien's poems set to music.

Donald Swann, best known for the musical revues, *At the Drop of a Hat* and *At the Drop of Another Hat,* first read *The Lord of the Rings* sometime around 1960 and continued to reread it at least once a year. "But when we went on tour we found the books were too heavy to take by air; and my wife suggested that I copy out some of the lyrics." Swann began setting some of Tolkien's poems to music when he was staying with Quaker friends at a boys' school in Ramanlah, Jordan, just outside Jerusalem. The first six songs were composed on a huge Steinway concert grand—which Swann speculated was the only such instrument in all Jordan—and the rest written in Europe and America. According to Swann, "the settings are in my own style, a sort of mixture of art song, ballad and folk song—right down the middle. The poems themselves are most moving and attractive and have a context outside the books: good poetry in the Georgian style." The music is for solo tenor with piano accompaniment; this delighted Edith Tolkien, since she was an excellent pianist and could play the songs herself (perhaps with Tolkien attempting to sing).[3]

Allen & Unwin arranged Swann's surprise concert at the anniversary party, with the composer at the piano and the tenor part sung by Michael Flanders, then appearing with Swann in *At the Drop of Another Hat* on the London stage. Tolkien appeared both flattered and awed. When the concert concluded, all he could say in uncharacteristic humbleness was "the words are unworthy of the music." According to Swann, "Professor Tolkien seemed to like it, and thought it brought out the words."

After the anniversary party, Tolkien and Swann got together to talk about the possibility of publishing a songbook and recording an album. Tolkien quickly gave his permission for Swann to use the music for public recital, and indeed the hobbit song, "I Sit Beside the Fire," was inserted in a Boston performance of *At the Drop of a Hat.* For the concerts—and later, the record album —Swann recruited a recent graduate of the Royal Academy of Music with the fantastically appropriate name of William Elven. Tolkien and Swann apparently developed a great rapport, and eventually a friendship, during the course of their collaboration. When Tolkien disagreed with Swann's version of an Elvish song because it didn't match the melody in his head, Swann asked the Professor to chant it as he thought it should be. The composer, after hearing it several times, whipped out a pen and copied it down, later adding his own accompaniment, also in the Gregorian manner. Once the song was finished, Tolkien instructed Elven on the correct way to chant Elvish, taking special care with proper pronunciation (especially how to roll the "Rs"). After several sessions perfecting and practicing the songs, Swann and Elven gave the first public performances at the Lakeland Theatre in Cumberland, England, in May and June of 1966. The concerts were tremendous successes, and Swann and Elven were invited to perform as part of the Camden Festival in London that summer. This led to an appearance on the BBC "Today" program, as well as other concerts throughout the country.

Tolkien and Swann also agreed to collaborate on a songbook and record album. The book, *The Road Goes Ever On: A Song Cycle*, was published by Allen & Unwin and Houghton Mifflin in 1967. In the introduction, Donald Swann tells of an encounter he had with a hard-core Tolkien addict: 'I was playing over the songs in this book to Dick Plotz, the president of the Tolkien Society of America, and he said 'It must be hard to write new tunes for these poems when there are already existing ones.' I was nonplussed by this for a moment, and there was a short silence. 'Where?' I said. 'In Middle-earth,' he replied.'' The Caedman record was also released in that year (although the official party honoring the two collaborators wasn't held until March, 1968), and was titled *The Road Goes Ever On.* Tolkien directly contributed to the album by reading some of his own works.

Although there was more than thirty years' age difference between the two, Tolkien and Swann became friends, above and beyond their professional collaboration. Donald Swann shared many interests and a common background with Tolkien: Swann had been a public school alumnus and an honors student at Christ Church, Oxford, with a degree in Russian and Modern Greek. Later, Swann and his wife periodically visited Tolkien. Their relationship was never intimate, but it was close enough, and Swann put his recollections and collaborations with Professor Tolkien in a book for Allen & Unwin.

On November 24, 1966, the Royal Society of Literature paid Tolkien its highest honor by awarding him the Benson Medal for *The Lord of the Rings.* (Tolkien was himself a Fellow of the Royal Society of Literature.) The Benson Medal—named after A.C. Benson, Master of Magdalen College, who endowed it—is England's most prestigious literary award, comparable to America's Pulitzer Prize, or the International Publishers' Prize. Past recipients include such distinguished authors as Lytton Strachey, George Santayana, Dame Edith Sitwell, E.M. Forster, and Harold Nicholson.

Now in his '70s, Tolkien began to feel the effects of age and an increasing distance from the modern world. To an interviewer he said, ''I'm an old man now, and I've got a short working day. I cannot go on working until two, as I used to.'' In a letter dated February 2, 1967, he expressed concern about ''my wife's ill health and my own weariness,'' and complained about all the responsibilities and commitments that were tiring him. ''I have far too much to do.''

He also noted in an interview some sort of personal accommodation to progress —which he had always hated—when he admitted that ''England's a small island with a large population, and it's getting bigger all the time. You have to build up. Either you build in the city and get uglier cities, or you destroy the countryside.'' He sadly lamented that ''there's no choice.''

''A person my age is exactly the kind of person who has lived through one of those quickly changing periods known to history. The world's a totally different place now, changing at a speed that anyone over seventy years surely now feels. Surely there has never been so much in seventy years:

> The old order changeth
> Yielding to the new
> And God fulfills Himself in many ways.''[4]

After 1965, Tolkien was hard pressed to preserve the privacy so essential for his creative work. He dealt with the problems of correspondence and interviews on a catch-as-catch-can basis that was anything except orderly. He would write ten-page letters to persistent admirers to explain why it was impossible for him to answer their letters. He dropped correspondence even with old friends, and often lost contact with them altogether.[5] Even with the help of part-time secretaries, the unanswered mail piled up. The constant interruptions meant little time for writing and no time for reading (Tolkien complained that he never had the time to read all the fairy stories that he wanted to). In desperation, Tolkien finally asked his publisher to provide some sort of relief and assistance; otherwise, he would never finish *The Silmarillion*. Since Tolkien was by that time Allen & Unwin's most successful author, and the financial interest in *The Silmarillion* was enormous, they acceded and appointed a young employee named Joy Hill to act as the professor's part-time secretary and personal assistant.

At first Joy Hill did not view her new job with pleasure; according to her own recollection the emotion was more one of terror. That was because the subject of Tolkien and *The Lord of the Rings* came up in conversation almost every day in the office, as did constant reminders, in the form of letters, parcels, gifts, telephone calls, and personal visits from his admirers. All this made him more than human—a demigod. Ms. Hill's first assignment was to bring Tolkien some of the accumulated mail. She feared this visit to the house in Headington, not only because of the aura of greatness around him, but because she was virtually the only person at Allen & Unwin who had never read *The Lord of the Rings*. When Tolkien asked her the inevitable question as to what she thought about the book, there was a pause, followed by silence. ''*Why not!*'' Tolkien boomed when he finally realized that she had not read it. She explained that ever since joining the firm, she had been oversaturated with Tolkien and *The Lord of the Rings*, and it had all turned her off. Tolkien chuckled at her confession and murmured ''quite right too.'' She did manage to read the trilogy before her second visit, however.

In February, 1968, Tolkien was finally persuaded to permit the BBC to make a documentary film about him. This represented quite a concession, since Tolkien had become almost completely inaccessible to the media. (A *Life* magazine writer had been turned away at the door, and had to console himself with an interwiew with Prime Minister Harold Wilson, who was apparently easier to see than the Oxford professor.) The director of the three-man camera crew was a talented young Oxford graduate named Leslie Megahey, who also happened to be an avid Tolkien fan. In an interview with the Oxford *Mail*, Megahey explained what he hoped to accomplish by filming Tolkien: ''The scope of the subject is simply enormous, and it would have been stupid and impossible to show the whole image of Professor Tolkien's work. That is why we chose to film him in his academic settings in Oxford, to show the man behind the marvelous epic living in his own environment, chatting at his home about his work, wandering around his old college, Merton, and to intersplice the interviews with things that illustrate the special qualities of his work, like the light and magic of the firework display. [Part of the documentary had been filmed at the Dragon School for boys, with Tolkien and the students watching a bonfire and fireworks.]

''I've shot miles and miles of film this week—much more than I can use. But Professor Tolkien has never been recorded on film before and I thought it was important to get as much as we could of him for the archives. There's tremendous interest in him. Since we started preparing this program, we've had inquiries coming in from all over the world.''

Tolkien did not enjoy being filmed. He thought it artificial and contrived. ''They filmed me at my fireside where I don't sit, with a glass of beer at my elbow, which I don't drink.[!] It's all rather bogus—like that show at the Dragon School, which they called a firework display. . . . It was terribly muddy. The smoke from those wretched magnesium flares made your throat sore. Whoever heard of putting paraffin on a bonfire? And they let the rockets off for the television cameras, not for us.'' (Apparently the students didn't think much of Tolkien and his protestations, and some thought him ''older and grumpier'' than they had expected.)

Although Megahey and his camera crew shot hours of film, the televised segment that finally appeared on the BBC-2 program, ''Release,'' ran only twenty minutes. According to Megahey, the reason why so little footage was shown was that much—most—of Tolkien's speech was incomprehensible.

The film editor could only splice together twenty minutes' usable footage. This is the only film documentary of Tolkien ever made, and the program was repeated on January 2, 1972, to celebrate Tolkien's eightieth birthday.

By 1968, living in Oxford had become untenable for Tolkien. The rose garden in Headington had been trampled underfoot by uninvited interlopers with cameras and tape recorders, the curtains had to be constantly drawn against the public, and infrequent trips out of the house were planned with the precision of a military campaign in order to avoid being followed or accosted. Tolkien finally became fed up with all this ''foolishness,'' and decided that the only way he could get any peace and quiet was to leave Oxford for parts unknown. With the aid of friends in Devon, the Tolkiens located a modest bungalow in the seaside town of Bournemouth at 19 Lakeside Road. The Tolkiens had taken their annual holidays at the Miramar Hotel for many years, and Edith Tolkien felt especially comfortable in the popular English seaside resort. The house at 76 Sandfield Road was sold, and Tolkien and his wife quietly left the city.

There was a great deal of secrecy involved in the move. For example, all Tolkien's neighbors on Lakeside Road knew about him was that he was ''somebody famous'' who wanted to be left alone. This tends to indicate that the Tolkiens used a false name in Bournemouth, or at the very least refused to give their last name to those who asked for it. Allen & Unwin tightened this web of secrecy by declining all inquiries for interviews and giving Tolkien's new address only to a select few. So concerned were they about keeping his Bournemouth residence from being discovered that whenever Joy Hill would collect the mail at the office before leaving to visit the Professor, she would return to her flat, change her clothes, and slip out the back door to avoid being followed to the train station.

The Tolkiens lived in self-imposed seclusion for several years, interrupted only by infrequent trips for business or pleasure to Oxford and London, and several holidays on the continent. Their children, grandchildren, and even great-grandchildren regularly visited them at their seaside bungalow, but it appears that their primary contact with the outside world was Joy Hill. ''He was like a father to me,'' she once said. Once, when Joy Hill brought a new dust jacket design for Tolkien's approval, he became quite cross and launched a tirade to vent his disapproval. Joy Hill in turn became agitated at Tolkien's animated criticism, and was about to say something when Mrs. Tolkien shot her a sympathetic warning against contradicting the professor in such moments. She decided to ignore the motherly advice and defended herself quite vigorously, pointing out that it wasn't *her* design, and that he had no right to take out his anger on her. There was silence for a few seconds; instead of the expected outburst at Joy Hill's presumption, Tolkien instantly apologized and became quite charming, trying to compensate for his momentary outburst of temper.

Shortly before moving from Oxford, Tolkien fell down the stairs in his Headington house and broke his hip. He was rushed to a hospital, and a large plaster cast reaching from ankle to thigh had to be applied. Tolkien asked for help from Allen & Unwin, and Joy Hill was dispatched to look after both the professor and his wife. After the move, the bungalow was in great disarray, the library in shambles, and both husband and wife ailing. Joy Hill took charge, unpacking his library from crates on the floor, hanging tapestries and paintings sent by fans, ferreting out books for Tolkien, and looking after the housework. After Tolkien's recovery he often walked with a cane.

Tolkien tried as best he could to continue writing, but it appears he accomplished little in preparing *The Silmarillion* for publication. Apparently, the last time anyone else read the manuscript was in 1967, when Christopher Tolkien saw it, at which time it was far from completion. Dr. Clyde Kilby of Wheaton College had assisted Tolkien the year before for several months and therefore knew the problems involved. Hal Lynch, of the Tolkien Society of America, had either seen portions or learned of its content in 1967; he confidently declared that it was an actual narrative "like *Paradise Lost.*" Raynor Unwin may also have seen the work in progress, since he was reported to have said that Tolkien "very consciously cut himself off, since his retirement as a don" to work on the book. The indications, however, are that few significant advances were made in the work after 1967, despite all the appearances of sustained writing activity.

Edith Mary Tolkien died in her eighty-second year on November 29, 1971. Although she had been ill for some years, the immediate cause of her death had been an inflamed gall bladder. She passed away in Bournemouth, but was buried in the Wolvercote Cemetary in north Oxford. Her final resting place was in a new section of the Catholic corner of the cemetery, in a family plot destined to be Tolkien's burial ground as well.

Edith Mary's death was a profound loss to Tolkien. They had been married fifty-five years, and although quite different in spirit and interests, their love for one another had been both real and enduring. His grief was deep and long-lasting, and the months following her death seemed intensely lonely. According to William Cater, "he didn't show external changes, but his wife's death was a deep blow. But then, a man of his generation didn't show outward feelings (the stiff upper lip). He did say that he missed her very much, but that was in a gruff aside to me, as if not wanting to dwell on it." One friend felt

Tolkien would have broken down completely if it hadn't been for his religious faith and his continuing joy and responsibility as a father. Although a regular church-goer, Tolkien began attending Mass every day, a practice he had partially abandoned because of his wife's illness and his own infirmities. His children and their children (and even *their* children) endeavored to visit him as often as possible. Christopher and Priscilla were still nearby in Oxford, but Michael had become headmaster of a Jesuit school in distant Stonyhurst, Lancashire, and John had become a secular priest in Stoke-on-Trent in the north country. In addition, Tolkien's friends went down to Devon to see him, or invited him to stay and visit with them.

In January, 1972, Tolkien's friends threw him an eightieth birthday party at the Eastgate in Oxford that must have resembled Bilbo's famous eleventy-first birthday party at Bag End. His happy response to the whole affair was ''you know, I do like perks!'' Apparently he used that visit to Oxford to return to his old college, Merton, where he had been elected an emeritus fellow seven years earlier. Now that his wife was gone, he expressed an interest in returning to Oxford to live out his final years. The warden and fellows at Merton College took the hint and quickly offered him rooms at 21 Merton Lane. In May of the following year, they accorded him another high honor by electing him an honorary fellow.

When Tolkien returned to Merton on March 22, 1972, he remarked that ''coming back to Oxford is like returning to a metropolis from a desert island.'' When asked of his future plans, he replied, ''I shall not be doing any teaching —I've come here hoping for a time of peace, without interruptions, in which to pick up the threads of my life.'' Tolkien was given rooms on the second floor of a large nineteenth century house—away from the main entrance, but not too many steps to walk. The suite had been slightly modified to accommodate the famous man in that a private foyer and individual bell had been installed. Also, an emergency bell that would ring in the basement flat to summon help was rigged up by Tolkien's bed. He never used it. The rooms may be described as small and smaller, with the latter being used as the bedroom and the former as a sitting room and study. But they overlooked a small, pleasant garden, which must have pleased Tolkien.

Various pieces of furniture cluttered up the flat, tapestries and small paintings from admirers hung on the walls, and hundreds of books were stuffed into the white bookshelves in the sitting room. The suite had no radio, record player, or television, though there was a telephone on top of the desk. Unfortunately, the Oxford telephone directory by mistake listed both his telephone number and address in the 1972 directory. That made any hope for total privacy slim.

Merton College was delighted to have one of their own return, and most members took an active interest in Professor Tolkien's welfare and well-being. He was cordially greeted whenever he slipped on his long black robe and sat at high table for dinner, or when he accepted one of the many invitations for social affairs at the Merton Senior Common Room. Everyone— from the domestic bursar, Rear Admiral Derick Hetherington, to Charles Carr, the servant at 21 Merton—tried to be friendly but unobtrusive, helpful but not overbearing. Tolkien, too, tried to keep mainly to himself and not to burden anyone with looking after him. He made few requests and demands of anyone, preferring to do things for himself.

According to Charles Carr, Tolkien was a man of regular habits. He rose at 8:00 each morning, and took his breakfast in his rooms at 9:00. While eating, Tolkien would always ask Carr something about current affairs or college goings-on; he seemed to need human contact to get him started each day, no matter what the subject or pretext. After breakfast and the inevitable ten or fifteen minute conversation with Carr, Tolkien lit up his pipe and read the London *Daily Telegraph* (apparently he never bothered with the local papers). After this morning ritual, Tolkien would get down to work (which was quite difficult), or sit and chat with Joy Hill (who would come up from London several times a week to help out with correspondence and business matters, and to type for him), or take a walk. About once a month, he would take the morning train to London to visit Allen & Unwin. In his last years Tolkien felt terribly alone; he often complained to the Carrs that he missed his wife almost more than he could bear. When he didn't work or go out, he often did nothing more than sit in his room and stare out the window, occasionally whistling or singing to himself. To help alleviate the loneliness, Tolkien took to visiting other elderly people at the Old Age Pensioners Club on George Street, the Jeune Street Day Center, or the Barton Old Folks Lunch Club. He became quite friendly with Dr. Muir Grey from the Oxfordshire Health Authority, and through him became acquainted with the financial problems experienced by some of the local organizations for the elderly. Characteristically, Tolkien donated money from time to time—anonymously—to the Jeune Street Day Center and the Barton Old Folks Lunch Club[6] (which his donations had helped establish). The amounts generally were not large, but they helped.

Charles and Mavis Carr, lifelong college servants, not only looked after Tolkien, but provided much-needed companionship. It is a favorable reflection on Tolkien's personality that he apparently neither felt nor intimated any condescension in his relationship with the Carrs, despite the social and educational gap. Tolkien greatly enjoyed conversing with Mavis Carr in her native Welsh; according to her, his command of that language was excellent. Whenever the

Carrs' children dropped in for a visit in their basement flat, Tolkien came downstairs to play with them. Once when the youngsters became excited over some horseplay with Tolkien, they began crying out "more, Tolkien, more!!" Mavis Carr heard their overly familiar outbursts, and rushed out of her room, reminding them to call him either "Professor Tolkien" or "Professor T." Tolkien smiled at her and said, "Mavis, please—Tolkien!"

Since Tolkien's address was publicly known through the telephone directory error, it was Carr's responsibility to intercept the steady stream of uninvited visitors who showed up at Merton Street. He usually told them that the Professor was too busy to receive visitors, but he would take messages and requests for audiences to him. Often the requests were for Tolkien to autograph one of his books, and if they happened to have a book ready, he would usually sign it. When he was busy, he would ask "is it one of our boys, Charlie?"— referring to the many Merton College members who wanted autographed copies. Departing from an earlier attitude, Tolkien frequently granted interviews to admirers who asked for permission in the proper manner.

On January 12, 1972, the *Guardian* published a letter critical of Tolkien by Alan Chedzoy, a senior lecturer at the College of Education in Weymouth, Dorset. It read:

> In my work I meet a number of young students who profess an admiration—even an adulation—for Tolkien's writings. Such students, and I understand there are many of them in England and the United States, share certain personality traits, in my observation. On the whole, they are rather timid in human relationships, rather orthodox in attitude. They prefer escapism to genuine emotional self-exploration. They usually do not like literature. . . . Frequently they are scientists or mathematicians with a preference for crossword complexities within a firm frame of traditional values. . . . Tolkien is the supreme ostrich writer of our time . . . . Perhaps we need to think how to wean students from Tolkien.

The ensuing outcry against Chedzoy's letter led to one of the *Guardian's* "biggest, angriest mailbags ever" as hundreds lept to the professor's defense. One letter said, "the students he [Chedzoy] describes seem perfectly healthy. It is healthy to be insecure and unhappy in this frightening world. It is reasonable and ordinary to enjoy reading travel books to escape into one's imagination." Another thought, "if there is something wrong in reading Tolkien, the fault is not with him or the readers, but the world seems so attractive besides it."

Tolkien probably agreed with most of his defenders, especially since the world had turned into something barely recognizable and quite undesirable. Oxford had grown to more than ten thousand students, and by the early '70s had been streamlined by abolishing gate hours, compulsory Latin, academic robes outside college, and even allowing several colleges to become coeducational. The emphasis on the classics had been abandoned for science, medicine, and other professional curricula, and the antiquated rules of behavior had been buried in long hair, the sexual revolution, and the drug culture. Tolkien was distressed by many of the changes, but he retained a fond affection for the students. Once when he was walking with William Cater, he passed ''an exceedingly grubby'' student repairing a broken-down bicycle outside Merton House. Tolkien waved to the student and said a few friendly words of greeting, and then commented that the lad happened to be proficient in Elvish, and even had his name written in Elvish on the staircase.

The university followed tradition when it awarded an honorary doctorate (D.Litt.) to Professor Tolkien on June 3, 1972. It was his fourth of five honorary doctorates and the one he valued most. The degree was awarded with great pomp in the Sheldonian Theatre by the University Vice-Chancellor, Sir Alan Bullock. The Oxford Public Orator, Colin Hardie, said that Tolkien ''had alone created a new mythology such as took the Greek people centuries to elaborate. . . . Now he has come back to us from retirement, whereby he eluded his intrusive fans. We are happy to salute him in his eightieth year.''

But the award that pleased Tolkien most was the Order of the British Empire (OBE), which he received in early 1973. This medal, bestowed by Queen Elizabeth in Buckingham Palace, was one rank below knighthood, and undoubtedly if Tolkien had lived longer, or had his works become popular sooner, he would have become Sir Ronald Tolkien. A half hour after Tolkien arrived back at Oxford following the ceremony, he left the OBE medal in his rooms and went off to dine. When he returned, it had been stolen as a souvenir by an unprincipled admirer. Tolkien was greatly depressed over its loss. Happily, the thief's conscience prevailed and after a time the medal was returned.

The last literary award that Tolkien received was the French Prize in February, 1973, for the best foreign novel of the year. *The Lord of the Rings* had been published for the first time in French the previous year, and it edged out an Italian novel by Leonardo Sciascia titled *The Context* for the prestigious award. Unfortunately, the octogenarian Professor was too ill to travel to Paris to receive his award, and it had to be sent to him at a later date.

Tolkien's health was generally good for an eighty-one-year-old man, and except for occasional stomach pains from eating too much rich food and head colds from the damp Oxford weather, he had few complaints. But he grew more tired, especially after his wife's death. When Lord Snowden took the photograph for the 1974 Tolkien Calender (and an article in the *Sunday Times* magazine), some of the dons teased him, saying that it looked as if he had got drunk and fallen down. Because of his tired look, there was some concern about his well-being. Once when Joy Hill telephoned to check on the Professor, she was unable to get an answer. She tried again—and again—with the same results. Acting in panic, and fearing that he might have become ill, she rushed up to Oxford on the train. It turned out that Tolkien had been downstairs in the Carrs' flat watching Wimbledon tennis on their color television set.

By the summer of 1973, Tolkien apparently had virtually abandoned all work on *The Silmarillion*. He looked forward to frequent visits from his family and afternoon chats with friends and college fellows; the breaks in the loneliness were probably welcome as an excuse, as well as a justification, for not working. Perhaps Tolkien had a premonition that he would never live to complete *The Silmarillion*, and wanted to use what little time was left enjoying what was most beautiful to him in this world. During that summer he took long walks around Oxford, covering distances that would tax even a younger man. On one such outing with his friend Lord Halsbury, he visited his favorite place in the area, the Botanical Gardens. On that occasion, he turned to Lord Halsbury and said, ''this is how you must communicate with a tree.'' Then ''he stood up to the tree, put his forehead against the bark, put both hands on either side of the bowl of the tree, and was absolutely silent with his eyes shut, for a little while.'' After communing with the tree, he turned to his astonished companion in great excitement and reported the ''message'' that the tree had given him. (Lord Halsbury refuses to reveal the ''message,'' saying that that ''would be giving away the game.'')

Not long afterward, Tolkien took Joy Hill to the same spot. ''I used to have a routine when visiting him, about doing the work first and getting it over with, and then it was talk. And this time, strangely, he flapped his hands and said 'Oh no no no, we won't do any work just yet. Have a drink.' So we had a drink. Then he said we would go for a walk, and we went for a very long walk. It was really *very* long, and I kept saying 'wouldn't you like to sit down?' because I was tired; he wasn't. He said 'Oh no, we're going to see all my favorite trees.' And this we did, and we looked at all the trees in the Botanical Gardens, and we went down by the river to look at the willows. And then we came back again and did the trees all over again.'' Tolkien then asked her to take pictures for him in September, when they would walk next, after he returned from visiting friends in Bournemouth.

On August 27, 1973, Tolkien had lunch with his daughter Priscilla (probably at the Eastgate), and she gave him presents she had brought back from a recent holiday in Austria. He put the bottle of liquor away (Tolkien had been put on a strict, liquor-free diet in 1972 when his ulcer began to worsen), but proceeded to eat all the fine chocolates one by one. The next morning, Tolkien packed his own bags for the Bournemouth visit, and was ready to leave when Carr came up to tell him the taxi was waiting downstairs. Tolkien smiled, walked with Carr downstairs and got into the car. As the driver started the engine, Carr bid the professor goodbye and wished him a pleasant journey and holiday. Tolkien replied, *"I feel on top of the world!"*

Five days later, on September 2, 1973, John Ronald Reuel Tolkien, his son John and daughter Priscilla by his side, died in a Bournemouth hospital of pneumonia, complicated by a gastric ulcer.

THE IMMORTAL

T HE BRILLIANT September morning sunlight poured in through the stained glass windows of the new church, illuminating the rows of dignitaries, friends and colleagues in a surreal swirl of colors. Outside, respectful groups of people silently watched and waited, not so much as mourners as to pay homage to a great writer. The church itself was literally overflowing with wreaths from friends and admirers around the world. Those flowers that could not be placed inside leaned against the outside walls. The memorial mass was performed in English by the Reverend John Tolkien, assisted by an old family friend, the Reverend John Murray, S.J., and the parish priest, Monsignor Wilfred Dornan. According to Vera Chapman of the British Tolkien Society, "the church was so full of light that the service was completely unconvincing. You couldn't really feel that anything was happening, because no one ever expected Professor Tolkien to go."

After the service, the entourage wound its way from Headington through the length of Oxford to the Wolvercote Cemetery, where Tolkien was buried beside his wife. The headstone bore a simple inscription, and had the names of Beren and Luthien, the lovers from Middle-earth, chiseled upon it. The grave is well-attended, and visitors still place flowers in the rose vase alongside the rough granite stone.

On his passing, the *Guardian* said Tolkien "stands as a unique figure in literature. While drawing inspiration from the style and mode of Celtic, Norse and Teutonic folklore, based on a lifetime's professional practice of textual criticism, he revived for himself, after a thousand years' lapse, the role of epic minstrel; took up again, to popular acclaim in the twentieth century, the immemorial theme of the Quest: the heroic attempt of puny mortals to resolve the agelong cosmic conflict of good and evil." *The National Review* described

156

The Lord of the Rings as easily "the best book of the century, though the greatest is *Ulysses,* and Lewis' *The Human Age* is the book we deserve most to be remembered for." Tolkien himself once said "if I could be remembered by *The Lord of the Rings,* I'd take it. It would be rather like Longfellow, wouldn't it? People remember Longfellow wrote *Hiawatha* and one or two other things, but quite forgot that he was a professor of modern languages."

The university paid its last respects in a November, 1973, memorial service in Merton Chapel. College deans, wardens, rectors, and fellows joined with the pro vice-chancellor, other university representatives, and personal friends in the Church of England service. The lessons from the Book of Job were read by Professor Nevill Coghill and the Reverend John Tolkien.

Tolkien left a net estate of £144,159 ($345,981) after taxes and death duties. From this figure, one may speculate that *The Lord of the Rings* earned its author approximately $4 million during his lifetime. Most of the money had been given away to relatives, friends and charities before Tolkien's death in order to avoid paying the high English inheritance taxes. The bulk of the estate, including all literary papers, the library, unpublished works, and copyrights, was left to a family trust, to be dispensed and used by Tolkien's children, grandchildren, and great-grandchildren. Tolkien left £1,000 to the Birmingham Oratory, in memory of Father Morgan, and relatively small amounts to Exeter College and Pembroke College. He also left £500 to Trinity College for the use of impoverished students, acknowledging the college's generosity in assisting one of his sons in a period of financial difficulty. In addition, Tolkien left a series of small bequests to individuals, including a godson.

After Tolkien's death, Raynor Unwin described the unfinished *Silmarillion* manuscript as "beads without a thread." He confidently announced at that time that "it is Tolkien at his very best, very moving, very fine. The historical scale of years is all there, but the linking passages are missing." Raynor Unwin's initial optimism was premature, and a careful inspection indicated that the work was far from completion. Christopher Tolkien took upon himself the task of finishing the work. Perhaps no one other than Tolkien himself was as qualified, since Christopher had followed in his father's footsteps as a philologist and lover of the sagas. In 1975, Christopher Tolkien wrote to Glen GoodKnight of the Mythopoeic Society, "you will like to know that my work on the preparation of *The Silmarillion* is progressing quite well, and that I hope before long to be able to devote more time to it than I have been able to hitherto." Later he told GoodKnight that he intended to leave Oxford and move to the south of France in order to lessen the distractions and provide a good working environment in which to finish his father's book.

Tolkien also left several other manuscripts to be completed. One is the verse play *The Homecoming of Beorhtnoth — Borehnoth's Son,* based on an earlier published work. There is a book entitled *Akallabêth* which has been included in the published version of *The Silmarillion.* Two other brief works, *Ainulindale* and *Valaquenta,* were also included in *The Silmarillion* because they related to the Middle-earth mythology. According to Christopher Tolkien, there are additional fragments, narratives, genealogies, and reference material that may be published at some future date.

It is impossible to estimate exactly how many people have read *The Lord of the Rings* since it was first published, but it seems safe to say that the trilogy is among the most popular works of fiction written during this century. Even today, more than twenty years after publication, it continues to sell extraordinarily well, and is bound to attract still more admirers as it becomes available in other languages. The work has inspired ballets, operas, and musical suites; scholarly analysis and criticism; would-be imitators and continuers of hobbit tales; serious attempts to expand and popularize the Elvish languages; Tolkien societies, clubs, and magazines; untold thousands of sketches, drawings, and paintings of Middle-earth characters and scenes; and at least fifteen published books on Tolkien and his mythology.

Perhaps the best final word on John Ronald Reuel Tolkien and his world of Middle-earth is told by an unknown admirer, an Oxford electrician who liked *The Lord of the Rings* so much that he named his tools after characters from the book (his wrench was "Smaug's Horde"). The man had been called in to repair some wiring in the English faculty library, and as he began working, he noticed the bronze bust of Professor Tolkien by Christoper Tolkien's ex-wife Faith that had been completed at the time of Tolkien's retirement. Without hesitation or embarrassment, he downed his tools, walked over to the bust and clapped his arm around the bronze shoulder.

"Well done, Professor," he said, addressing the bust as if it were a living person. *"You've written a smashing good yarn!"*

EPILOGUE:
THE SILMARILLION

ON SEPTEMBER 19, 1977, Allen & Unwin in Great Britain and Houghton Mifflin in the United States simultaneously published J.R.R. Tolkien's long-awaited posthumous work, *The Silmarillion*. Incidentally, the publication date, either by coincidence or design, was almost exactly sixty years after young Lt. Tolkien had begun scribbling the first fragments of his "dark and brooding" tale into a notebook while convalescing in an army hospital in Birmingham.

Of course, Tolkien had not completed *The Silmarillion* when death overtook him, and the task of preparing the manuscript for publication fell to his son Christopher. In his Foreword, Christopher Tolkien assures us that his father worked on the tale continually for well over a half century, and that throughout Tolkien's "long life he never abandoned it, nor ceased even in his last years to work on it." This, however, appears very unlikely. During Tolkien's last decade of life, when his publisher and public automatically assumed that he was hard at work on *The Silmarillion*, Tolkien had in reality done virtually no new writing. Apparently, the manuscript was almost unchanged since the mid-'60s, when the American scholar, Dr. Clyde Kilby, had assisted Tolkien in preparing certain revisions. Kilby, who is on the faculty of Wheaton College in Illinois, wrote a small book entitled *Tolkien and The Silmarillion* in 1976.[1] He revealed in November, 1977, that while he had not yet read the published version of *The Silmarillion*, a close colleague of his who had read portions of the original manuscript and the final book had concluded that the two were virtually identical. If true, this would mean that Tolkien had neither revised nor rewritten most of the manuscript after 1966.

Why had Tolkien gone to great lengths to create the impression that he was working on *The Silmarillion* when in fact he was not? One possible explanation is that Tolkien, after unsuccessfully laboring over the work for most of his adult life, had simply given up in frustration. Another possibility is that he was either too old or too tired to bear up under the daily discipline of writing and revising such a challenging and unrewarding work. Whatever the truth—and it is likely a combination of both tiredness and disinterest—Tolkien apparently did not want to disappoint anyone by announcing that he had abandoned work on *The Silmarillion.* He therefore gave the *appearance* of industry up to the time of his death.

Shortly after Tolkien died in September, 1973, Raynor Unwin of Allen & Unwin believed *The Silmarillion* was nearly completed and could be published within a year or two. But after Christopher Tolkien examined the jumble of notes, drafts and versions of *The Silmarillion*—some of which went back all the way to 1917—it quickly became apparent that the work was far from ready. Unwin revised his timetable and announced that it might be years before *The Silmarillion* could be published. Christopher Tolkien, as estate executor and a philologist in his own right, decided to take over the task of editing and preparing the final version.

The challenge was formidable. There were many fragments from which to choose, and because they had been written at different times over a period of many years, their quality and continuity varied widely. While some chapters were well-written and self-contained, they could not be incorporated in the final version because they did not agree with the overall story line. Other sections were written in a clearly inferior style, but because they were integral to the story line, they had to be included. Transitions from one section to the next were missing and had to be written. Names and places had to be carefully checked to make certain that the same spellings were used throughout. And like *The Lord of the Rings,* an index and appendix of proper names and their meanings had to be prepared. Since *The Silmarillion* also demanded a map, Christopher Tolkien drew one as best as he could to conform with his father's physical descriptions of terrain and distance.

But the hardest task was to alter the complete text in order to provide a smooth internal consistency. In essence, this meant that if, for example, a character is described as having blue eyes on page 44, he couldn't be later described on page 389 as having brown eyes. Such obvious contradictions were relatively easy to eliminate, but because *The Silmarillion* contains such a wealth of names, places and events, and because entire chapters would have to be substantially rewritten in order to fit exactly into the correct time sequence or story line, many contradictions had to be left in. Christopher Tolkien explained that ''a complete consistency (either within the compass of *The Silmarillion* itself or between *The Silmarillion* and other published writings of my father's) is not to be looked for, and could only be achieved, if at all, at heavy and needless cost." Christopher Tolkien then admits some of the more serious inconsistencies, such as shifting tenses and viewpoints, differences in portrayal and tone, and uneven detail; but what he does not mention, is how events and names in *The Silmarillion* contradict familiar facts told in the text and appendices of *The Lord of the Rings.* Nor has he attempted to add his own annotations or notes to indicate where the unpublished versions differ. The main reason for this intended oversight, according to Christopher Tolkien, is that "there is indeed a wealth of unpublished writing by my father concerning the Three Ages, narrative, linguistic, historical, and philosophical, and I hope that it will prove possible to publish some of this at a later date."

Also included in *The Silmarillion* are four related, "but wholly separate and independent" works. Christopher Tolkien states that "they are included according to my father's explicit intention." The longest and best of these is *Akallabêth,* which is a revised version of one of Tolkien's early unpublished works, *Númenor.* The last is entitled *Of the Rings of Power,* and it was probably written in the mid-1950s, some time after the publication of *The Lord of the Rings.* The other short sections, the *Ainulindalë* and *Valaquenta,* are placed at the beginning, and although they appear to have been written some time between the first drafts of *The Silmarillion* and *The Lord of the Rings,* they are meant to precede both. Since the style and language of both *Ainulindalë* and *Valaquenta* are markedly different from either *The Silmarillion* or *The Lord of the Rings,* it is probable that Christopher Tolkien wrote most of the final published versions himself, using notes and fragments, rather than simply editing existing texts.

Christopher Tolkien remained at Oxford for two years after his father's death. Much of his time was taken up with academic duties and management of the Tolkien estate, as well as working with Humphrey Carpenter, who had been selected by the Tolkien family to write the "authorized" biography of the creator of Middle-earth. Work on *The Silmarillion* had to be relegated to a part-time devotion, and although Christopher Tolkien was assisted by Guy Kay, the book's progress proceeded too slowly for anyone's satisfaction. In 1975, Christopher Tolkien resigned his position as a don at University College and moved with his family to France. He told people that the change had been necessary in order to devote his undivided attention to completing *The Silmarillion.*

When *The Silmarillion* was finally finished, it was tentatively scheduled for publication on September 15, 1977. In June of that year, Houghton Mifflin announced to the trade that there would be a first edition of 150,000—an unusually large print run for any hardbound book. The publisher had correctly anticipated that the widespread continuing interest in *The Lord of the Rings* would stimulate significant sales. On the other hand, the tremendous stylistic difference between the new work and Tolkien's acknowledged masterpiece was thought to insure that *The Silmarillion* could never become the runaway best-seller that *The Lord of the Rings* had been. Furthermore, *The Silmarillion* had been selected as an alternate offering of Book of the Month Club, which usually means diminished hardbound sales for the original publisher. The paperback rights had been sold to Ballantine—which had published Tolkien's trilogy in paperback—and millions of youthful admirers were expected to purchase the relatively inexpensive paperback version rather than pay a $10.95 list price for the original edition.

However, Houghton Mifflin had badly underestimated the size and anticipation of Tolkien's reading audience. Within days of the first public announcement, the publisher was flooded with an unprecedented groundswell of advance orders by booksellers throughout America. Houghton Mifflin immediately increased its first edition to 325,000 copies, but when the advance orders exceeded even *that* figure, the publisher went back to press for an additional four printings. Instead of a first edition of 150,000, Houghton Mifflin scheduled a total of 700,000 copies prior to the publication date. In order to do this, the publisher had to subcontract the work, and then keep the presses running 24 hours a day. (Even so, the printers didn't catch up until the end of October.) And to be fair to booksellers, Houghton Mifflin had to begin rationing orders. According to Richard B. McAdoo, Senior Vice-President and Director of Houghton Mifflin's trade division, "we did not fill on a first-come-first-served basis. We tried to treat all orders equally, filling with the maximum number of titles we thought an account would need for the initial sales." The balance of the orders were shipped as new stock became available. It was even reported that a brisk black market developed as booksellers began offering premium prices for additional copies of *The Silmarillion*. A complex international agreement made it mandatory that the books be shipped to all bookstores at the same time. This, coupled with the fact that production was slowed because each map had to be pasted into each book by hand, caused the publication date to be pushed back four days to September nineteenth. Nevertheless, Houghton Mifflin warned that a further five weeks would pass before all American bookstores would receive their full orders. To squeeze out a few hundred extra copies, Houghton Mifflin also eliminated most of the bound galleys that are traditionally sent out to book reviewers weeks and even months before the publication date. Nor did they send out finished copies of the book to many reviewers until months after the initial release.

What was happening was completely unprecedented in publishing history. Never before had a novel created such intense advance interest, or promised such high sales. The only book that came close to it was the *Standard Revised Version of the Bible*, which in 1952 had advance sales approaching a half million. "It's like the fire storm that feeds on the draft," commented Houghton Mifflin's editor-in-chief, Austin Olney. Most booksellers who received their orders a few days in advance of publication immediately put the books on the shelves; many sold out within hours. Within a week, *The Silmarillion* had easily outdistanced every other book being sold in America and England; within two weeks, it had far surpassed in total sales Colleen McCullough's *The Thorn Birds*, a novel which had rested comfortably at the top of the best-seller list for many months. Within three weeks, Houghton Mifflin was confidently predicting that there would be over one million copies of *The Silmarillion* in print by early 1978. (They reached that goal in early December, however.) Whether *The Silmarillion* will ever outsell *The Lord of the Rings* may not be known for years, but if the first few months after publication are an accurate indication, it will certainly come close.

In an advance review, the trade magazine, *Publisher's Weekly*, said, "Four years after Tolkien's death his son has performed a difficult service exceedingly well, bringing together previously unpublished material that serves as a background to *The Lord of the Rings*. . . . All the writing throughout is as rich and resonant as that in *The Lord of the Rings* and should not be missed by Tolkien lovers." Other than that brief but glowing mention, almost all the major reviewers in America and England unequivocally panned the book. The *Times Literary Supplement* of London declared it "unreadable. . . . Least bearable is the diction. Where [*The Lord of the Rings*] occasionally plunged into elevated speech, [*The Silmarillion*] falutes stratospherically. The language has crossed the boundary between mythology and scripture, and has lost its head entirely." The *New York Review of Books* called it "an empty and pompous bore. . . . *The Silmarillion* is a commercial and perhaps a social phenomenon of some interest, but not a literary event of any magnitude." And *Time* pointed out that "There are moments when Tolkien sounds as if he were writing a parody of Edgar Rice Burroughs in the style of the *Book of Revelations*."

The problem in determining whether *The Silmarillion* is a smashing success or a stunning failure is that it must be measured in context. When compared to *The Lord of the Rings* it fails, and fails badly. Missing are the wit, charm, and readability; the snatches of detail that made characters come alive; and a sense of the movement of time. Readers are frequently distracted by lengthy lists of virtually unpronounceable proper names, as well as curious archaic phrases and repetitious recitations. The writing is wildly uneven—Christopher Tolkien's hand clearly shows through, and is far inferior to that of his father—the lapses in continuity are confusing, and the remoteness and inaccessibility of it all do not draw readers into the drama.

But *The Silmarillion* should no more be compared to *The Lord of the Rings* than *The Lord of the Rings* should be compared to *The Hobbit*. Tolkien wrote *The Hobbit* as a children's bedtime story, pure and simple; that he incorporated components of his Middle-earth mythology seems almost incidental (but fortuitous). Certainly *The Hobbit* wasn't the only bedtime tale he had concocted for his growing children; it just happened to have been committed to paper, and only because it was superior to the other stories. Despite Tolkien's later protestations to the contrary, *The Hobbit* was conceived, published and sold strictly as small-time fare. When Sir Stanley Unwin suggested that Tolkien follow up his initial success as an author of children's books, the result was *The Lord of the Rings*. Tolkien began to write it at a time when his youngest son and daughter were teenagers, and while the scholarship is adult, and the story gave him an opportunity to further expand his own private predilection for making up languages and exploring the process of creating new mythologies, the style and approach are clearly aimed for an adolescent reader. Had this not been true, it is extremely unlikely that *The Lord of the Rings* would ever have become one tenth as popular as it did.

The Silmarillion, on the other hand, was first written at a time when Tolkien had no children. It was conceived during the bloodiest war in history, nurtured in an intense academic environment, and expanded towards the approach of old age. *The Silmarillion,* unlike *The Lord of the Rings,* was not meant to be read for enjoyment or escapism; it was Tolkien's greatest attempt to write an English language epic in the classic style of the Old Norse sagas. And there lies the problem: the book should have been reviewed not by Tolkien scholars and lovers—who had, after all, certain expectations and therefore experienced inevitable disappointments—but by Old Norse or Anglo-Saxon scholars.

To the degree that the Old Norse sagas are stilted and unreadable to the general public, so too is *The Silmarillion*. It even appears that the narrative was specifically written not to be read as a book, but rather to be read *aloud* as a heroic epic. After all, the ancient sagas were not primarily preserved through written documents, but oral traditions. The language and the alliterative style of *The Silmarillion*—however imperfect it may be due to the uneven interaction of author and editor—suggest that Tolkien intended his vast mythology to be recited over a blazing yule log or on a forest green by a storyteller or balladeer.

The most unsatisfactory sections of the book, from almost any point of view, are the opening works, *Ainulindalë* and *Valaquenta.* Tolkien apparently divided his priorities between inventing a brand new myth of creation and a non-Christian explanation of The Fall, and in exercising his remarkable talent for making up names. Unfortunately, the result, as Eric Korn of the *Times Literary Supplement* laconically describes it, reads like "an archangelic *Who's Who.*" Since the language is significantly different from anything else that Tolkien published, it appears likely that there is much more of Christopher than J.R.R. Tolkien in it.

The Silmarillion itself can only loosely be described as a novel only because it happens to be a work of fiction (unlike *The Lord of the Rings,* which, despite its length, treatment, and inclusion of frequent verse, follows the traditional format of the modern novel rather closely). Thus the standard literary criteria for judging it, such as character development, story line, and the like, cannot be accurately applied. A much more relevant point of reference would be a work like *Beowulf* or the *Elder Edda* in a sixteenth-century English translation.

According to those criteria, *The Silmarillion* is an astonishingly rich and imaginative work, an epic that spans the Age of the World to the Age of Man, or the thread of continuity from the past to the present. It reveals the pantheon of gods as reflections of the best and the worst of ourselves, while it unerringly equates natural law with a God-given inherent sense of absolute right and wrong. Against this literary fabric, all other (well-deserved) criticism can not only be forgiven, but forgotten.

Some autobiographical strains can be gleaned from a careful reading of *The Silmarillion.* One chapter, "Of Beren and Luthien," is a thinly veiled metaphorical account of Tolkien's own romance with Edith Mary Bratt. Beren, a great and mighty warrior, happens to be from the race of Man while Luthien, fairest in all Middle-earth, is an Elf. Luthien's brother, King Thingol, is filled with anger when he learns of the ill-matched lovers, and but for a promise that he made to his sister, he would have slain Beren for his presumption. Instead, Thingol makes a bargain with Beren to obtain one of the Silmarils, the precious gems that had been stolen by the most evil persona in Middle-earth, Morgoth. Beren agrees to this impossible quest in order to win Luthien's hand.

After many trials and tribulations, Beren and Luthien manage to wrest one of the Silmarils from Morgoth's iron crown, but at the eventual cost of

Beren's life. However, Beren is favored by Iluvatar (God), and Luthien is given the choice of either joining her lover in death or giving up her Elf immortality to live as a mortal with a resurrected Beren. She chooses the latter, and they live out the normal span of life in perfect happiness.

Tolkien, a Catholic orphan with few prospects, fell in love with Edith Mary, a Protestant girl several years his senior. Their romance was actively discouraged by both sets of guardians, and Tolkien was given what seemed at the time an impossible ban: he was not to see or communicate with Edith Mary until his twenty-first birthday. This he did. Then the Great War came, and no man knew whether he would live or die; Tolkien survived the bloody Battle of the Somme, and returned as one risen from the dead. In their day and age, the religious difference was an almost insurmountable barrier, and the only way to breech it was for one of them to convert to the other's faith; Edith Mary, after considerable pressure from Tolkien, agreed to become a Catholic.

Of interest to admirers of *The Lord of the Rings* is the brief section entitled *Of the Rings of Power and the Third Age*. Tolkien probably wrote this some time after the publication of *The Lord of the Rings*, and it was meant to be a bridge between *The Silmarillion* and the trilogy. It details the continued rise of Sauron, and the war that broke his power. The creation of magic rings of power and how the ruling ring came to be lost, which had been briefly outlined in *The Lord of the Rings*, is briefly detailed here. At long last, after struggling through literally hundreds of new and virtually unpronounceable names, we finally encounter familiar ones like Gandalf, Galadriel and the Ringwraiths. Frodo is briefly mentioned too, not as a Hobbit but as one of the Mithrandir, or Halflings. Unfortunately, the transitional section is far too brief to become animated, and it still leaves many questions unanswered. For example, what happened to the company of Hobbit warriors who marched off to fight Sauron at the end of the Second Age, or where did the Hobbits or Hobbiton come from? Tolkien's failure to make his entire mythology complete and self-contained is disappointing.

The remaining section, *Akallabêth*, is a revised version of a work that Tolkien had written back in the 1920s called *Numenor*. It is Tolkien's attempt to write a mythology based on the stories of Atlantis, a subject with which he had been obsessed since his teens. It is likely that the original *Numenor* was only loosely associated with Tolkien's Middle-earth mythology, but subsequent revisions (both by Tolkien and his son Christopher) transformed it into a sequel to *The Silmarillion*. (C.S. Lewis borrowed from the Numenor myth when he wrote his *Out of the Silent Planet* trilogy; apparently his intent was to encourage his friend Tolkien to take up the work again and expand it.)

EPILOGUE: THE SILMARILLION

With the publication of *The Silmarillion*, J.R.R. Tolkien has finally completed the myth of Middle-earth. There will be no more forthcoming because Tolkien did not leave any large works behind him that expanded the mythology. Undoubtedly there are fragments of mythologies and germs of stories which may make their way into print in future years, but they will not substantially increase our knowledge of Middle-earth.

It is possible, however, that Christopher Tolkien may attempt to continue the myth by writing his own Middle-earth stories, based upon his father's works and characters. This is a long-established literary tradition, but one that is rarely, if ever, successful. If Christopher Tolkien's work on *The Silmarillion* is an accurate indication of his literary abilities, then it can be stated with some degree of certainty that he simply will not succeed in capturing the spirit, wit, and charm that made *The Lord of the Rings* such a unique work. Nor could any other writer succeed, since it would take the special talents of a philologist and an Anglo-Saxon scholar to imitate and expand Tolkien's private mythology.

We are informed, however, that there will be additional posthumous fragmentary writings from the pen of J.R.R. Tolkien, including a few short stories, translations of Middle English poems, appendices, genealogies and explanatory notes to both *The Lord of the Rings* and *The Silmarillion*. How and when these fragments are published will probably be determined by Tolkien's continued popularity; as long as he has a loyal audience which will buy anything bearing his name, such material will be published.

AUTHOR'S NOTE

I first read J.R.R. Tolkien's *The Lord of the Rings* in 1968 when I was flatsitting over the Christmas holidays for a geneticist friend in Cambridge, England. Like most other English academics' flats, it was ill-heated, tiny, and cluttered from floor to ceiling with books, papers, clothing, and other domestic paraphernalia. Whenever I enter a room for the first time, I usually amble over to the bookshelves and inspect the titles: one can learn much about a person from the books he reads. My friend Julian Heartley is a serious scientist, and in addition to scientific studies and political treatises, he also possessed many books of fantasy, mythology, and science fiction.

I was already familiar with a number of the science fiction novels, but to me, fantasy was bedtime fare for little children, and mythology an academic exercise in memorizing all the Greek gods and legends. Perhaps that was the reason that I somehow escaped the great Tolkien explosion on campus during the mid-'60s. I remember visiting relatives several years later, about 1967, and asking my fifteen-year-old cousin what her ''FRODO LIVES'' button meant. She looked at me as if I were a troglodyte just out of hibernation. Later, I asked a less reticent literary friend the same question, and he explained that Frodo was a character from a fantasy novel titled *The Lord of the Rings,* written by an Oxford professor named J.R.R. Tolkien.

This information I promptly forgot—until the day I spied a beautiful three-volume boxed edition of *The Lord of the Rings* on Julian's shelf. For the first few chapters, it seemed only an adult fairy tale, and not particularly engrossing either. But I persevered, and soon saw more significant things. The writing was exceptional, the scholarship impeccable, but what finally swayed me was the author's incredible imagination. Tolkien had created not only an entire world, but a *cosmology* whose totality was absolutely staggering. Middle-earth

168

had a history, a language, a culture so complete—and its continuity so detailed—that it was difficult for me to believe it did not exist—indeed, had never existed save in the author's imagination. Once hooked, I read all three volumes of *The Lord of the Rings* nonstop. It was only after I finished the last volume, on Christmas Day, that I noticed how worn Julian's hardbound edition was; it had obviously been read many times.

But what was the meaning of *The Lord of the Rings?* I immediately began searching for historical parallels, events in our own past upon which Frodo's quest to return the evil ring of power to its place of creation/destruction could possibly be based. There were none. I then considered a Freudian alternative, that the trilogy was symbolic of some stage of our evolution or development; or an allegory about the quixotic romantic having to adapt to our modern world; perhaps the characters represented personality traits in our psyche. But such speculation seemed like trying to fit round pegs into square holes. I even tried to relate *The Lord of the Rings* to my own research into phenomenology. (I know now that my work and Tolkien's novel had much in common. I failed to realize this at the time because I was still searching for meaning in the *content* of the story, and not paying particular attention to the *form*. But more about that later.)

I overlooked, of course, what was obvious to the millions of Tolkien admirers throughout the world. *The Lord of the Rings,* as well as *The Hobbit,* were written for the sheer pleasure of it all. Indeed, Michael Tolkien confirmed this in a letter to me, saying ''my father wrote primarily for his family and for his own amusement and was only persuaded against his will to publish at all.'' Tolkien, a distinguished philologist and acknowledged authority on Nordic mythology, wrote the books simply in order to entertain, and to satisfy a need to express the highly imaginative ideas and insights that his cross-discipline gave him. In short, there is no deep philosophical or cabalistic meaning in what is essentially an exercise in creativity.

And yet, this explanation somehow disturbed me. Something was still missing, and I felt that Tolkien would remain an enigma to me forever unless I discovered a deeper significance. At the time, I overlooked an important clue—if only I had thought of just why *The Lord of the Rings,* and a well-read edition at that, was sitting in my friend's library among the political tomes and revolutionary literature.

Not long afterward, I had to interrupt my idyllic research at Cambridge and return to professional life as a freelance writer and journalist. And so it was that I ended up in the short-lived breakaway state of Biafra at the height of the Nigerian civil war in the spring of 1969. Back then, I would definitely have characterized myself as pro-Biafran, because I sincerely thought that I had a thorough grasp of the *reality* of the war—its origins, issues, participants, and the probable consequences of a Nigerian victory. But by January, 1970, as Biafran resistance collapsed, and the long-feared massacres and reprisals against the Ibo tribe didn't happen, and humanitarian aid was given by the victorious to the vanquished, I had to admit that most of my carefully constructed conceptions about the war had been completely wrong.

The unexpected humanitarian response by the Nigerian military government greatly surprised and even shocked me. The collapse halted, nearly in midsentence, progress on the large novel I had been writing about the Biafran-Nigerian war. Before I could write another word, I had to find an explanation for my obvious, but to me obviously impossible error in judgment.

Over the next three years, I slowly began to discover my mistake. Like many other journalists involved in the Nigerian Civil War, I had unquestioningly accepted "facts" about the conflict I thought were established beyond question. The massacres, the coups, the secret political agreements, the military savagery, the harsh treatment of different ethnic and religious minorities—all of them, my colleagues and I thought, were well-defined, beyond controversy, and provable by eyewitness reports, physical evidence, commission inquiries, and the like. But, as America's experience in Indo-China has finally taught us, such "evidence" is often subjective, conflicting, or totally fabricated.

Political mythology, as I have experienced it, means the incorporation of events that may never have happened, or distorted accounts of events that have happened, into the accepted body of known facts. Rumors can transform an internecine squabble between neighbors into a bloody fistfight, then into a riot, and finally into an insurrection. Fifteen people killed in a disaster can quickly grow to fifty as the rumor grapevine does its duty, and that figure may ultimately become five hundred in a wire service bulletin or press report. Myths—at least, *political* myths—are created out of the necessity to discredit one side or enhance the other for tactical or strategic advantage. Biafra was my first experience with mythology of this sort, and I, like others, fell prey to the lies, half-truths, and distortions that helped create a nonobjective bias in favor of the Biafran side.

That I was guilty of allowing myself to be misled is understandable (though not really excusable); however, I should have been forewarned by my knowledge of Josef Goebbels' Nazi propaganda machine, which misled entire nations. I should have been alerted by my philosophical studies as well, especially by the concept of *reification*—treating ideas and abstractions as if they were things, objects. We reify experience all the time, adding adrenalin-charged mental pictures while reading an exciting novel, or becoming emotionally involved in a weepy Hollywood production. On another level, reification means that through some propagandistic sleight-of-hand, total fabrication can become absolute truth.

Perhaps Tolkien's trilogy can now be perceived in another perspective by applying the concept of reification. *The Lord of the Rings* is much more than a sophisticated fairy story; this despite Tolkien's frequent protestations to the contrary. Tolkien himself said that "as for any inner meaning or 'message,' it has in the intention of the author none. It is neither allegorical nor topical." Most critics agree that Tolkien's adamant disavowals cannot be accepted as absolute. Colin Wilson, in his book *Tree by Tolkien*, writes that "Edmund Wilson quotes a statement prepared for his publishers in which Tolkien refers to *The Lord of the Rings* as a philological game. The 'stories were made rather to provide a world for the languages than the reverse.' This, it seems to me, is a red herring, like James's description of *The Turn of the Screw* as 'a fairy tale, pure and simple.' Tolkien may well have derived enormous pleasure from giving the book another dimension of realism with the invention of Elvish and other 'languages,' but this modest statement of its aims is plainly an attempt to disarm hostile critics—as it partly disarmed Wilson." If this be so, then one may also question Michael Tolkien's comment that *The Lord of the Rings* is only a brilliant fairy story. "I feel certain that it was, in the first place, on account of our enthusiasm for stories *told* and invented by my father that the inspiration came to him to put in permanent shape what he so rightly regarded as the type of fairy story *real* children *really* want," wrote Michael Tolkien in the London *Daily Telegraph*. "Thus I maintain that it was through his own children that the literary and imaginative genius of my father was brought to a level from which it could be communicated in terms of quest and adventure, overlaid with brilliant characterization, to the world in general, with the publication of *The Hobbit,* now the necessary introduction to the *Ring* masterpiece." We may also challenge Michael Tolkien's premise because *The Lord of the Rings* was first read, not to children, but to learned literary men over most of the course of the almost fourteen years it took to complete the work.

I believe that Tolkien told the truth when he said that the story had no inner meaning or allegorical significance. The story, plot, and theme are really quite irrelevant to what I feel was his *real* purpose in writing *The Lord of the Rings*. And that purpose was the conscious effort by a benevolent genius to discover for himself the *process* of creating myths. It is one thing to lecture about the possible origin and importance of a given mythology, but quite another to build one yourself, from beginning to end. Tolkien said that his purpose in writing *The Lord of the Rings* was "to modernize the myths and make

171

them credible.'' This means that he had to discover and use the process of reification that would lead to, in Coleridge's words, ''the willing suspension of disbelief.''

The story of Middle-earth is, objectively, unreal. It exists only on paper, through the medium of printing. But ask any Tolkien reader what he felt or thought as he read about Frodo's flight from the dark horsemen, Gandalf's desperate life-and-death struggle with the Balrog, or Éowyn's slaying of the Nazgûl, and you are likely to discover fear, fright, anticipation, anger, desperation—very human emotions that are usually produced by experiences in the objective world.

Somewhere, somehow, Tolkien was able to transform a tale into real flesh-and-blood emotions and responses; the reader makes an unconscious agreement with the writer to allow imagination to become reality. In earlier times, mythology played an important cultural role in reifying past events—real and imagined—into points of reference in the present world. To hear how mighty Odin wielded a sword, or fleet-footed Hermes dashed across the heavens, was to hear something more than mere nighttime stories for small children. It was a viable link to the past, which provided heroes, gods, and acceptable explanations for natural events. If the truth had been told, that man is puny, terribly weak, alone, and helpless against nature, the effect would have been devastating. Perhaps this is how, or why, mythological figures were eventually elevated to the realm of the gods, making them larger than life, stronger than man—something, or someone, greater than oneself to believe in.

But precisely *how* does an invented tale become a myth? This is a problem that apparently occupied Tolkien for some years, one that I think he eventually believed he had solved. In his famous Andrew Lang Lecture, ''On Fairy-Stories,'' Tolkien expressed the opinion that fairy stories (and, by extension, myths) become most ''real'' to us through what he called ''sub-creation.'' This means to create a world not wholly unlike our own, and to people it with creatures not unlike ourselves, but to make it different enough so that it cannot be historically anachronistic or recognized as an inaccurate parallel to our own development on this planet. The writer cannot hope to make his readers suspend their disbelief and accept his tale as real if he thinks of ''ten impossible things before breakfast'' (as the Red Queen told Alice) that could never happen anywhere because they violate scientific principle, natural law, or common sense. One can possibly accept a world in which intelligent dragons converse with hobbits, but not a world in which five-ton elephants fly by merely flapping their ears.

To make mythology believable, a mythmaker has to convince us that his characters *could* exist, or have existed, somewhere in the universe. Tolkien attempted to do this by making Middle-earth close enough to ours in terms of flora, fauna, geology, and geography, but different enough that it wouldn't be recognizable as a place that had ever existed.

Because so much more scientific and historical knowledge is known today than when the great Norse sagas were written, we cannot accept without question the existence of demigods and avatars, or contradictions to the laws of physics. Tolkien recognized this and circumvented the problem by creating an archeology, a paleontology, an evolution, an historical and linguistic development that fit the form of academic scholarship, and therefore give added authority to the tale. He could have told us, for example, the history of the Elves in straightforward narrative, but by making it appear that a professional historian rather than a mere storyteller had constructed the history, we are all the more willing to accept it.

The process of reifying mythology is quite complex, but appears to have the following elements: a world like our own, but different enough that it cannot be specifically identified; a pseudo-scholarly exposition of the natural, historical, cultural, and linguistic background of that world; the formula of a "rediscovered" rather than an invented world; a world that may not conform to all the known laws of nature, but does not obviously contradict them; a lengthy tale that would allow enough time in which to express all the aforementioned.

I do not profess to be a Tolkien scholar, or purport to know the entire process of reifying myths. But I do feel that most Tolkien critics have missed the point because they couldn't see the forest for the trees. *The Lord of the Rings* was primarily written as a literary *tour de force* through which the author wished to try out his own theories on how the *process* of mythmaking works in an age when the old myths are no longer acceptable. Such a literary theory conforms to most of the information that I discovered in the course of researching this biography. I also believe that Tolkien could only be certain that he had succeeded in creating the process if someone other than himself discovered and recognized his attempt. This is why he deliberately decided to cover his tracks by publicly affirming that the work had no meaning—a misleading clue that was technically true, but which would also bring the real intent to the attention of those perceptive enough to find it. If he failed in his effort, if his theories of modern mythmaking were wrong, then no one would recognize his intent or call attention to his failure.

Mythmaking is still alive and well in the modern world; it has simply changed its form and purpose. Instead of insulating us against the unknown dangers of nature, we are protected against the harsh political realities of global *realpolitik*. Trying to separate myth from objective reality on the television news is a near-impossible task for persons unaware of the dynamics of media, and probably an unrewarding job for those who are. Identifying and understanding "real" events in our modern world becomes increasingly important to the informed citizen in an age when we are flooded with information and misinformation. But perhaps it may become easier to perceive the truth if we have a better understanding of how nonevents and distorted accounts of real events are translated from myths to facts. This may be Tolkien's contribution to the world, above and beyond the mere enjoyment of a story well told: a new dimension of meaning and an aid to understanding the mythmaking process.

During the course of researching this book, I received a friendly, informative letter from Professor T.V. Benn, one of Tolkien's former students. He concluded by saying "I don't envy you in your task—making a record of a writer, which will remain when the writer is no longer a best-seller." Professor Benn's statement proved quite accurate, because writing this biography proved a longer, much more arduous task than my publishers and I had anticipated. One major problem was that Tolkien himself refrained from giving out any bio graphical data during his lifetime. He wrote to a would-be biographer in 1967, "I dislike being written about, and the results to date have caused me both irritation and distaste. I vetoed being treated in one of the series *Contemporary Writers in Christian Perspective* published by Eerdmans. I will not attempt to do the same in regard to your project. But I hope you will make it literary (and as critical of that aspect as you like) and not personal. I have no inclination, in fact must refuse, to provide information about myself, family and family origin. In any case this would be a matter of considerable labor if it was to be any more use than the sufficient facts found in the English *Who's Who?*"

This position is quite understandable for a living author who wishes to protect his privacy, but not defensible after his death. A world-famous literary figure who allowed his works to be published generates considerable interest on the part of his readers, who naturally wish to know more about the man. But I found there was still considerable resistance to releasing information by the Tolkien family. Michael Tolkien, responding to my request to interview him, wrote, "I am well aware of the world-wide interest in my father's work and the great admiration for it that exists in almost every country where it has been published, and I am in fully sympathy with all this. But it is my policy to keep all discussion about my father himself as far as possible strictly within the fami ly, or those so long associated with it as to be virtually part of it. . . . if people want to write about my father and his work I cannot stop them (much as I would like to!), but all I have seen published so far seems to me to be extraordinarily inaccurate and ill-informed."

I could therefore count on no assistance from the family; hence, I did not have access to Tolkien's literary papers, letters, and other records. Matters became doubly difficult when I learned that the family had requested Tolkien's close friends and associates to refrain from releasing information, out of respect for Tolkien's memory. I suppose I could dismiss this as sour grapes, but in all fairness, the family had commissioned a Mr. Humphrey Carpenter to write an "official" biography, which was published in June, 1977, with the title *Tolkien*, and they understandably wished to keep a monopoly on information about Tolkien's life. Such a practice is ethically tenuous, but economically practical. Fortunately for me, enough people who knew Tolkien agreed with my position—that his readers are entitled to information about his life—to assist me in my research. Furthermore, since the publication of the first edition of this book in 1976, my publishers and I have received much additional information from readers, enabling us to make this new edition more complete and accurate.

A few words are in order about the style of this book. In writing, I have had to assume that the reader has read *The Lord of the Rings,* or at least has a passing knowledge of the trilogy. It is, of course, possible to read and (I hope) enjoy this biography without having read Tolkien, but I think it will mean more to those who have already traveled through Middle-earth.

Because of the aforementioned problems in researching the book, there are still, quite naturally, gaps in information. Such detailed information as birthdays and school grades may seem important to readers obsessed with detail, but I feel that such can be safely deleted. When information from two or more sources conflicted, or simply was unavailable, I tried to indicate this in the text, just as I have attempted to separate my educated guesses from mere speculation. But I felt justified in engaging in speculation at times when the data justified it. For example, I really don't know exactly when the Tolkien family came to England (I do know it was in the eighteenth century), or why they changed their name to an Anglicized spelling. However, knowing of the large German migration to England that accompanied the Hanoverian kings' appointment to the vacant throne, and the unpopularity of "German George" at the end of his reign, and the fact that many Germans changed their names because of it, I speculated that this could have been the reason. I hope that I have not overstepped the bounds of integrity either in speculating or in making educated guesses.

All the spellings and punctuations have been Americanized for consistency and convenience, even when a text is taken from the printed page. I supplied the punctuation (and interpretation of Tolkien's difficult speech) to the spoken interviews myself, trying to keep them as close to the intended inflection as possible.

The text is heavily footnoted because, after trying various methods of introducing relevant, but discontinuous material wherever it seemed warranted, footnoting proved the only practical method. I have tried to make footnotes as readable as possible, and though it may upset scholars, I have not inserted textual or source footnotes. This biography is not written for scholars or academics alone, but for all those who enjoy and admire Tolkien.

I feel now, as I write this, that J.R.R. Tolkien's *The Lord of the Rings* is probably the one work that will survive our century. Of the literature written over the years, only a precious few are still widely read as living works and not curious anachronisms or class assignments. *The Lord of the Rings* has an appeal that transcends geographical and temporal limits; it creates and satisfies that wistful longing for a time when the world seemed less complicated. Perhaps, too, if we have a choice as to how we would like to be remembered by future generations, we would describe our era not as one of world wars, nuclear weapons, and social convulsions, but as the century in which Middle-earth was created.

Daniel Grotta
Philadelphia, Pennsylvania

176

REFERENCE NOTES

The Young Lad: 1892–1911

1 (p. 23)   Shortly after the publication of *The Lord of the Rings*, Tolkien discussed his early literary tastes and mentioned that George MacDonald had been his favorite writer. But more than a decade later, he apparently changed his mind and said that he had had little interest in fairy stories as a child, and could not bear to read MacDonald. ''I was, and remained, primarily interested in the world about me,'' he said to one interviewer, implying his early disinterest in fairy stories and fantasy.

2 (p. 30)   At Oxford and Cambridge, an exhibitioner is a student who has been awarded a fixed sum to pay for his college and tuition expenses by demonstrating, or exhibiting, superior knowledge or ability. The closest American equivalent is the Merit Scholarship winner.

The Exhibitioner: 1911–1915

1 (p. 32)   At Oxford, the academic year is divided into four six-week terms: Michaelmas (autumn); Hilary, or Lent (winter); Easter; and Trinity (spring). There is a ''short vac'' of one month between Michaelmas, Hilary, and Easter, but no break between Easter and Trinity. The ''long vac'' between Trinity and Michaelmas runs from June through September, at which time new students traditionally come up. Cambridge, incidentally, recognizes only three terms, but they roughly coincide with Oxford's schedule.

2 (p. 32)   In England, a commoner is also a person who is neither royalty nor nobility. This definition did not apply, since many commoners at Oxford had titles. Technically speaking, even the Prince of Wales, who

was a student at Magdalen College in Tolkien's day, was a common student.

3 (p. 32) To "read" in England means to study; it also refers to the student's "major" subject, for which his degree will be granted.

4 (p. 32) In 1902, Oxford University rejected a proposal to drop Greek as a compulsory prerequisite for matriculation, but in 1904 a motion was carried—but later defeated—allowing students to substitute a science, mathematics, or a modern language for Greek. The Greek requirement wasn't dropped until the 1920s, and Latin as a prerequisite survived until 1971.

5 (p. 33) Oxbridge is used to describe Oxford and Cambridge whenever they share something in common.

6 (p. 34) Also called Oxonia, Oxenforde, or Oxonforde, all indicating that the area was a cattle crossing point at the confluence of the rivers Thames (Isis) and Cherwell.

7 (p. 35) Even All Soul's College, one of the oldest and best-known Oxford colleges, is technically not part of the university. Nor are many of the ecclesiastical colleges or the "halls," (several dating back to the thirteenth century) in which students resided and were tutored prior to entry into one of the University colleges. In Tolkien's day, the university did not officially recognize the four women's colleges— Lady Margaret Hall, Somerville, St. Hugh's, and St. Hilda's— although their students were permitted to attend university lectures and tutorials, as well as their examinations. They were not permitted to grant degrees until 1920, and were not accorded equal status to the male colleges until 1960.

8 (p. 36) A committee of self-righteous Victorians changed all these ancient names during the nineteenth century, but the Oxford city fathers decided to revert to the original names after the Second World War.

9 (p. 36) The most famous "progging" story occurred when Tolkien was resident in Oxford from 1918 to 1921, at the time women were first officially recognized by the university. One night, the proctor and his bulldogs, tapped an unescorted young lady—an offense—on the shoulder and asked her the dreaded question: Are you a member of the university? The quick-thinking student instantly retorted, "I'm sorry—I never speak to strange men in the street!," hopped on her bicycle and sped away from the flabbergasted officials.

10 (p. 37) Atheism still was not officially recognized in Tolkien's time, although it was almost a century after the poet Shelley had been "sent down" from University College for officially proclaiming it.

11 (p. 37) Dons refer to fellows, tutors, professors, and any other senior members of either the university or the colleges.

12 (p. 38)   No relation to the nineteenth century writer.

13 (p. 38)   The term ''Oxonians'' specifically refers to both present and past members of the University, but popular usage has been expanded to include anyone living in Oxford or from Oxford, whether he or she ever had an association with the university.

14 (p. 38)   As might be expected, the university courts were especially lenient with members who were accused of offenses against the townspeople, and harsh against townspeople who committed offenses against members; this blatant double standard of justice caused great resentment among the townspeople, which occasionally precipitated riots and retaliatory murders.

15 (p. 39)   At Oxford and Cambridge, the Master of Arts degree is *honorary* rather than academic, and is automatically granted to those with bachelor's degrees after several years' postgraduate residence. All M.A.s automatically become lifelong senior members of the university.

16 (p. 39)   At Oxford the college servant is called a scout. He administers to the needs of a set number of college members, which in Tolkien's day was usually eight.

17 (p. 39)   Lord Roseberry, a brilliant student and later a famous politician, owned a racehorse and was given an ultimatum to either leave or get rid of the horse. To everyone's astonishment, he left Oxford, and the horse made him a small fortune with its winnings.

18 (p. 39)   One student at the beginning of the eighteenth century was so outraged at not being able to keep a stable of hunting dogs that he kept a chained bear, which was not mentioned in the rules.

19 (p. 40)   Although there were relatively few students from working-class families who were members of the university before World War I, the newly-opened Ruskin College was predominantly working-class and socialist. It was not, however, and still is not, part of the university.

20 (p. 40)   In 1924, Prince Chicibu of Japan studied at Magdalen College for two years. When he first arrived at Oxford, he was greeted with great ceremony. The vice-chancellor asked the prince what he would like to be called. ''Not Chicibu, if you please. It means 'the son of God.' '' The vice-chancellor nodded and replied without any embarrassment ''That's all right. We've had the sons of many famous people here. ''

21 (p. 40)   Today at Oxbridge the highest degree is a first-class degree, equivalent to a *magna cum laude*; a second-class degree is quite honorable, equivalent to a ''B'' average; the third-class degree is ''C'' or below.

22 (p. 41)   Most students at that time lived in the college rather than in

(approved) bed-sitters or flats in the town. Today, however, because of the large student population, many students are only able to live one year in the college, and must share at that. Fellows who are not resident in the colleges (having either houses or flats outside) must also share rooms for tutorials in many instances.

23 (p. 42) I have been unable to discover precisely what a four-in-nine is, but from the context it appears to be a golf bag or some other sort of sporting apparel or equipment.

The Soldier: 1915–1925

1 (p. 47) Tolkien frequently told interviewers that all but one of his close friends had been killed, the sole survivor being Christopher Wiseman. But Tolkien apparently overlooked, or did not know, that Harold Trimmingham, who had volunteered in 1914, lived on for many years afterward, eventually moving to Bermuda.

2 (p. 51) *Dulce et decorum est pro patria mori* translates from the Latin ''How sweet and honorable it is to die for one's country.'' The Latin phrase was written by Horace, who may have been paraphrasing *The Iliad* of Homer, in which one passage translates ''It is not unseemly for a man to die fighting in defense of his country.''

3 (p. 53) Orc is originally from the Latin *orcus*, or hell. It became *orcneas* in Anglo-Saxon, and appears in *Beowulf*. The seventeenth century English poet John Milton used the word *orc* in *Paradise Lost*, but that particular word was from the Greek *oryga* and the Middle French *orque*, meaning whale, and later any monster, giant, or ogre. Tolkien adapted many obsolete, archaic, and foreign words for his names in *The Lord of the Rings*. Another example is the word Mordor, which comes from the Anglo-Saxon word *morthor*, or murder. The wargs that Bilbo fought in *The Hobbit* also come from the Anglo-Saxon, the word *wearg*, which means wolf.

4 (p. 57) In the spring of 1975, Tolkien's daughter Priscilla told members of the British Tolkien Society that her father had been evacuated from France on the Lusitania, which had been converted into a hospital ship, and that the vessel had been torpedoed on its very next journey. Miss Tolkien, however, appears to have confused the Lusitania with another ship, since the liner had been sunk off the Irish coast nearly a year and a half earlier and in any event had never been pressed into service as a hospital ship.

The Scholar: 1919–1925

1 (p. 60) This is not to say that all but three hundred university members had

been killed, since many students came up and left after 1914. The figure of 2,700 also includes dons.

2 (p. 60) When C.S. Lewis came up to University College for one term in 1916 (in order to insure an army commission), he noted that "Hall is in the possession of the blue-coated wounded." At that time, the college had twelve members, only five of whom were undergraduates; most colleges also experienced such depletions of both junior and senior members.

3 (p. 61) Actually temporary first lieutenant at that time, and technically still attached to the service.

4 (p. 61) The name of the elves' hidden city in *The Silmarillion*.

5 (p. 62) For a more detailed analysis of this sort of tongue-in-cheek scholarship, see Paul Kocher's *Master of Middle Earth*.

6 (p. 64) At English universities, there is only one professor for each subject or chair; there are no assistant or associate professors.

7 (p. 65) Stewart later became an Oxford don and a member of the English School. He also became an extremely popular writer of adventure and spy novels, using the *nom de plume* of Michael Innes. Actually, Oxford dons writing popular fiction on the side is an old tradition at Oxbridge, as is the use of pseudonyms.

8 (p. 65) A research student at an English university is a graduate student going for a Ph.D. or other advanced degrees.

9 (p. 65) Published by the Oxford University Press.

10 (p. 65) Mallory, a fifteenth century knight from Warwickshire, probably wrote *Le Morte d' Arthur* while in prison, where he was incarcerated in 1451 and 1452 after a quarrel with the powerful Earl of Warwick. The work became famous, and is probably one of the best examples of late Medieval literature in England.

11 (p. 66) Four decades later Tolkien translated *Pearl* into modern English, and it was published along with his own modern English translation of *Sir Gawain and the Green Knight* in 1967.

12 (p. 66) Tolkien must have been delighted when Charles Williams read his long poem *Taliessin Through Logres* to the Inklings during the period in which Tolkien was struggling to complete the first two books of *The Lord of the Rings*. *Taliessin* was based on the Arthurian legend, as was *Gawain*, but Williams's poem was so complex and difficult that he later began *Arthurian Torso* in order to "explain" his poem. C.S. Lewis finished *Arthurian Torso* after Williams's death in 1945.

13 (p. 66) In 1936, a book entitled *Songs for the Philologists* was privately printed by the Department of English at University College, London,

which contained songs by Tolkien, E.V. Gordon, and others. Undoubtedly some of these were sung at the Leeds dinner parties.

14 (p. 66)   Tolkien was usually called "Tolkien" by his friends and colleagues, as was the custom of the time. In private conversation he was John, and later Ronald, although his two Christian names seemed to have been used interchangeably. But he was "Tolk" to his students (not to his face, however).

15 (p. 67)   One of the students who attended his Oxford seminars was Katherine Ball, who later became a professor at the University of Toronto. She remembered that "He came in lightfully and gracefully, I always remember that, his gown flowing, his fair hair shining, and he read *Beowulf* aloud. We did not know the language he was reading, yet the sound of Tolkien made sense of the unknown tongue and the terrors and the dangers that he recounted—how I do not know—made our hair stand on end. He read like no one else I have ever heard. . . . He was a great teacher, and delightful, courteous, ever so kindly."

16 (p. 67)   According to T.V. Benn, Tolkien gave his seminars in a "large tiered lecture room in the Old Baines Wing. This room, which could hold about one hundred students, is now a physiology research lab."

17 (p. 69)   A kind of handball played by two to four participants. It is also erroneously known as both the Eton Game and the Rugby Game (a mistake probably only committed by alumni from those two famous public schools).

18 (p. 69)   Tolkien disliked being compared to Lewis Carroll, (Dodgson's nom de plume), whose *Alice in Wonderland* he dismissed as "A satire on chess." About Ariosto he said, "I don't know Ariosto and I'd loathe him if I did;" about Cervantes, "He was a weed-killer to romance;" and about Dante, "He's full of spite and malice. I don't care for his petty relations with petty people in petty cities." In later life, Tolkien did not care to read any modern writer of fairy stories, but preferred science fiction and, of course, rereading his own works.

19 (p. 69)   A pastiche of English nursery rhymes that later found its way into *The Lord of the Rings*, where it is recited by Frodo at the Prancing Pony.

The Professor: 1925–1937

1 (p. 75)   At both Oxford and Cambridge, the colleges are the largest landlords because of their extensive property holdings. Such houses are usually rented at nominal sums to dons and other M.A.'s.

2 (p. 76)   Bosworth also endowed £10,000 in 1867 to the University of Cambridge in order to establish a chair of Anglo-Saxon, which he named after himself.

REFERENCE NOTES

3 (p. 81)   Tolkien admitted to a fondness for intelligent lizards in a radio interview when he said, "Dragons always attracted me as a mythological element. They seem to comprise human malice and bestiality together, a sort of malicious wisdom and shrewdness. Terrifying creatures."

4 (p. 83)   This is much earlier than the date Tolkien himself frequently gave for the incident, but Michael Tolkien is convinced it took place in 1928. "I first heard it at the age of 7, when John, my elder brother was 10, and Christopher 3. My sister was not even born then." Since Michael Tolkien had been born in November, 1920, this would place the time at summer, 1928. However, it is possible that Tolkien was referring to the time when *The Hobbit* was being typed in manuscript form, which was years later.

5 (p. 84)   Tolkien once said that he had made his hobbits small "because of reach of imagination and not strength of power." This makes sense when one considers that the hobbits were modeled upon rustics from Sarehole and common soldiers under his command, who did their duty unfailingly, despite the dangers, but were always followers rather than leaders. As to hobbits having been modeled after rabbits (who, after all, also lived in holes in the ground), Tolkien had this to say: "I don't like small creatures. Hobbits are three to four feet in height. You can see people like that. If there was anything I detested it was all that Drayton stuff; hideous. All that hiding in cowslips. Shakespeare took it up because it was fashionable, but it didn't invite his imagination at all. He produced some nice, funny names like Cobweb, Peaseblossom and so on; and some poetic stuff about Titania, but he never takes the slightest notice of her. She makes love to a donkey."

6 (p. 84)   One of Tolkien's favorite books, which is understandable when one considers that Lewis' Babbit is a smug bourgeois character who reflects all of the middle class values that Tolkien also held dear.

7 (p. 85)   An example of this is found in Tolkien's treatment of religion in *The Lord of the Rings*: "The man of the twentieth century must have gods in a story of this kind, but he *can't* believe in gods like Thor and Odin, Aphrodite, Zeus. I couldn't possibly construct in my mythology *lupus* or Asgards on the terms in which the people who worship those gods believed in. God is supreme, the Creator, outside the *transcendent*. The place is well taken by angelic spirits created by God, created before the particular time sequence of the world which now exists. Those are the battles of the powers—it is a construction of mythology in which a large part of the demographic has been handed over to the powers which are created on the other hand of the One. It is slightly and more elaborately thought out than C.S. Lewis' business, *Out of the Silent Planet*, where you have a demogod that is actually in command of the planet Mars and the idea that Lucifer was in charge of the world in which he fell."

8 (p. 85)   Despite this, Tolkien said he modeled his dwarfs after the Jews, and not after the Norse dwarfs.

The Mythmaker: 1937–1953

1 (p. 92)   As far as this author has been able to ascertain, only one woman ever attended any of the Inkling meetings—the novelist Dorothy Sayers, creator of the Lord Peter Wimsey detective stories. Apparently she sat in on a few meetings during World War II when she was visiting Oxford, and then only on nights when Tolkien was absent. According to Lewis, it is doubtful that the two ever met.

2 (p. 95)   According to Randel Helms, in his book *Tolkien's World*, Tolkien gently parodied the rhyming style of *Taliessin Through Logres* in Bilbo's poem "Errantry" in *The Lord of the Rings*, as well as in *The Adventures of Tom Bombadil*. There is, in fact, a marked similarity in that both Williams and Tolkien rhymed words in the middle of the line. Since Tolkien often parodied other works in his trilogy, it is quite likely that he did so with Williams's poem.

3 (p. 95)   Tolkien once said that "hobbits have what you might call universal morals. I should say that they are examples of natural philosophy and natural religion." He also revealed that "the book is about the world that God created—the actual world of this planet."

4 (p. 97)   Tolkien created the concept of the "sub-creator" to explain the role of a mythmaker who has "discovered" another world or universe. For a more detailed explanation, read Tolkien's "On Fairy-Stories" in *The Tolkien Reader* (Ballantine).

5 (p. 97)   Kilby knew Tolkien and assisted him in the summer of 1966 in trying to prepare *The Silmarillion* for publication.

6 (p. 98)   According to Tolkien, C.S. Lewis had read some of his earlier writings; this probably includes *The Silmarillion* in incomplete manuscript form.

7 (p. 98)   Númenor, or Dúnedain, was the powerful kingdom that arose during the Second Age of Middle-earth, and was ultimately destroyed in an Atlantis-like deluge. Although Númenor plays no direct part in *The Lord of the Rings*, it is central to *The Silmarillion*.

8 (p. 99)   In a 1968 BBC television documentary, Tolkien said that "a new language is like a new wine. I can write in Elvish, but I think that my writing is very inferior to the elves'." At that point, interviewer Leslie Megahey asked Tolkien to say something in Elvish, which he did. He suddenly stopped in midsentence, paused for long seconds, and said in an embarassed, almost inaudible voice, "Oh God . . . I made a mistake, didn't I?" Then he proceeded to pronounce the correct Elvish.

9 (p. 100) Tolkien had originally promised to deliver a lecture on fairy stories to an undergraduate society at Worcester College in 1938, but apparently he never gave it. It is likely that the 1939 Andrew Lang lecture on the same subject was an extended version of the one he had written, but never delivered, the year before.

10 (p. 101) Tolkien himself applied the rules of Faërie to *The Lord of the Rings* in that Middle-earth was quite close to our own world in many respects. As Paul Kocher observes in his book, *Master of Middle Earth*: "Middle-earth is a place of many marvels. But they are carefully fitted into a framework of climate and geography, familiar skies by night, familiar shrubs and trees, beasts and birds on earth by day, men and manlike creatures with societies not too different from our own. Consequently the reader walks through any Middle-earth landscape with a security of recognition that woos him on to believe in everything that happens. Familiar but not too familiar, strange but not too strange. This is the master rubric that Tolkien bears always in mind when inventing the world of epic."

11 (p. 102) C.S. Lewis once wrote to a friend that "Tolkien's book is not an allegory—a form he dislikes. You'll get nearest to his mind by studying his essay on Fairy Tales . . . His root idea of narrative art is 'sub-creation'—the making of a secondary world. What you would call 'a pleasant story for children' would be to him *more serious* than an allegory. . . . *My* view would be that a good myth . . . is a higher thing than allegory. . . . Into an allegory a man can put only what he already knows; in a myth he puts what he does not know and could not come by in any other way."

12 (p. 103) After *The Lord of the Rings* was published, Tolkien quietly revised key sentences in later editions of *The Hobbit* that dealt with Bilbo, Gollum, and the ring. This tightened the continuity between the two works by giving the ring a more sinister and secret aura than it had originally possessed. It also showed that providence and pity had stayed Bilbo's hand in sparing Gollum, thus insuring his future involvement with the ring. Incidentally, one of the major problems in Tolkien's rewriting and revising *The Silmarillion* was precisely this question of continuity, of making it more closely conform to both *The Hobbit* and *The Lord of the Rings*. Paul Kocher believes that Tolkien failed to link the two works together. He writes, "Despite its surface connections with *The Lord of the Rings* the two works are so unlike fundamentally as to be different in kind. . . . Each work has virtues . . . , but they had better be read independently of each other as contrasting, if related, specimens of the fantasy writer's art."

13 (p. 106) Paul Kocher notes Tolkien's disdain for machines: "Tolkien's usual vendetta against our machine age shows through his remarks in *The Hobbit* about goblins, that they love wheels and engines: 'It is not unlikely that they invented some of the machines that have since

troubled the world, especially the ingenious devices used for killing large numbers of people at once.' . . . Tolkien was an ecologist, lover of handicrafts, detester of war long before such attitudes became fashionable.''

14 (p. 109) When Michael Tolkien transferred from the army to the RAF, he was required to fill out innumerable forms and questionnaires. After completing dozens of them, he came to yet another blank asking for his father's profession. In that blank he wrote the word WIZARD.

15 (p. 112) Tolkien's friendship with Lewis had slightly cooled when Lewis had been passed over for the Merton professorship. Lewis believed that Tolkien had been in a position to cast the deciding ballot, and had voted against his old friend.

16 (p. 112) During the war, the British government instituted both a *de facto* censorship and a system of publication priorities, for both political and security reasons and because of the lack of supplies. All books had to be passed by a board and those deemed to have the most merit were allotted paper first. Both *The Hobbit* and *Farmer Giles of Ham* had been passed for press in 1946, but paper still had not been found for the latter.

17 (p. 113) In 1948, Tolkien wrote, ''We still have a hope of crossing the water, but so far arrangements have not advanced. One difficulty is that though legislation to give professors 'sabbatical' leave has at last gone through, I need a *rest*. And I cannot yet envisage a bout of teaching and lecturing in a new milieu!''

18 (p. 113) In the original introduction to *The Lord of the Rings* (1954), Tolkien wrote, ''For if the labor has been long (more than fourteen years), it has been neither orderly nor continuous. But I have not had Bilbo's leisure. Indeed much of that time has contained for me no leisure at all, and more than once for a whole year the dust has gathered on my unfinished pages. I only say this to explain to those who have waited for this book why they have had to wait so long. I have no reason to complain.''

19 (p. 113) Incidentally, the final draft of the map of Middle-earth used in the published work was drawn up by Tolkien's son, Christopher.

20 (p. 114) In another version of the story, Tolkien submitted the manuscript to Milton Waldman of Collins even *before* giving it to Allen & Unwin. Apparently Tolkien was dissatisfied with the way Allen & Unwin had handled the new edition of *The Hobbit*, and remembering the earlier rejection of *The Silmarillion*, therefore felt no particular love or loyalty for his original publisher.

The Author: 1953–1966

1 (p. 119) Hughes wrote, ''What can I say then? For *width* of imagination it

almost beggars parallel, and it is nearly as remarkable for its vividness and for the narrative skill which carries the reader on, enthralled, for page after page.'' Naomi Mitchison said, ''It's odd, you know, one takes it as seriously as Mallory.''

2 (p. 122) A turn-of-the-century American who wrote and illustrated a number of books for children. His best-known work is *The Merry Adventures of Robin Hood*.

3 (p. 123) Vera Chapman, Secretary and founder of the British Tolkien Society, thinks that ''Tolkien just wasn't interested in females. He had a story to tell and the female element just wasn't necessary, except towards the end when his children, for whom he was writing, were growing up, and he felt it was necessary to write in a female character somewhere. So you get the character of Éowyn, who, although his daughter (Priscilla) doesn't bear it out, was Tolkien's asking himself what's in it for the girls, and then writing in a female character for his teenage daughter.''

4 (p. 130) Tolkien later claimed that he had never been advised of the Ace edition before publication, and that it had come as a complete surprise and shock. That seems unlikely, however, since Wollheim had nothing to gain from fabricating the story of the negotiations, and Tolkien had something to lose in admitting his foreknowledge.

The Recluse: 1966–1973

1 (p. 138) Even Tolkien and his wife had Middle-earth names—Beren and Luthien, lovers from *The Silmarillion*. W.H. Auden's Middle-earth name was Gimli, the dwarf.

2 (p. 139) In 1931, Tolkien had written a long poem, which is still unpublished, entitled ''Mythopoeia.'' In context, the word means ''the making of myths.''

3 (p. 144) Edith Tolkien had been preparing for a career as a piano teacher before she met her husband-to-be. Although she never played or taught professionally, one of her greatest pleasures was playing the piano for herself and her family.

4 (p. 146) A misquote from Tennyson's poem, *Idylls of the King*.

5 (p. 146) When Allen Barnett and his wife Sarah visited Oxford to see Tolkien, they were told he was no longer in the city. Several days later they learned that he was indeed home, but seeing neither friend nor stranger.

6 (p. 151) The first time Tolkien went to the Old Age Pensioners Club, he made an ostentatious show of secrecy. He asked Carr ''Where do you think

I'm going?'' and then confided his destination. At the OAP Club, he then was greeted by a man who asked him to guess his age. When Tolkien said eighty, the old man grinned and remarked how young Tolkien looked (the man was in fact eighty-seven).

Epilogue: The Silmarillion

1 (p. 159) Christopher Tolkien asked Dr. Kilby to delete a chapter in his book that summarized *The Silmarillion* on the grounds that it might jeopardize sales of the posthumous work by revealing beforehand what the story was about. Although Kilby had both the moral and legal right to retain the summarization, he reluctantly deleted it in order not to offend Christopher Tolkien, the reason being that Kilby is writing a book about the Inklings and needs his continued good will.

FURTHER READINGS

A Guide to Middle-earth, by Robert Foster. New York: Ballantine Books, Inc., 1974. 291 pp. $6.95.

This indispensable book has appeared in various forms since it was first compiled in 1966 for the literary journal *Niekas.* It is a concordance to *The Lord of the Rings,* with page references to the Ballantine paperback edition. The book contains a directory to all the proper names that appear in the trilogy, as well as those in *The Hobbit, The Adventures of Tom Bombadil* and *The Road Goes Ever On,* and is cross-indexed for convenience. Foster's work is essential for scholars and academics; for Tolkien lovers in general, it is simply fun to read.

J.R.R. Tolkien, by Robley Evans. New York: Warner Books, Inc., 1972. 205 pp. $1.50.

This, one of the *Writers For the '70s* series, is written by an academic, but manages to avoid being pedantic and preachy. Evans discusses fantasy and fantasy writers who share common themes with Tolkien, and the book is peppered with many interesting, but often not very relevant literary references. In fact, it is less about Tolkien and *The Lord of the Rings* than about literary fantasy in general.

Master of Middle-earth: The Fiction of J. R. R. Tolkien, by Paul H. Kocher. Boston: Houghton Mifflin Co., 1973. 247 pp. $3.25.

An excellent, penetrating study of Tolkien's major fictional works. Especially good are the two chapters dealing with cosmic order and the races that make up the Fellowship of the Ring. Despite the book's occasional weaknesses, it remains the best basic work I have read on Tolkien.

Modern Heroism, by Roger Sale. Berkeley: University of California Press, 1973. 261 pp. $10.00.

This is the only book included in this bibliography that is not exclusively devoted to Tolkien. Professor Sale postulates what he calls the Myth of Lost Unity—that the age of heroism is over and we must reach into the past for our heroes—and presents D.H. Lawrence, William Empson, and J.R.R. Tolkien as examples of writers who defied the Myth by creating heroes of their own. On first reading, I found it difficult to understand what these three writers were supposed to have in common, but later I found I had somewhat missed Professor Sale's point. He wishes only to demonstrate each writer's individual approach to heroism.

Professor Sale's fast-moving account of Frodo's journey is almost as exciting to read as Tolien's account in *The Lord of the Rings.* Instead of joining the number of scholars and critics who have meticulously analyzed characters and specific events, Sale carefully pays homage to Tolkien's claim that his book is only a story by pointing out some of the more ridiculous attempts to read nonexistent meanings into *The Lord of the Rings.* I greatly enjoyed the Tolkien section by itself, but less so when read in the context of the entire book.

Tolkien: A Look Behind The Lord of the Rings, by Lin Carter. New York: Ballantine Books, Inc., 1975. 212 pp. $1.75.

A rambling, informal, but very readable personal perspective on Tolkien and his importance in fantasy literature. It often becomes embroiled in interesting irrelevancies, and although some of Carter's insights into Tolkien's possible source materials and meanings are questionable, the book is a healthy relief from heavier critical analysis. Actually, it would have been better as two books: one on Tolkien, and the other a history of fantasy in literature. Purists may be offended by Carter, because he tries to prove how much of Tolkien's names, themes, and ideas were appropriated from the old Norse sagas.

Tolkien and the Critics, edited by Neil D. Isaacs and Rose A. Zimbardo. Notre Dame: University of Notre Dame Press, 1968. 296 pp. $3.45.

This is the sort of book Tolkien disliked and chided: a collection of scholarly essays by eminent academics and critics analyzing the ''meaning'' of *The Lord of the Rings.* (It includes contributions from his friend C. S. Lewis and arch-supporter W. H. Auden.) I find myself disagreeing with Tolkien, however; no matter that they may or may not have missed the point, most of the essays are interesting and thought-provoking. Perhaps the critics are reading more into *The Lord of the Rings* than Tolkien ever consciously wrote into it, but most of them present good arguments for their hypotheses.

The Tolkien Reader, writings by J.R.R. Tolkien. New York: Ballantine Books, Inc., 1974. 200 pp. $.95.

I have included this book in the bibliography of books *on* Tolkien because, in addition to some lesser-known works of fiction and poetry, it contains what is perhaps Professor Tolkien's single most important essay, ''On Fairy-Stories.'' To properly understand the motivation behind *The Lord of the Rings,* one must first digest Tolkien's own thoughts on the purpose and pleasure of fairy stories and mythology. This essay was first delivered at St. Andrew's University in 1939, when Tolkien was struggling with the first chapters of his great work, and first printed by the Oxford University Press in 1947 in *Essays Presented to Charles Williams.*

The Tolkien Relation, by William B. Ready. Chicago: Henry Regnery Co., 1973. 184 pp. $3.95.

This is an odd sort of book: not quite criticism, not quite biography, but nevertheless readable and interesting. Ready apparently set out to include everything he thought one might like to know about Tolkien and his work, which, to my taste, is really not enough. Because he tries to cover a rather broad subject in only 184 pages, the book seems rather superficial; its redeeming grace is that he does manage to cover the most interesting and relevant information about Tolkien in a manner that makes the reader clamor for more. *The Tolkien Relation* may be read as a sort of adult Tolkien primer.

Tolkien's World, by Randel Helms. Boston: Houghton Mifflin Co., 1974. 167 pp. $3.95.

Since I dislike reviewing bad books, my initial feeling was not to include Randel Helms's book in this list. On the other hand, because my 1974 review of this work in the *Philadelphia Inquirer* indirectly led to the writing of my own book, I should at least mention its existence. For my taste, *Tolkien's World* misses the point of the work entirely by attempting to apply Freudian analysis to the characters and themes of *The Lord of the Rings.* It is dogmatic in the extreme, as well as pedantic, but without the scholarship to back it up. It seems that Mr. Helms couldn't make up his mind whether to publish a scholarly work or a book of popular criticism, and the writing reflects his indecision.

At the moment, there are so many Tolkien societies, journals, and ''fanzines'' throughout the world that it would be impractical to list them all. And since many ''fanzines'' have exceedingly brief lives, such a list is likely to be inaccurate and outdated by the time this book is published. Also, it is unlikely that readers will want to rush out and join such exotic organizations as the West Borneo Tolkien Society, or wish to know how to obtain a pirate edition of *The Lord of the Rings* in Vietnamese.

I would, however, like to list the addresses of the two best-known Tolkien societies. In Britain, the Tolkien Society is a loosely-knit, informal group that meets at the Carpenter's Arms Pub at Whitfield Street in London's West End on the first Saturday of the month. The British Tolkien Society also publishes a bi-monthly journal called *Amon Hen* and a yearly journal, *Mallorn,* and holds yearly banquets and ''Oxonmoots,'' during which members spend a weekend in Oxford visiting some of Tolkien's favorite spots and former houses. Jessica Yates is Secretary of the Society, whose address is 14, Norfolk Avenue, London, N15, 6JX.

In America, the original Tolkien Society founded by Richard Plotz has been absorbed by the California-based Mythopoeic Society. The Mythopoeic Society is ''devoted to the study, discussion, and enjoyment of the works of J.R.R. Tolkien, C.S. Lewis, and Charles Williams. It believes these authors provide an excellent introduction to the realms of myth, fantasy, and imaginative literature.'' The Society was created in 1967 by Glen H. GoodKnight, and has approximately thirty local chapters throughout the United States. Besides the twice-yearly costume picnics, the Society sponsors a yearly convention known as Mythcon, at which awards are presented for the best fantasy work and best scholarly work on fantasy for the preceding year. The Society's monthly newsletter, *Mythprint,* is included with the $8.00 annual membership, and is, I believe, tax deductible, since the society is a literary nonprofit, tax-exempt organization. For information and the address of the nearest local chapter write to: The Mythopoeic Society, Post Office Box 4671, Whittier, California 90607.

INDEX

INDEX